Unlocking the Power of Vulkan: A Journey into AI and Machine Learning

Kameron Hussain and Frahaan Hussain

Published by Sonar Publishing, 2023.

While every precaution has been taken in the preparation of this book, the publisher assumes no responsibility for errors or omissions, or for damages resulting from the use of the information contained herein.

UNLOCKING THE POWER OF VULKAN: A JOURNEY INTO AI AND MACHINE LEARNING

First edition. October 22, 2023.

Copyright © 2023 Kameron Hussain and Frahaan Hussain.

ISBN: 979-8223497097

Written by Kameron Hussain and Frahaan Hussain.

Table of Contents

2. AI-driven Procedural Content Generation

3. Generative Adversarial Networks (GANs)

4. Real-time AI Training

5. Cross-Platform VR and AR

6. AI-powered Animation

7. Quantum Computing Integration

8. Machine Learning in Rendering

9. AI-enhanced Artistic Tools

10. Neuromorphic Hardware

Section 18.2: Machine Learning Advancements

1. Efficient Deep Learning Models

2. Transfer Learning and Pretrained Models

3. On-Device Inference

4. Federated Learning

5. Explainable AI (XAI)

6. AI Hardware Acceleration

7. AI-powered Content Creation Tools

8. Real-time Data Augmentation

9. AI-driven Dynamic Level of Detail (LOD)

10. AI in VR and AR Interactions

Section 18.3: Vulkan API Updates

1. Vulkan Extensions for AI

2. Multi-GPU Support

3. API Abstraction Layers

4. Advanced Descriptor Indexing

5. Pipeline Cache and State Management

6. Dynamic Resource Allocation

7. Cross-Vendor Compatibility

Section 18.4: Industry Applications

1. Gaming Industry

2. Automotive Simulations

3. Healthcare and Medical Imaging

4. Manufacturing and Industrial Automation

5. Aerospace and Defense

6. Entertainment and Media

7. Education and Training

8. Scientific Research

9. Finance and Investment

10. Retail and E-Commerce

Section 18.5: The Intersection of AI and Graphics

1. Synergy between Vulkan and AI

2. Enhanced Realism and Immersion

3. Personalization and User Engagement

4. Rapid Prototyping and Content Generation

5. Real-Time Analytics and Decision Support

6. Accessibility and Inclusivity

7. Challenges and Ethical Considerations

8. Education and Research

9. Collaboration and Innovation

10. Continued Evolution

Chapter 19: Case Studies and Success Stories

Section 19.1: AI-driven Graphics Projects

1. Enhancing Video Games with AI

2. AI-powered Content Creation

3. Real-time Object Detection in AR

4. Medical Imaging and AI

5. AI in Art and Creativity

6. AI-driven Simulation and Training

7. Educational Tools and AI Tutors

8. AI for Financial Analysis

Section 19.2: Vulkan in Industry Solutions

1. Automotive Industry

2. Manufacturing and Robotics

3. Energy and Utilities

4. Agriculture

5. Retail and E-commerce

6. Environmental Monitoring

7. Logistics and Supply Chain

8. Healthcare and Telemedicine

Section 19.3: Real-world Applications

1. Gaming Industry

2. Medical Imaging

3. Language Processing

4. Finance and Trading

5. Entertainment and Animation

6. Space Exploration

7. Educational Technology

8. Aerospace and Defense

Section 19.4: Lessons Learned and Best Practices

1. Start with a Strong Foundation

Chapter 1: Introduction to Vulkan

1.1 The Evolution of Graphics APIs

In the ever-evolving world of computer graphics, the development of graphics APIs (Application Programming Interfaces) has played a pivotal role in shaping the way we interact with and harness the power of GPUs (Graphics Processing Units). To understand the significance of Vulkan, it's crucial to trace the evolution of graphics APIs and appreciate the challenges they've addressed over the years.

From Ancient Beginnings to Modern Realism

The history of graphics APIs dates back to the early days of computer graphics when systems were rudimentary, and graphics capabilities were limited. Early graphics libraries were often tied closely to specific hardware and lacked portability. As a result, developers faced considerable challenges when attempting to create cross-platform applications.

Over time, graphics APIs evolved to provide more abstraction and portability. Libraries like OpenGL emerged, offering a standardized way to interact with GPUs. OpenGL's cross-platform nature made it a popular choice for game developers and other graphics-intensive applications.

The Need for Efficiency

While OpenGL and similar APIs served a crucial role in advancing graphics technology, they also had their limitations. These APIs were designed in an era when single-threaded, sequential execution was the norm. As the hardware landscape evolved with the rise of multi-core processors, the need for more efficient and scalable graphics APIs became evident.

Efficiency was particularly critical in the gaming industry, where every ounce of performance mattered. Developers sought ways to minimize CPU overhead and maximize GPU utilization to achieve smooth, high-performance graphics. This led to the development of APIs like DirectX 12 and Metal, which introduced lower-level access to hardware and multithreading capabilities.

Enter Vulkan: The Next Evolution

Vulkan, introduced by the Khronos Group in 2016, represents the next significant evolution in graphics APIs. It was built from the ground up with a focus on performance, efficiency, and cross-platform compatibility. Vulkan's architecture empowers developers with unprecedented control over GPU resources, enabling them to squeeze every ounce of performance from modern graphics hardware.

One of the defining features of Vulkan is its explicit nature. Instead of relying on the driver to manage resource allocation and synchronization, developers have direct control over these aspects. This level of control allows for fine-grained optimization and efficient multi-threading, making Vulkan an ideal choice for high-performance applications, including games and simulations.

Conclusion

The evolution of graphics APIs has been a journey from early, hardware-specific libraries to modern, efficient, and cross-platform solutions like Vulkan. In the chapters that follow, we will delve deeper into the world of Vulkan, exploring its architecture, benefits, and how to harness its power to create stunning graphics and integrate machine learning for enhanced experiences.

1.2 What Is Vulkan?

Vulkan, often referred to as the Vulkan API, is a high-performance, cross-platform graphics and compute API. It was developed by the Khronos Group, an industry consortium known for creating open standards in graphics and computing. Vulkan was designed to address the shortcomings of previous graphics APIs and provide developers with more control, efficiency, and portability.

A Low-Level Graphics API

One of the key distinctions of Vulkan is its low-level nature. Unlike higher-level APIs like OpenGL, Vulkan gives developers direct control over GPU resources and parallelism. While this level of control can be more challenging to work with, it offers significant advantages in terms of performance and optimization.

Vulkan's low-level design allows developers to:

- Explicitly manage memory allocation and synchronization.

- Efficiently utilize multiple CPU cores through multithreading.

- Minimize driver overhead, leading to reduced CPU usage.

- Optimize rendering pipelines and shaders for specific hardware.

Cross-Platform Compatibility

Vulkan was developed with cross-platform compatibility in mind. It is designed to work on a wide range of devices, including desktop computers, mobile devices, gaming consoles, and embedded systems. This cross-platform support is achieved through a combination of clear specifications and the availability of Vulkan drivers for various platforms.

By targeting Vulkan, developers can write code that runs on multiple platforms with minimal modifications. This reduces the need to rewrite large portions of code for different operating systems or hardware configurations, making it an attractive choice for game developers and applications requiring high-performance graphics.

Vulkan's Popularity in the Gaming Industry

Vulkan has gained significant popularity in the gaming industry due to its performance advantages and cross-platform capabilities. Many game developers have adopted Vulkan as their graphics API of choice, especially for Linux-based systems and Android platforms. Vulkan's support for high-performance rendering, efficient multi-threading, and reduced CPU overhead aligns well with the demands of modern games.

In addition to its use in traditional gaming, Vulkan has found applications in other areas, such as virtual reality (VR) and augmented reality (AR) development. Its efficient resource management and low-level access to hardware make it a valuable tool for creating immersive VR and AR experiences.

Ecosystem and Development Tools

To support developers working with Vulkan, a robust ecosystem of tools, libraries, and extensions has emerged. These resources simplify the development process and offer solutions for common tasks. For example, the Vulkan SDK provides essential tools for development, including validation layers for debugging and code validation.

Vulkan also offers extensions that enable advanced graphics features, such as ray tracing and machine learning integration. These extensions allow developers to push the boundaries of what is possible in graphics and compute applications.

In summary, Vulkan is a powerful graphics and compute API designed for performance, efficiency, and cross-platform compatibility. Its low-level nature and explicit control over GPU resources make it a versatile choice for a wide range of applications, from video games to scientific simulations. In the following chapters, we will explore the fundamental concepts and practical aspects of using Vulkan to create high-performance graphics and integrate machine learning for enhanced experiences.

1.3 Benefits of Using Vulkan

Vulkan offers a range of compelling benefits for developers and applications that require high-performance graphics and compute capabilities. In this section, we'll explore some of the key advantages of using Vulkan as your graphics and compute API of choice.

1. Performance Optimization

Vulkan's low-level nature provides developers with granular control over GPU resources and execution. This level of control allows for fine-tuning and optimization of graphics pipelines, shaders, and resource management. By minimizing CPU overhead and efficiently utilizing the GPU, Vulkan can lead to significant performance improvements in graphics-intensive applications.

For example, in gaming, Vulkan's reduced driver overhead and support for multithreading can result in higher frame rates and smoother gameplay. In scientific simulations, Vulkan's performance benefits enable researchers to process complex calculations more quickly, accelerating their work.

2. Cross-Platform Compatibility

Developers often face the challenge of targeting multiple platforms with their applications. Vulkan addresses this challenge by offering cross-platform compatibility. Whether you're developing for Windows, Linux, macOS, Android, or other platforms, Vulkan provides a consistent API that allows you to write code that runs across a wide range of devices.

This cross-platform support reduces the need to maintain separate codebases for different platforms, streamlining development and reducing costs. It also ensures that your application can reach a broader audience, making it an ideal choice for games, graphics software, and applications targeting diverse hardware.

3. Explicit Control

Vulkan's explicit nature means that developers have direct control over GPU resources and synchronization. This level of control enables developers to optimize their code for specific hardware configurations, ensuring that applications perform optimally across a variety of devices.

Explicit control also allows for efficient multithreading, which is crucial for modern applications that need to leverage the full power of multi-core CPUs. Developers can create highly parallelized rendering pipelines, resulting in better CPU utilization and overall performance.

4. Rich Graphics Features

Vulkan supports a wide range of graphics features and extensions, enabling developers to create stunning visuals and effects. Whether you're working on realistic rendering, dynamic lighting, or complex simulations, Vulkan provides the tools and extensions needed to implement these features efficiently.

Additionally, Vulkan's support for ray tracing has opened up new possibilities for real-time, cinematic-quality graphics. Developers can harness the power of hardware-accelerated ray tracing to create lifelike reflections, shadows, and global illumination in their applications.

5. Extensibility and Innovation

Vulkan's extensible architecture encourages innovation in graphics and compute applications. The Vulkan community actively develops and shares extensions that expand the capabilities of the API. These extensions cover a wide range of areas, including machine learning, virtual reality, and advanced rendering techniques.

Developers can leverage these extensions to push the boundaries of what's possible in their applications. For example, Vulkan's machine learning extensions enable the integration of AI and neural networks directly into graphics pipelines, opening up new opportunities for AI-powered graphics enhancements.

6. Open and Cross-Industry Standard

Vulkan is an open standard developed by the Khronos Group, a consortium of industry leaders. Being an open standard means that Vulkan is not controlled by a single company, fostering a collaborative and inclusive development environment. This openness encourages innovation and ensures that Vulkan remains accessible to developers and hardware manufacturers alike.

In conclusion, Vulkan offers a wide range of benefits, including performance optimization, cross-platform compatibility, explicit control, rich graphics features, extensibility, and adherence to open standards. These advantages make Vulkan a compelling choice for developers looking to create high-performance graphics and compute applications across diverse platforms and industries. In the subsequent chapters, we will delve deeper into the practical aspects of using Vulkan to harness these benefits effectively.

1.4 Getting Started with Vulkan

Now that we've explored the advantages of using Vulkan, let's take a closer look at how you can get started with Vulkan development. This section provides an overview of the essential steps and tools you'll need to begin creating graphics and compute applications with Vulkan.

1. Install Vulkan SDK

The first step in getting started with Vulkan is to install the Vulkan SDK (Software Development Kit) on your development machine. The Vulkan SDK provides essential tools, libraries, and header files for Vulkan development. You can download the SDK from the official Khronos Group website or from a package manager if it's available for your platform.

2. Set Up a Development Environment

Before writing Vulkan applications, you need to set up a development environment. This typically involves configuring your development IDE (Integrated Development Environment) and build system to work with Vulkan. Popular development environments like Visual Studio, CLion, and Visual Studio Code offer Vulkan integration through extensions and plugins.

3. Create a Vulkan Instance

In Vulkan, you start by creating a Vulkan instance, which represents the connection between your application and the Vulkan library. The Vulkan instance is a critical initialization step that provides information about your application to the Vulkan runtime. It includes details such as the application name, version, and extensions required.

Here's a simplified example of creating a Vulkan instance in C++:

```cpp
#include <vulkan/vulkan.h>

int main() {

// Create a Vulkan application instance

VkApplicationInfo appInfo{};

appInfo.sType                                    = VK_STRUCTURE_TYPE_APPLICATION_INFO;

appInfo.pApplicationName = "My Vulkan App";

appInfo.applicationVersion = VK_MAKE_VERSION(1, 0, 0);

appInfo.pEngineName = "No Engine";

appInfo.engineVersion = VK_MAKE_VERSION(1, 0, 0);

appInfo.apiVersion = VK_API_VERSION_1_0;

VkInstanceCreateInfo createInfo{};
```

```cpp
createInfo.sType = VK_STRUCTURE_TYPE_INSTANCE_CREATE_INFO;

createInfo.pApplicationInfo = &appInfo;

VkInstance instance;

if (vkCreateInstance(&createInfo, nullptr, &instance) != VK_SUCCESS) {

// Handle instance creation failure

return -1;

}

// ...

// Destroy the Vulkan instance when done

vkDestroyInstance(instance, nullptr);

return 0;

}
```

4. Query and Select a Physical Device

After creating a Vulkan instance, you need to query and select a physical device (GPU) to work with. Vulkan supports multiple GPUs, so your application can choose the most suitable device based on your requirements, such as performance capabilities and features.

You can enumerate available physical devices and select one based on your criteria. Here's a simplified example:

```cpp
// Enumerate physical devices
```

```cpp
uint32_t deviceCount = 0;

vkEnumeratePhysicalDevices(instance, &deviceCount, nullptr);

if (deviceCount == 0) {

// No suitable Vulkan devices found

return -1;

}

std::vector<VkPhysicalDevice> physicalDevices(deviceCount);

vkEnumeratePhysicalDevices(instance,              &deviceCount,
physicalDevices.data());

// Select a suitable physical device (e.g., based on properties and features)

VkPhysicalDevice selectedDevice = VK_NULL_HANDLE;

for (const auto& device : physicalDevices) {

// Check device properties and features

// ...

if (suitable) {

selectedDevice = device;

break;

}

}

if (selectedDevice == VK_NULL_HANDLE) {

// No suitable device found
```

```
return -1;
```

```
}
```

5. Create a Logical Device and Queues

Once you've selected a physical device, you can create a logical device, which represents an interface to that physical device. The logical device allows you to create Vulkan objects, such as command buffers, pipelines, and buffers.

You can also create queues associated with the logical device. Vulkan queues are used for submitting command buffers for execution on the GPU. You typically create multiple queues with different capabilities, such as graphics, compute, and presentation queues.

```
// Create a logical device and queues

VkDeviceQueueCreateInfo queueCreateInfo{};

queueCreateInfo.sType                                    =
VK_STRUCTURE_TYPE_DEVICE_QUEUE_CREATE_INFO;

queueCreateInfo.queueFamilyIndex = queueFamilyIndex; // Specify
the queue family

queueCreateInfo.queueCount = 1; // Create one queue

float queuePriority = 1.0f; // Queue priority (0.0 to 1.0)

queueCreateInfo.pQueuePriorities = &queuePriority;

VkDeviceCreateInfo deviceCreateInfo{};

deviceCreateInfo.sType                                   =
VK_STRUCTURE_TYPE_DEVICE_CREATE_INFO;
```

```cpp
deviceCreateInfo.queueCreateInfoCount = 1; // Number of queue create infos

deviceCreateInfo.pQueueCreateInfos = &queueCreateInfo;

deviceCreateInfo.enabledExtensionCount = 0; // Number of enabled extensions

deviceCreateInfo.ppEnabledExtensionNames = nullptr;

deviceCreateInfo.pEnabledFeatures = nullptr; // Optional device features

VkDevice logicalDevice;

if (vkCreateDevice(selectedDevice, &deviceCreateInfo, nullptr, &logicalDevice) != VK_SUCCESS) {

// Handle device creation failure

return -1;

}
```

These are the initial steps to set up a basic Vulkan development environment and create a Vulkan instance, select a physical device, and create a logical device with queues. In the upcoming chapters, we will explore Vulkan's concepts and features in greater detail, allowing you to dive deeper into graphics and compute application development with Vulkan.

1.5 Setting Up Your Development Environment

Before diving into Vulkan development, it's essential to set up a robust development environment that allows you to efficiently create, test, and debug your Vulkan applications. In this section, we will explore the key components of a Vulkan development environment and how to configure them for your needs.

1. Development IDE

Choosing the right Integrated Development Environment (IDE) is crucial for productive Vulkan development. Several popular IDEs offer excellent support for Vulkan:

- **Visual Studio**: If you're developing on Windows, Visual Studio is a popular choice. It provides a comprehensive development environment with debugging tools and extensions for Vulkan development.

- **CLion**: CLion is a cross-platform IDE that supports C++ development, making it suitable for Vulkan development on various platforms.

- **Visual Studio Code (VS Code)**: VS Code is a lightweight, open-source code editor that offers extensions for Vulkan development. It is available on multiple platforms, making it a versatile choice.

- **Qt Creator**: Qt Creator is another cross-platform IDE with support for C++ and Vulkan development. It provides a range of features for GUI-based applications.

Choose an IDE that aligns with your platform and development preferences. Ensure that you install any necessary extensions or plugins to enable Vulkan support within your chosen IDE.

2. Vulkan SDK

The Vulkan SDK is a fundamental tool for Vulkan development. It includes essential libraries, header files, and tools for compiling and debugging Vulkan applications. To set up the Vulkan SDK:

1. Download the Vulkan SDK from the official Khronos Group website or a package manager that supports your platform.
2. Install the SDK according to the provided instructions for your platform.
3. Ensure that your IDE is configured to use the Vulkan SDK. This typically involves setting the SDK's path in your IDE's project settings.

3. Graphics Drivers

Up-to-date graphics drivers are essential for Vulkan development, as they provide the necessary runtime support for Vulkan applications. Make sure that you have the latest graphics drivers installed for your GPU. Check the website of your GPU manufacturer (e.g., NVIDIA, AMD, or Intel) for driver updates.

4. Validation Layers

Validation layers are crucial for debugging Vulkan applications. They help identify and diagnose issues in your code, such as invalid API usage or memory leaks. To enable validation layers:

1. Ensure that the Vulkan SDK includes validation layers. Most Vulkan SDK installations come with a set of standard validation layers.
2. Set the VK_LAYER_PATH environment variable to the path where the validation layers are located. This allows

Vulkan to find and load the validation layers when running your application.

3. Enable validation layers in your Vulkan application by specifying them in the instance creation process. This helps catch errors during development.

5. GPU Debugging Tools

For efficient debugging of Vulkan applications, consider using GPU debugging tools provided by GPU manufacturers, such as NVIDIA Nsight or AMD Radeon GPU Profiler. These tools offer insights into GPU performance and allow you to diagnose GPU-related issues.

6. Version Control

Using a version control system, such as Git, is advisable for managing your Vulkan project. Version control helps track changes, collaborate with team members, and revert to previous states if issues arise. Platforms like GitHub, GitLab, and Bitbucket offer hosting and collaboration tools for Vulkan projects.

7. Tutorials and Resources

Lastly, take advantage of Vulkan tutorials, documentation, and online communities. The Vulkan community is active and provides valuable resources for learning and troubleshooting. Refer to official Vulkan documentation and explore online forums and communities for guidance.

In conclusion, setting up your development environment for Vulkan is a crucial initial step in your journey toward creating high-performance graphics and compute applications. Choose the right IDE, install the Vulkan SDK, keep your graphics drivers up-to-date, use validation layers for debugging, leverage GPU debugging tools, employ version control, and tap into available tutorials and resources. With a well-configured development environment, you'll be well-prepared to explore the power of Vulkan in the subsequent chapters of this book.

Chapter 2: Understanding Graphics Pipelines

2.1 Overview of Graphics Pipelines

In the world of computer graphics, a graphics pipeline is a fundamental concept that governs the process of transforming data into pixels displayed on your screen. Understanding how graphics pipelines work is essential when working with Vulkan or any other graphics API. This section provides an overview of graphics pipelines and their components.

1. What Is a Graphics Pipeline?

A graphics pipeline is a series of stages through which graphics data flows to produce a final image on the screen. Each stage of the pipeline performs a specific operation, such as transforming 3D coordinates into 2D screen space, applying textures, and performing shading calculations.

2. Stages of a Graphics Pipeline

A typical graphics pipeline consists of several stages, each responsible for a specific aspect of rendering:

- **Vertex Input:** This stage takes the vertex data as input, including vertex positions, colors, normals, and texture coordinates. It prepares this data for further processing.

- **Vertex Shader:** The vertex shader processes each vertex in the input data, performing transformations like translation, rotation, and projection. It also passes data to the next stages.

- **Tessellation Control Shader and Tessellation Evaluation Shader:** These stages are optional and are used for tessellation, a technique for adding detail to surfaces.

- **Geometry Shader:** This stage is also optional and allows for geometry manipulation. It can generate additional vertices or primitives based on the input.

- **Rasterization:** Rasterization converts geometric shapes into individual pixels. It determines which pixels are covered by the primitives.

- **Fragment Shader:** The fragment shader calculates the color of each pixel and may apply texture mapping, lighting, and other shading techniques.

- **Raster Operations (Raster Ops):** This stage performs depth testing, stencil testing, and blending. It determines which fragments are drawn and in what order.

- **Frame Buffer Operations:** Finally, the results are written to the frame buffer, which is the memory representing the displayed image on the screen.

3. Data Flow in a Graphics Pipeline

Data flows through the graphics pipeline from one stage to another, and each stage processes the data and may modify it. The output of one stage becomes the input for the next. This flow of data ensures that each stage operates on the correct information and contributes to the final image.

Here's a simplified representation of the data flow in a graphics pipeline:

1. Vertex data is input into the vertex input stage.
2. The vertex shader processes vertex data and passes it to the next stage.
3. Tessellation stages (optional) may further modify the data.
4. The geometry shader (optional) operates on the data.
5. Rasterization determines which pixels are covered by primitives.
6. Fragment shader calculates pixel colors.
7. Raster Ops and depth/stencil tests are performed.
8. The result is written to the frame buffer.

4. Parallelism and Optimization

Graphics pipelines are designed to be highly parallel, allowing for the efficient use of modern GPUs, which have many cores. This parallelism enables the simultaneous processing of multiple vertices and fragments, making real-time rendering possible.

Graphics pipelines are also optimized for performance. Developers can use various techniques to streamline the pipeline, such as culling invisible objects, reducing overdraw, and applying level-of-detail (LOD) techniques.

In summary, a graphics pipeline is a series of stages through which graphics data flows to create a final image. Understanding the stages and data flow in a graphics pipeline is essential when working with Vulkan, as it provides insight into how rendering is accomplished and how to optimize the process for real-time graphics applications.

2.2 Vertex Shaders in Vulkan

Vertex shaders play a central role in the graphics pipeline, responsible for processing individual vertices of 3D objects. In Vulkan, as in many other graphics APIs, vertex shaders are a crucial component for transforming raw vertex data into their final positions on the screen. In this section, we'll delve into vertex shaders in Vulkan, exploring their purpose, structure, and how to use them effectively.

1. Purpose of Vertex Shaders

The primary purpose of a vertex shader is to perform transformations on vertex data. These transformations include:

- **Model-View-Projection (MVP) Transformation:** Converting object space coordinates to view space and then projecting them to screen space. This step positions the vertices correctly in the 3D scene.

- **Normal Transformations:** Transforming normals to ensure proper lighting calculations.

- **Other Vertex Attributes:** Modifying other vertex attributes, such as color, texture coordinates, or custom data.

Vertex shaders are programmable, allowing developers to define custom transformations and manipulate vertex data as needed. This programmability is what makes vertex shaders so powerful and versatile.

2. Structure of a Vertex Shader

In Vulkan, vertex shaders are typically written in the SPIR-V (Standard Portable Intermediate Representation for Vulkan) language. SPIR-V is a binary intermediate language used by Vulkan that allows for efficient execution on GPUs. Here's a simplified example of a vertex shader in SPIR-V assembly-like notation:

```
; Vertex Shader Example

; Input: Vertex position (vec4)

; Output: Transformed position (vec4)

; Vertex Shader Function

; Main entry point for the vertex shader

; Vertex positions are transformed using an MVP matrix

func main() {

; Load the input vertex position

; Input location is specified in the shader pipeline layout

in_position = load_input(0)

; Apply the MVP transformation

transformed_position = mvp_matrix * in_position

; Store the transformed position as output

; Output location is specified in the shader pipeline layout

store_output(0, transformed_position)

}
```

In this example, the vertex shader takes a 4D vertex position as input, applies an MVP transformation, and stores the transformed position as output. Note that the specific syntax and operations may vary depending on the shading language used (e.g., GLSL or HLSL).

3. Compiling Vertex Shaders

To use a vertex shader in a Vulkan application, you need to compile it into SPIR-V bytecode. You can do this using specialized tools like glslangValidator, which can convert shaders written in GLSL (a high-level shading language) into SPIR-V. Once compiled, you can load and use the resulting SPIR-V bytecode in your Vulkan application.

Here's an example of how you might compile a GLSL vertex shader to SPIR-V using glslangValidator:

glslangValidator -V vertex_shader.glsl -o vertex_shader.spv

This command takes the GLSL vertex shader file vertex_shader.glsl and compiles it into SPIR-V, saving the result as vertex_shader.spv.

4. Binding Vertex Shaders in Vulkan

To use a compiled vertex shader in your Vulkan application, you must create a Vulkan pipeline and specify the vertex shader as one of its stages. You do this by creating a VkPipelineShaderStageCreateInfo structure and associating it with the pipeline.

Here's a simplified example of how you might bind a vertex shader in Vulkan:

VkPipelineShaderStageCreateInfo vertexShaderStageInfo{};

```
vertexShaderStageInfo.sType                                    =
VK_STRUCTURE_TYPE_PIPELINE_SHADER_STAGE_CREATE_I

vertexShaderStageInfo.stage                                    =
VK_SHADER_STAGE_VERTEX_BIT;

vertexShaderStageInfo.module = vertexShaderModule; // Compiled
SPIR-V module

vertexShaderStageInfo.pName = "main"; // Entry point function
name

// Create other shader stages (e.g., fragment shader) similarly

VkPipelineShaderStageCreateInfo         shaderStages[]         =
{vertexShaderStageInfo, /*... other stages ... */};

VkPipelineCreateInfo pipelineInfo{};

pipelineInfo.stageCount = 2; // Number of shader stages

pipelineInfo.pStages = shaderStages; // Array of shader stage info

// Create the Vulkan pipeline with the specified shader stages

if (vkCreateGraphicsPipelines(device, VK_NULL_HANDLE, 1,
&pipelineInfo, nullptr, &pipeline) != VK_SUCCESS) {

// Handle pipeline creation failure

}
```

In this example, we create a VkPipelineShaderStageCreateInfo structure for the vertex shader, specifying its stage, compiled SPIR-V module, and entry point function name. We then include this structure in the array of shader stages when creating the Vulkan pipeline.

With the vertex shader bound to the pipeline, you're ready to use it in your rendering process. The vertex shader will be invoked for each vertex in your geometry, performing the necessary transformations and producing the transformed vertex positions for further stages in the pipeline.

Understanding vertex shaders and how to use them effectively is essential for developing graphics applications with Vulkan. These shaders allow you to manipulate vertex data and prepare it for rendering, making them a critical component of the graphics pipeline.

2.3 Fragment Shaders and Rasterization

In the graphics pipeline, after vertices have been transformed by the vertex shader and primitive assembly has taken place, the next critical stage is the fragment shader. Fragment shaders are responsible for determining the color and other attributes of each pixel, also known as fragments, in the rasterized primitives. In this section, we'll explore fragment shaders, their role in Vulkan, and the process of rasterization.

1. Purpose of Fragment Shaders

Fragment shaders are the pixel-level counterparts of vertex shaders. While vertex shaders operate on vertices, fragment shaders operate on individual fragments generated during the rasterization process. Their primary purpose is to determine the final color of each pixel on the screen.

In addition to color, fragment shaders can compute other attributes, such as depth values for depth testing, texture coordinates for texture sampling, and custom per-pixel data for various effects.

2. Rasterization

Before we delve deeper into fragment shaders, let's understand the rasterization process, as it directly affects the input to fragment shaders. Rasterization is the process of converting geometric primitives (such as triangles or lines) into individual pixels on the screen.

During rasterization:

- The vertices of the primitive, previously transformed by the vertex shader, are converted into fragments based on their position within the primitive and the screen's resolution.

- Each fragment represents a pixel on the screen, and its position, depth, and other attributes are interpolated from the vertices.

- Fragments that fall within the primitive's boundaries are processed by the fragment shader, while fragments outside the primitive are discarded.

3. Structure of a Fragment Shader

Fragment shaders in Vulkan, like vertex shaders, are typically written in the SPIR-V shading language. A fragment shader's main task is to determine the color of the fragment, which will be displayed on the screen. Here's a simplified example of a fragment shader:

; Fragment Shader Example

; Input: Interpolated data from vertex shader

; Output: Fragment color (vec4)

```
; Fragment Shader Function

; Main entry point for the fragment shader

func main() {

; Interpolated data from the vertex shader

interpolated_color = load_input(0)

interpolated_texture_coords = load_input(1)

; Sample a texture using the interpolated texture coordinates

texture_color = texture_sampler(interpolated_texture_coords)

; Combine the interpolated color and texture color

final_color = interpolated_color * texture_color

; Store the final color as output

store_output(0, final_color)

}
```

In this example, the fragment shader takes interpolated data from the vertex shader, which may include color and texture coordinates. It then samples a texture using the interpolated texture coordinates and combines it with the interpolated color to produce the final fragment color.

4. Raster Operations (Raster Ops)

After fragment shaders have determined the color and other attributes of fragments, the raster operations stage takes place. Raster operations include depth testing, stencil testing, and blending.

- **Depth Testing:** Depth testing compares the depth value of the fragment with the depth value already stored in the depth buffer. If the fragment is closer to the camera than the existing depth value, it is considered "in front" and is written to the frame buffer. Otherwise, it is discarded.

- **Stencil Testing:** Stencil testing involves comparing a fragment's stencil value with the stencil buffer's value. Stencil testing can be used for various effects, such as masking or creating stencil shadows.

- **Blending:** Blending combines the fragment's color with the color already in the frame buffer. This is crucial for transparency effects and rendering techniques like alpha blending.

5. Output to the Frame Buffer

Finally, fragments that have passed all previous stages are written to the frame buffer. The frame buffer is the memory area representing the final image that will be displayed on the screen. Each fragment contributes its color (and possibly other attributes) to the corresponding pixel in the frame buffer.

In summary, fragment shaders play a critical role in determining the color and attributes of individual pixels in the rasterized primitives. They operate on fragments generated during the rasterization process and are essential for rendering realistic and visually appealing graphics in Vulkan applications. Understanding fragment shaders and how they integrate with rasterization and other pipeline stages is key to creating stunning visual effects in graphics programming.

2.4 Combining Shaders in Pipelines

In Vulkan, shaders are essential components of the graphics pipeline, responsible for performing various tasks, including vertex transformations, fragment color calculations, and more. To create a complete graphics application, shaders must be organized and combined into pipelines. In this section, we will explore the process of combining shaders in Vulkan pipelines and how these pipelines are used in rendering.

1. Shader Modules

Before shaders can be used in pipelines, they need to be compiled into Vulkan-compatible shader modules. Shader modules represent the compiled bytecode of shaders in a format that Vulkan understands. These modules can be created and loaded into your Vulkan application.

Here's a simplified example of how to create and load a shader module in Vulkan:

```cpp
VkShaderModule createShaderModule(VkDevice device, const std::vector<uint32_t>& code) {

VkShaderModuleCreateInfo createInfo{};

createInfo.sType = VK_STRUCTURE_TYPE_SHADER_MODULE_CREATE_INFO;

createInfo.codeSize = code.size() * sizeof(uint32_t);

createInfo.pCode = code.data();

VkShaderModule shaderModule;
```

```cpp
if    (vkCreateShaderModule(device,    &createInfo,    nullptr,
&shaderModule) != VK_SUCCESS) {

// Handle shader module creation failure

}

return shaderModule;

}
```

In this example, we create a shader module using the bytecode of the shader stored in a vector of uint32_t.

2. Shader Stages in Pipelines

Vulkan pipelines are created by specifying shader stages. Each shader stage corresponds to a particular shader type, such as vertex, fragment, or geometry shader. When creating a pipeline, you specify which shader modules should be used for each stage.

Here's a simplified example of how to specify shader stages when creating a Vulkan graphics pipeline:

```cpp
VkPipelineShaderStageCreateInfo vertexShaderStageInfo{};

vertexShaderStageInfo.sType                                        =
VK_STRUCTURE_TYPE_PIPELINE_SHADER_STAGE_CREATE_I

vertexShaderStageInfo.stage                                        =
VK_SHADER_STAGE_VERTEX_BIT;

vertexShaderStageInfo.module = vertexShaderModule; // Shader
module for vertex shader

vertexShaderStageInfo.pName = "main"; // Entry point function
name
```

```cpp
VkPipelineShaderStageCreateInfo fragmentShaderStageInfo{};

fragmentShaderStageInfo.sType =
VK_STRUCTURE_TYPE_PIPELINE_SHADER_STAGE_CREAT

fragmentShaderStageInfo.stage =
VK_SHADER_STAGE_FRAGMENT_BIT;

fragmentShaderStageInfo.module = fragmentShaderModule; // Shader module for fragment shader

fragmentShaderStageInfo.pName = "main"; // Entry point function name

// ... Other shader stages (e.g., geometry shader) can be added similarly

VkPipelineShaderStageCreateInfo shaderStages[] = {vertexShaderStageInfo, fragmentShaderStageInfo, /* ... other stages ... */};

VkPipelineCreateInfo pipelineInfo{};

pipelineInfo.stageCount = 2; // Number of shader stages

pipelineInfo.pStages = shaderStages; // Array of shader stage info

// Create the Vulkan graphics pipeline with the specified shader stages

if (vkCreateGraphicsPipelines(device, VK_NULL_HANDLE, 1, &pipelineInfo, nullptr, &pipeline) != VK_SUCCESS) {

// Handle pipeline creation failure

}
```

In this example, we specify two shader stages: vertex and fragment shaders. We associate the corresponding shader modules with each stage and provide the entry point function names.

3. Shader Inputs and Outputs

Shaders communicate with each other and the graphics pipeline through inputs and outputs. For example, data passed from the vertex shader to the fragment shader is interpolated and passed as inputs to the fragment shader. Similarly, fragment shaders output colors, which are then written to the frame buffer.

You can define input and output variables in your shaders to facilitate data transfer between shader stages. Vulkan provides mechanisms for specifying input and output variables and their locations.

4. Shader Specialization

Shader specialization allows you to customize shader behavior without creating entirely separate shader modules. With specialization constants, you can change shader behavior at runtime by providing specific values for these constants when creating a pipeline. This can be useful for creating flexible and efficient shaders.

5. Dynamic Pipeline Creation

In some cases, you may need to create pipelines dynamically based on specific requirements. Vulkan allows you to modify shaders, shader modules, and pipeline configurations at runtime, providing the flexibility needed to adapt to changing rendering scenarios.

In conclusion, combining shaders in Vulkan pipelines is a fundamental aspect of graphics programming. Shader modules represent the compiled bytecode of shaders, and Vulkan pipelines are configured with specific shader stages. Shaders communicate with each other and the pipeline through inputs and outputs. Vulkan's support for shader specialization and dynamic pipeline creation enables developers to create versatile and efficient graphics applications that can adapt to a wide range of rendering scenarios. Understanding how to organize and use shaders in Vulkan pipelines is essential for creating complex and visually appealing graphics applications.

2.5 Optimizing Graphics Pipelines

Optimizing graphics pipelines is a critical aspect of developing high-performance graphics applications in Vulkan. Efficient pipelines can make the difference between smooth, responsive graphics and slow, laggy rendering. In this section, we'll explore various optimization techniques and best practices for Vulkan graphics pipelines.

1. Pipeline State Objects (PSOs)

Pipeline State Objects (PSOs) in Vulkan encapsulate the configuration of graphics and compute pipelines. Creating and switching between PSOs can be expensive, so it's essential to minimize PSO changes when rendering multiple objects with similar characteristics. Reuse PSOs whenever possible to reduce overhead.

2. Descriptor Sets and Layouts

Descriptor sets are used to bind resources (e.g., textures, buffers) to shader stages. Efficiently managing descriptor sets can significantly impact performance. Consider the following tips:

- Group resources with similar lifetimes in the same descriptor set to reduce set updates.

- Use descriptor set layouts and descriptor set pools efficiently to minimize descriptor allocation overhead.

3. Dynamic State

Vulkan allows for dynamic state changes, which can be more efficient than recreating pipelines with different states. For example, you can change viewport or scissor settings dynamically instead of creating separate pipelines for each configuration.

4. Pipelining and Multithreading

Modern GPUs are highly parallel, so take advantage of parallelism:

- Use command buffers effectively to record and submit multiple rendering commands in parallel.

- Consider using multiple threads for command buffer recording and submission when dealing with complex scenes.

5. Culling and LOD Techniques

Implement culling techniques like frustum culling and occlusion culling to skip rendering objects that are not visible. Additionally, use Level-of-Detail (LOD) techniques to reduce the complexity of distant objects.

6. Vertex and Index Buffers

Optimize vertex and index buffers:

- Use vertex and index buffer binding efficiently to minimize data transfers.

- Consider using Vertex Buffer Objects (VBOs) and Index Buffer Objects (IBOs) for better memory management.

7. Shader Optimization

Shader performance is crucial. Follow these shader optimization tips:

- Minimize branching in shaders to avoid divergent execution paths.

- Optimize texture sampling by using texture atlases and mipmapping.

- Avoid unnecessary calculations and memory accesses.

- Profile and test shaders to identify bottlenecks.

8. Render Passes

Vulkan render passes define how rendering operations interact with attachments (e.g., frame buffer images). Optimize render passes:

- Use subpasses within a render pass when possible to reduce memory bandwidth.

- Avoid render pass creation during runtime. Define render passes at initialization.

9. Memory Management

Efficient memory management is crucial for pipeline performance:

- Use Vulkan's memory management features like memory pools and transient memory.

- Minimize memory transfers between the CPU and GPU by keeping data on the GPU as much as possible.

10. Validation Layers

While validation layers are essential during development for debugging, disable them in production builds to reduce overhead.

11. GPU Profiling

Use GPU profiling tools provided by GPU vendors to identify performance bottlenecks. Profiling can help pinpoint areas that require optimization.

12. Resource Recycling

Reusing resources like buffers and textures can reduce memory allocations and deallocations, improving performance.

13. Pipeline Caching

Cache pipeline objects to avoid recreating them when they have the same configuration.

14. Push Constants

Push constants are a way to pass small amounts of data to shaders quickly. Use them for frequently changing data instead of using uniform buffers.

15. Shader Modules

Reuse compiled shader modules to avoid unnecessary recompilation.

16. Reduce Overdraw

Minimize overdraw (rendering pixels that are later hidden) by using techniques like depth testing and occlusion queries.

17. GPU Synchronization

Avoid excessive synchronization between the CPU and GPU, as it can introduce delays. Use synchronization wisely, and use Vulkan's asynchronous capabilities.

18. Driver Updates

Keep GPU drivers up-to-date, as newer drivers often include performance improvements and bug fixes.

19. Profiling and Benchmarking

Regularly profile and benchmark your application to identify performance issues and track improvements over time.

Optimizing Vulkan graphics pipelines is an ongoing process that requires careful analysis, testing, and iteration. By implementing these best practices and techniques, you can maximize the performance of your Vulkan applications and deliver smooth, responsive graphics experiences to users.

Chapter 3: Vulkan Basics

3.1 Vulkan Objects and Layers

Vulkan introduces several key concepts and abstractions that form the foundation of the API. Understanding these concepts is crucial for effectively using Vulkan to develop graphics applications. In this section, we will explore Vulkan objects and layers, providing an overview of the essential elements that make up the Vulkan ecosystem.

1. Vulkan Objects

Vulkan represents GPU resources and operations using various objects. These objects are created, configured, and managed to perform rendering and compute tasks efficiently. Some of the essential Vulkan objects include:

- **Instance:** The starting point for interacting with the Vulkan API. It represents the connection between the application and the Vulkan runtime. Each Vulkan application typically has one instance.

- **Physical Device:** A physical GPU device present in the system. Vulkan applications query and select a physical device to use for rendering. A system may have multiple physical devices, each with its capabilities.

- **Device:** A logical representation of a physical device, including its selected features and properties. Most Vulkan operations are performed through a logical device, which manages resources and queues.

- **Queue:** Queues are used for issuing commands to the GPU. Vulkan devices have multiple queues, each with a specific purpose (e.g., graphics queue, compute queue).

- **Command Buffer:** Command buffers contain sequences of rendering and compute commands that are executed on the GPU. Applications record commands into command buffers and submit them for execution.

- **Framebuffer:** Framebuffers represent the attachments and configurations needed for rendering a frame. They are used to specify where the output of rendering operations should be written.

- **Swap Chain:** Swap chains are used for presenting rendered images to the screen. They manage the display of images in a way that avoids tearing and ensures synchronization with the screen's refresh rate.

- **Descriptor Sets:** Descriptor sets are used to bind resources like textures and buffers to shaders. They facilitate communication between the CPU and GPU about which resources are accessed during rendering.

- **Pipeline:** Pipelines define how rendering and compute operations are processed. They include graphics pipelines for rendering and compute pipelines for non-rendering tasks.

- **Semaphore and Fence:** Semaphores and fences are synchronization primitives used to coordinate work between CPU and GPU or between GPU queues.

2. Layers and Extensions

Vulkan introduces the concept of layers and extensions to provide flexibility and extensibility:

- **Layers:** Layers are optional components that can be added to the Vulkan runtime to perform validation, debugging, and other tasks. Validation layers, for example, help identify errors and misuses in Vulkan applications during development.

- **Extensions:** Extensions add extra functionality to Vulkan. They allow Vulkan to be extended with new features without modifying the core API. Extensions can be platform-specific or vendor-specific.

3. Instance Creation

Creating a Vulkan instance is the first step in setting up a Vulkan application. During instance creation, you specify the application and engine information, enable validation layers for debugging, and request specific Vulkan extensions. Here's a simplified example of instance creation:

```
VkApplicationInfo appInfo{};

appInfo.sType                                                    =
VK_STRUCTURE_TYPE_APPLICATION_INFO;

appInfo.pApplicationName = "My Vulkan App";

appInfo.applicationVersion = VK_MAKE_VERSION(1, 0, 0);

appInfo.pEngineName = "My Vulkan Engine";

appInfo.engineVersion = VK_MAKE_VERSION(1, 0, 0);
```

```cpp
appInfo.apiVersion = VK_API_VERSION_1_0;

VkInstanceCreateInfo createInfo{};

createInfo.sType                                    =
VK_STRUCTURE_TYPE_INSTANCE_CREATE_INFO;

createInfo.pApplicationInfo = &appInfo;

// Enable validation layers (only in debug builds)

#ifdef NDEBUG

const          char*          validationLayers[]    =
{"VK_LAYER_KHRONOS_validation"};

createInfo.enabledLayerCount = 1;

createInfo.ppEnabledLayerNames = validationLayers;

#else

createInfo.enabledLayerCount = 0;

createInfo.ppEnabledLayerNames = nullptr;

#endif

// Specify required extensions

uint32_t glfwExtensionCount = 0;

const char** glfwExtensions;

glfwExtensions                                      =
glfwGetRequiredInstanceExtensions(&glfwExtensionCount);

createInfo.enabledExtensionCount = glfwExtensionCount;
```

```
createInfo.ppEnabledExtensionNames = glfwExtensions;

// Create Vulkan instance

VkInstance instance;

if (vkCreateInstance(&createInfo, nullptr, &instance) !=
VK_SUCCESS) {

// Handle instance creation failure

}
```

In this example, we configure the application and engine information, enable validation layers (only in debug builds), and specify the required extensions for GLFW, a popular windowing library.

Understanding Vulkan objects and layers is fundamental for working with the API effectively. These objects represent GPU resources and operations, while layers provide additional functionality and validation. Properly configuring the Vulkan instance is the first step in setting up a Vulkan application for graphics rendering.

3.2 Command Buffers and Queues

In Vulkan, command buffers and queues are fundamental components of the rendering process. They play a crucial role in issuing commands to the GPU, allowing developers to control the execution of rendering and compute operations. In this section, we'll explore the concepts of command buffers and queues in Vulkan and how they work together to orchestrate GPU tasks.

1. Command Buffers

Command buffers in Vulkan are objects used to record sequences of commands that will be executed on the GPU. These commands can include rendering operations, resource updates, and synchronization instructions. There are two types of command buffers in Vulkan:

- **Primary Command Buffers:** Primary command buffers are top-level command buffers that can be submitted directly to queues for execution. They typically contain the main rendering commands for a frame.

- **Secondary Command Buffers:** Secondary command buffers are sub-level command buffers that can be included within primary command buffers. They are useful for encapsulating reusable rendering tasks or complex objects within a scene.

2. Command Buffer Recording

Recording commands into command buffers is a critical part of the rendering process. Vulkan provides a rich set of commands for tasks like drawing, clearing framebuffers, and updating resources. Command buffer recording follows these steps:

- **Begin Recording:** Before recording commands, a command buffer must be put into the recording state using the vkBeginCommandBuffer function.

- **Recording Commands:** During the recording phase, developers issue Vulkan commands to the command buffer. For example, to draw a triangle, you would use the vkCmdDraw command.

- **End Recording:** Once all desired commands are recorded, the command buffer is closed using the vkEndCommandBuffer function.

3. Command Buffer Submission

Command buffers are submitted to Vulkan queues for execution. Vulkan supports multiple types of queues, each with its capabilities and purposes. Common queue types include:

- **Graphics Queue:** Used for graphics rendering commands.

- **Compute Queue:** Used for compute shader and general computation tasks.

- **Transfer Queue:** Used for data transfers between CPU and GPU.

To submit a command buffer to a queue, you use the vkQueueSubmit function. Submission allows multiple command buffers to be processed in parallel, providing opportunities for optimization and parallelism.

4. Synchronization and Semaphores

To ensure correct execution and avoid data hazards, Vulkan provides synchronization mechanisms. Synchronization is essential when working with command buffers and queues. Key synchronization objects include:

- **Fences:** Fences are used to synchronize CPU and GPU operations. They can be signaled by the GPU when a command buffer completes execution, allowing the CPU to wait for GPU tasks to finish.

- **Semaphores:** Semaphores are used to synchronize operations within the GPU and between queues. They are often used for ensuring correct rendering order or managing resource transitions.

5. Command Buffer Lifecycle

Command buffers in Vulkan have a well-defined lifecycle:

- **Recording Phase:** During this phase, command buffers are in the recording state, and commands can be recorded into them.

- **Execution Phase:** Command buffers can be submitted to queues for execution during this phase.

- **Resetting Phase:** After execution, command buffers can be reset to the recording state for reuse. This is more efficient than creating new command buffers for each frame.

6. Example of Command Buffer Recording

Here's a simplified example of recording a primary command buffer in Vulkan:

```
// Begin command buffer recording

VkCommandBufferBeginInfo beginInfo{};

beginInfo.sType = VK_STRUCTURE_TYPE_COMMAND_BUFFER_BEGIN_INFO;
beginInfo.flags = 0; // Optional flags for special behaviors
```

```
beginInfo.pInheritanceInfo = nullptr; // For secondary command
buffers (nullptr for primary)

vkBeginCommandBuffer(commandBuffer, &beginInfo);

// Record rendering commands (e.g., drawing)

vkCmdBeginRenderPass(commandBuffer,          &renderPassInfo,
VK_SUBPASS_CONTENTS_INLINE);

// Issue drawing commands here

vkCmdDraw(commandBuffer,      vertexCount,      instanceCount,
firstVertex, firstInstance);

vkCmdEndRenderPass(commandBuffer);

// End command buffer recording

if (vkEndCommandBuffer(commandBuffer) != VK_SUCCESS) {

// Handle command buffer recording failure

}
```

In this example, we begin recording a primary command buffer, record rendering commands within a render pass, and end command buffer recording. The recorded commands can be submitted to a graphics queue for execution.

Command buffers and queues are fundamental to Vulkan's approach to GPU rendering. Understanding how to record and manage command buffers, as well as how to use queues for execution, is crucial for efficient graphics programming in Vulkan. These concepts allow developers to harness the power of modern GPUs for high-performance rendering.

3.3 Memory Management in Vulkan

Efficient memory management is a critical aspect of Vulkan programming. Vulkan provides explicit control over memory allocation and usage, allowing developers to optimize memory usage for their specific rendering needs. In this section, we will explore the memory management system in Vulkan and discuss best practices for handling memory efficiently.

1. Memory Heaps and Memory Types

In Vulkan, physical device memory is organized into memory heaps and memory types. Memory heaps are large blocks of memory with specific properties, such as device-local, host-visible, and coherent. Memory types, on the other hand, are defined by combining properties from one or more memory heaps. For example, a memory type can be device-local and host-coherent.

When allocating memory for resources like buffers and textures, developers need to choose the appropriate memory type based on their requirements, such as read/write access and memory access patterns.

2. Memory Allocation

Vulkan provides mechanisms for allocating and managing memory, primarily through the vkAllocateMemory and vkFreeMemory functions. To allocate memory, developers need to specify the memory type, size, and alignment requirements. It's essential to allocate memory efficiently to avoid fragmentation and maximize memory utilization.

3. Resource Memory Binding

Once memory is allocated, it needs to be bound to Vulkan resources like buffers and images. This binding process is essential for accessing and manipulating data within these resources. Memory binding is performed using the vkBindBufferMemory and vkBindImageMemory functions.

4. Memory Mapping

To read or write data from CPU code, Vulkan provides memory mapping. Memory mapping allows developers to access device memory from the CPU and perform operations like data initialization or reading the results of rendering operations. Memory mapping is performed using the vkMapMemory and vkUnmapMemory functions.

5. Buffer Usage and Memory Barriers

Vulkan requires developers to manage memory barriers explicitly. Memory barriers ensure proper synchronization between CPU and GPU access to memory. When transitioning data between different usages (e.g., from vertex data to shader uniform data), memory barriers are used to guarantee the visibility of data changes.

6. Staging Buffers

Staging buffers are temporary buffers used for efficient data transfer between CPU and GPU memory. When updating data frequently, it's more efficient to write changes to a staging buffer and then transfer the data to the final resource using memory barriers. This reduces the overhead of frequent memory mapping and unmapping.

7. Memory Pools

Vulkan allows developers to create memory pools, which are collections of memory allocated from the same memory type. Memory pools can help reduce memory allocation overhead by allocating and freeing memory from a pre-allocated pool, rather than requesting individual memory allocations.

8. Suballocation

Suballocation is a technique used to efficiently manage memory within a larger memory allocation. For example, instead of allocating separate memory blocks for small objects, developers can suballocate regions within a larger memory block. This reduces memory fragmentation and improves memory utilization.

9. Memory Budget and Monitoring

Vulkan provides mechanisms for querying the available memory and monitoring memory usage. This information can be crucial for optimizing resource management and avoiding out-of-memory errors.

10. Device-Local and Host-Visible Memory

Understanding the difference between device-local and host-visible memory is essential. Device-local memory is generally faster to access by the GPU but not directly accessible by the CPU. Host-visible memory can be accessed by both the CPU and GPU but may have slightly higher latency for GPU access.

11. Memory Allocation Best Practices

To optimize memory management in Vulkan, consider the following best practices:

- Allocate memory in larger chunks to reduce memory allocation overhead.

- Use memory pools for frequently allocated resources.

- Avoid excessive memory mapping and unmapping; prefer staging buffers for data transfers.

- Carefully manage memory barriers to ensure proper synchronization.

- Use suballocation for small, frequently used memory allocations.

- Monitor memory usage and be mindful of memory budgets.

Efficient memory management is a key aspect of achieving high-performance rendering in Vulkan. By carefully managing memory types, allocation, and synchronization, developers can make the most of the available hardware resources while avoiding common memory-related performance issues.

3.4 Synchronization and Semaphores

Synchronization is a fundamental aspect of Vulkan programming to ensure that rendering operations proceed in a coordinated and predictable manner. Vulkan provides mechanisms for managing synchronization between CPU and GPU and among different GPU operations. Semaphores are key components in Vulkan's synchronization system. In this section, we will explore synchronization and the use of semaphores in Vulkan.

1. Why Synchronization Is Necessary

Modern GPUs perform rendering and computation tasks in parallel with the CPU. To maintain data integrity and avoid race conditions, synchronization is required. Vulkan applications need to control the order of execution of GPU commands, ensuring that one set of commands doesn't read or write data while another set is modifying the same data.

2. Vulkan Synchronization Primitives

Vulkan provides several synchronization primitives to control the flow of operations:

- **Fences:** Fences are binary synchronization objects that signal when GPU commands have completed execution. They are typically used to synchronize CPU and GPU operations. For example, a fence can be signaled when a command buffer has finished rendering.

- **Semaphores:** Semaphores are similar to fences but are used for synchronization within the GPU. They signal the completion of specific GPU operations and can be used to coordinate between different queues or stages of a rendering pipeline.

- **Events:** Events are more flexible synchronization objects that can be set and reset by the CPU or GPU. They allow conditional synchronization and can be used to synchronize GPU operations based on specific conditions.

3. Semaphore Usage

Semaphores are commonly used to synchronize rendering tasks in Vulkan. Here's how they are typically used:

- **Acquisition Semaphores:** Before rendering a frame, a semaphore is used to signal that the rendering task has completed and the next frame can begin rendering. This ensures that the CPU doesn't start rendering the next frame until the previous one has finished.

- **Presentation Semaphores:** After a frame has been rendered, a presentation semaphore is used to signal that the image is ready for presentation on the screen. This synchronization step ensures that the image isn't presented before it's fully rendered.

- **Queue Family Ownership Transfer:** When using multiple queues (e.g., graphics and presentation queues), semaphores are used to transfer ownership of resources between different queue families. This ensures that resources are accessed and modified by the correct queues.

4. Semaphore Creation and Usage

Creating and using semaphores in Vulkan involves the following steps:

- **Semaphore Creation:** Semaphores are created using the vkCreateSemaphore function. For example:

```
VkSemaphoreCreateInfo semaphoreInfo{};

semaphoreInfo.sType                                    =
VK_STRUCTURE_TYPE_SEMAPHORE_CREATE_INFO;
```

```
VkSemaphore semaphore;
```

if (vkCreateSemaphore(device, &semaphoreInfo, **nullptr**, &semaphore) != VK_SUCCESS) {

// Handle semaphore creation failure

```
}
```

• **Semaphore Usage:** Semaphores are used in the submission of command buffers to queues. For example, when submitting a command buffer for rendering:

```
VkSubmitInfo submitInfo{};
```

```
submitInfo.sType                              =
VK_STRUCTURE_TYPE_SUBMIT_INFO;
```

// Set the wait semaphore to signal that the previous frame is complete

```
submitInfo.waitSemaphoreCount = 1;
```

```
submitInfo.pWaitSemaphores                    =
&imageAvailableSemaphore;
```

// Set the signal semaphore to indicate that rendering is complete

```
submitInfo.signalSemaphoreCount = 1;
```

```
submitInfo.pSignalSemaphores                  =
&renderFinishedSemaphore;
```

// Submit the command buffer to the graphics queue

```
if (vkQueueSubmit(graphicsQueue, 1, &submitInfo,
VK_NULL_HANDLE) != VK_SUCCESS) {

// Handle submission failure

}
```

- **Semaphore Cleanup:** After they are no longer needed, semaphores should be destroyed using the vkDestroySemaphore function.

5. Pipeline Barriers

In addition to semaphores, pipeline barriers are used to control synchronization between different stages of the graphics pipeline. Pipeline barriers allow you to specify memory dependencies and execution dependencies between sets of commands.

6. Synchronization Best Practices

To optimize synchronization in Vulkan, consider the following best practices:

- Use semaphores to synchronize rendering tasks and ensure proper order of execution.

- Minimize the use of pipeline barriers, as they can be expensive. Use them only when necessary to avoid over-synchronization.

- Avoid unnecessary synchronization, as it can impact performance. Vulkan provides mechanisms to control synchronization at a fine-grained level, allowing for efficient synchronization management.

Synchronization and semaphores play a vital role in ensuring that Vulkan applications execute correctly and efficiently. Proper synchronization ensures that rendering and compute tasks are executed in the correct order, leading to visually consistent and predictable results. By understanding and managing synchronization in Vulkan, developers can harness the full potential of the API for high-performance graphics rendering.

3.5 Debugging and Validation Layers

Debugging is a crucial part of Vulkan development, as it helps identify and rectify errors and issues in your graphics applications. Vulkan provides a robust system for debugging and validation through validation layers. In this section, we will explore the role of debugging and validation layers in Vulkan and how they can assist developers in building stable and error-free applications.

1. Why Debugging is Important

Graphics programming can be complex, with many opportunities for errors, including memory leaks, resource management issues, and synchronization problems. Detecting and diagnosing these issues can be challenging, especially when they lead to undefined behavior or crashes. Effective debugging is essential for the development of reliable and performant Vulkan applications.

2. Validation Layers

Vulkan validation layers are optional components that can be enabled during Vulkan instance creation. They provide extensive runtime validation and error checking, helping developers catch and address issues early in the development process. Validation layers offer the following benefits:

- **Error Detection:** Validation layers detect common errors, such as invalid API usage, incorrect state transitions, and resource leaks. When an error is detected, the application receives detailed error messages.

- **Performance Warnings:** Validation layers can provide performance warnings and suggestions for optimization. This helps developers identify potential bottlenecks and inefficiencies in their code.

- **Compatibility Checks:** Validation layers can verify that your application complies with the Vulkan specification and works correctly on different hardware and drivers.

3. Enabling Validation Layers

To enable validation layers in Vulkan, you need to specify them during Vulkan instance creation. Here's an example of how to enable validation layers:

```cpp
VkInstanceCreateInfo createInfo{};

createInfo.sType = VK_STRUCTURE_TYPE_INSTANCE_CREATE_INFO;

// Enable validation layers (only in debug builds)

#ifdef NDEBUG

const char* validationLayers[] = {"VK_LAYER_KHRONOS_validation"};

createInfo.enabledLayerCount = 1;

createInfo.ppEnabledLayerNames = validationLayers;
```

```
#else

createInfo.enabledLayerCount = 0;

createInfo.ppEnabledLayerNames = nullptr;

#endif
```

// Specify required extensions and create Vulkan instance

// (similar to previous Vulkan instance creation examples)

In this example, validation layers are enabled only in debug builds to avoid their overhead in release builds.

4. Common Validation Layer Messages

When using validation layers, you may encounter various types of messages, including:

- **Validation Errors:** These messages indicate critical issues that violate Vulkan's rules. They can lead to Vulkan functions returning error codes or undefined behavior.

- **Warnings:** Warnings indicate potential problems or inefficient usage but do not necessarily result in errors. Addressing warnings can improve your application's performance and stability.

- **Informational Messages:** These messages provide additional information about Vulkan's behavior and can be useful for debugging and understanding the API's operation.

5. Debugging Tools

In addition to validation layers, Vulkan developers can use various debugging tools and utilities provided by GPU vendors, such as:

- **RenderDoc:** A popular open-source graphics debugging tool that allows you to capture frames, inspect resources, and analyze rendering pipelines.

- **NVIDIA Nsight:** A suite of tools for GPU debugging and profiling, including Nsight Graphics and Nsight Compute.

- **AMD Radeon Developer Tools:** A collection of tools for AMD GPUs, including Radeon GPU Profiler (RGP) and Radeon Memory Visualizer (RMV).

- **Vulkan Debugging Extensions:** Some vendors offer Vulkan debugging extensions that provide advanced debugging and profiling capabilities.

6. Debugging Best Practices

To make the most of debugging and validation layers in Vulkan, consider the following best practices:

- **Enable validation layers during development:** Always enable validation layers during development and testing to catch errors and issues early.

- **Regularly check for validation messages:** Periodically check the validation layer messages and address any reported issues promptly.

- **Use debugging tools:** Utilize external debugging tools like RenderDoc or vendor-specific tools to inspect rendering frames and identify performance bottlenecks.

- **Profile and optimize:** Profiling your application using GPU-specific tools can help identify performance bottlenecks and areas for optimization.

- **Monitor memory usage:** Keep an eye on memory usage and resource management to prevent memory leaks and ensure efficient memory utilization.

Debugging and validation layers are essential components of Vulkan development, providing tools and mechanisms to identify and address errors and issues in graphics applications. By embracing these debugging practices, developers can create robust and high-performance Vulkan applications that deliver a smooth and error-free user experience.

Chapter 4: Building Your First Vulkan Application

4.1 Creating a Vulkan Instance

Creating a Vulkan instance is the first step in setting up a Vulkan application. The instance represents the connection between your application and the Vulkan runtime, and it is required to interact with the Vulkan API. In this section, we will walk through the process of creating a Vulkan instance, including specifying application information, enabling validation layers for debugging, and requesting Vulkan extensions.

1. Vulkan Application Info

Before creating a Vulkan instance, you need to provide information about your application. This information is encapsulated in a VkApplicationInfo structure, which includes details like the application name, version, and engine name and version:

```cpp
VkApplicationInfo appInfo{};

appInfo.sType = VK_STRUCTURE_TYPE_APPLICATION_INFO;

appInfo.pApplicationName = "My Vulkan App";

appInfo.applicationVersion = VK_MAKE_VERSION(1, 0, 0);

appInfo.pEngineName = "My Vulkan Engine";

appInfo.engineVersion = VK_MAKE_VERSION(1, 0, 0);

appInfo.apiVersion = VK_API_VERSION_1_0;
```

In the code above, we specify the application and engine names, along with their respective versions. The apiVersion field should typically be set to the Vulkan API version you intend to use.

2. Vulkan Instance Creation

To create a Vulkan instance, you need to populate a VkInstanceCreateInfo structure with information about the application and any desired extensions or validation layers:

```
VkInstanceCreateInfo createInfo{};

createInfo.sType                                        = VK_STRUCTURE_TYPE_INSTANCE_CREATE_INFO;

createInfo.pApplicationInfo = &appInfo;
```

In this example, we set the pApplicationInfo field to the previously defined VkApplicationInfo structure.

3. Enabling Validation Layers

Validation layers are crucial for debugging Vulkan applications during development. They help identify common errors and misuse of the Vulkan API. To enable validation layers, you can define an array of layer names and add it to the VkInstanceCreateInfo structure:

```
const         char*         validationLayers[]         = {"VK_LAYER_KHRONOS_validation"};

#ifdef NDEBUG

createInfo.enabledLayerCount = 0;

createInfo.ppEnabledLayerNames = nullptr;
```

```
#else
```

```
createInfo.enabledLayerCount = sizeof(validationLayers) / sizeof(validationLayers[0]);
```

```
createInfo.ppEnabledLayerNames = validationLayers;
```

```
#endif
```

In this code snippet, we define an array of validation layer names. In release builds (defined by the NDEBUG macro), we disable validation layers to optimize performance. However, in debug builds, we enable the specified validation layers.

4. Requesting Vulkan Extensions

Vulkan extensions provide additional functionality beyond the core API. You may need to request specific extensions based on your application's requirements, such as window system integration. To request extensions, you can set the enabledExtensionCount and ppEnabledExtensionNames fields in the VkInstanceCreateInfo structure:

```
uint32_t glfwExtensionCount = 0;
```

```
const char** glfwExtensions;
```

```
glfwExtensions = glfwGetRequiredInstanceExtensions(&glfwExtensionCount);
```

```
createInfo.enabledExtensionCount = glfwExtensionCount;
```

```
createInfo.ppEnabledExtensionNames = glfwExtensions;
```

In this code, we use GLFW, a popular windowing library, to retrieve the required extensions for platform-specific functionality.

5. Creating the Vulkan Instance

Finally, you can create the Vulkan instance by calling vkCreateInstance:

VkInstance instance;

if (vkCreateInstance(&createInfo, **nullptr,** &instance) != VK_SUCCESS) {

// Handle instance creation failure

}

In the event of a failure to create the instance, you should implement error handling to gracefully handle the issue.

Creating a Vulkan instance is a fundamental step in preparing your application to use Vulkan. By providing application information, enabling validation layers for debugging, and requesting the necessary extensions, you establish the foundation for interacting with the Vulkan API and building graphics applications.

4.2 Window and Surface Initialization

In a graphical application, the interaction between Vulkan and the windowing system is critical for rendering to a window or screen. To achieve this, Vulkan provides a mechanism to create a rendering surface that represents the window or display. In this section, we will explore the steps involved in initializing a window and creating a Vulkan surface for rendering.

1. Window Initialization

Before creating a Vulkan surface, you need to initialize a window or obtain a handle to an existing window. The specific steps for window initialization depend on the windowing system or framework you are using. Common libraries like GLFW, SDL, or platform-specific APIs can be used for window creation and management.

Here's a simplified example using GLFW to create a window:

```cpp
#include <GLFW/glfw3.h>

int main() {

// Initialize GLFW

if (!glfwInit()) {

// Handle initialization failure

return -1;

}

// Create a windowed mode window and its OpenGL context

GLFWwindow* window = glfwCreateWindow(800, 600, "Vulkan Window", NULL, NULL);

if (!window) {

// Handle window creation failure

glfwTerminate();

return -1;

}

// Main rendering loop

while (!glfwWindowShouldClose(window)) {
```

```
// Render here

// Swap front and back buffers

glfwSwapBuffers(window);

// Poll for and process events

glfwPollEvents();

}

// Cleanup and exit

glfwDestroyWindow(window);

glfwTerminate();

return 0;

}
```

In this example, we use GLFW to create a window with an OpenGL context. Vulkan can work alongside other graphics APIs like OpenGL, but for a pure Vulkan application, the OpenGL context is not necessary.

2. Vulkan Surface Creation

Once you have a window, you can create a Vulkan surface associated with it. The surface represents the connection between Vulkan and the windowing system and is essential for rendering.

The process of creating a Vulkan surface is platform-dependent because Vulkan must interact with the underlying windowing system. Here's an example of creating a Vulkan surface using GLFW for the X11 windowing system (Linux):

```cpp
#include <vulkan/vulkan.h>

#include <GLFW/glfw3.h>

int main() {

// Initialize GLFW

if (!glfwInit()) {

// Handle initialization failure

return -1;

}

// Create a windowed mode window and its OpenGL context

GLFWwindow* window = glfwCreateWindow(800, 600, "Vulkan
Window", NULL, NULL);

if (!window) {

// Handle window creation failure

glfwTerminate();

return -1;

}

// Create a Vulkan instance (as shown in Section 4.1)

// Create a Vulkan surface

VkSurfaceKHR surface;

if (glfwCreateWindowSurface(instance, window, nullptr, &surface)
!= VK_SUCCESS) {
```

```cpp
// Handle surface creation failure
glfwDestroyWindow(window);
glfwTerminate();
return -1;
}

// Main rendering loop (Vulkan rendering is not shown here)
// Cleanup and exit
vkDestroySurfaceKHR(instance, surface, nullptr);
glfwDestroyWindow(window);
glfwTerminate();
return 0;
}
```

In this code, after initializing the GLFW window, we create a Vulkan surface using glfwCreateWindowSurface and associate it with the Vulkan instance. The details of Vulkan instance creation (as discussed in Section 4.1) are assumed to be present in the code.

It's important to note that creating a Vulkan surface varies depending on the windowing system (e.g., X11, Wayland, Windows, macOS). You should use the appropriate platform-specific code or a library like GLFW that abstracts these details for you.

Once you have successfully created a Vulkan surface, you can use it to render graphics to the window, making it a crucial step in setting up a Vulkan application for rendering.

4.3 Swap Chain Creation

In Vulkan, the swap chain is a fundamental concept for presenting images to the screen or window. It manages the process of swapping (or presenting) rendered images to the display in a synchronized and efficient manner. In this section, we will delve into the creation of a swap chain in Vulkan, which involves defining its properties, selecting an appropriate surface format, and managing its images.

1. Swap Chain Properties

Before creating a swap chain, you need to determine its properties, such as the format of the images it will use, the presentation mode, and the extent (resolution) of the images. These properties are influenced by the capabilities of the physical device and the surface to which the swap chain will present.

Here's how you can query and set these properties:

// Query swap chain support

VkSurfaceCapabilitiesKHR capabilities;

vkGetPhysicalDeviceSurfaceCapabilitiesKHR(physicalDevice, surface, &capabilities);

// Choose a surface format

VkSurfaceFormatKHR surfaceFormat;

uint32_t formatCount;

vkGetPhysicalDeviceSurfaceFormatsKHR(physicalDevice, surface, &formatCount, **nullptr**);

if (formatCount != 0) {

```cpp
std::vector<VkSurfaceFormatKHR>
availableFormats(formatCount);

vkGetPhysicalDeviceSurfaceFormatsKHR(physicalDevice, surface,
&formatCount, availableFormats.data());

for (const auto& availableFormat : availableFormats) {

if (availableFormat.format == VK_FORMAT_B8G8R8A8_SRGB
&&                availableFormat.colorSpace                ==
VK_COLOR_SPACE_SRGB_NONLINEAR_KHR) {

surfaceFormat = availableFormat;

break;

}

}

if (surfaceFormat.format == VK_FORMAT_UNDEFINED) {

surfaceFormat = availableFormats[0];

}

}

// Choose a presentation mode

VkPresentModeKHR                presentMode                =
VK_PRESENT_MODE_FIFO_KHR; // V-Sync by default

// Choose swap chain extent (resolution)

VkExtent2D extent;

if (capabilities.currentExtent.width != UINT32_MAX) {
```

```
extent = capabilities.currentExtent;

} else {

int width, height;

glfwGetFramebufferSize(window, &width, &height);

extent.width = static_cast<uint32_t>(width);

extent.height = static_cast<uint32_t>(height);

extent.width                    =                    std::clamp(extent.width,
capabilities.minImageExtent.width,
capabilities.maxImageExtent.width);

extent.height                   =                    std::clamp(extent.height,
capabilities.minImageExtent.height,
capabilities.maxImageExtent.height);

}
```

In the code above, we first query the swap chain support and capabilities. Then, we select a suitable surface format, presentation mode (usually V-Sync), and extent based on the window size and capabilities.

2. Swap Chain Creation

With the swap chain properties defined, you can create the swap chain itself. The creation process involves specifying the properties, including the number of images in the swap chain and their format, as well as the presentation mode and extent:

```
VkSwapchainCreateInfoKHR createInfo{};
```

```cpp
createInfo.sType                                    =
VK_STRUCTURE_TYPE_SWAPCHAIN_CREATE_INFO_KHR;

createInfo.surface = surface;

createInfo.minImageCount = capabilities.minImageCount + 1;

createInfo.imageFormat = surfaceFormat.format;

createInfo.imageColorSpace = surfaceFormat.colorSpace;

createInfo.imageExtent = extent;

createInfo.imageArrayLayers = 1;

createInfo.imageUsage                               =
VK_IMAGE_USAGE_COLOR_ATTACHMENT_BIT;

// Handle case when graphics and presentation queues are different

uint32_t    queueFamilyIndices[]    =    {graphicsQueueIndex,
presentQueueIndex};

if (graphicsQueueIndex != presentQueueIndex) {

createInfo.imageSharingMode                         =
VK_SHARING_MODE_CONCURRENT;

createInfo.queueFamilyIndexCount = 2;

createInfo.pQueueFamilyIndices = queueFamilyIndices;

} else {

createInfo.imageSharingMode                         =
VK_SHARING_MODE_EXCLUSIVE;

createInfo.queueFamilyIndexCount = 0; // Optional
```

```cpp
createInfo.pQueueFamilyIndices = nullptr; // Optional
}

createInfo.preTransform = capabilities.currentTransform;

createInfo.compositeAlpha = VK_COMPOSITE_ALPHA_OPAQUE_BIT_KHR;

createInfo.presentMode = presentMode;

createInfo.clipped = VK_TRUE;

VkSwapchainKHR swapChain;

if (vkCreateSwapchainKHR(device, &createInfo, nullptr, &swapChain) != VK_SUCCESS) {
// Handle swap chain creation failure
}
```

In this code snippet, we set up a VkSwapchainCreateInfoKHR structure, specifying the surface, image format, color space, extent, and other properties. The code also takes into account cases where the graphics and presentation queues are different, using concurrent sharing mode.

3. Managing Swap Chain Images

After creating the swap chain, you need to retrieve its images and manage them. These images will be used for rendering:

```cpp
std::vector<VkImage> swapChainImages;

vkGetSwapchainImagesKHR(device, swapChain, &imageCount, nullptr);
```

```
swapChainImages.resize(imageCount);

vkGetSwapchainImagesKHR(device, swapChain, &imageCount,
swapChainImages.data());
```

Once you have the swap chain images, you can use them as rendering targets in Vulkan.

The swap chain is a critical component for presenting images to the screen in a Vulkan application. By defining its properties, creating it with appropriate settings, and managing its images, you ensure that your application can efficiently display rendered frames on the screen or window.

4.4 Rendering Passes and Framebuffers

In Vulkan, rendering passes and framebuffers play a crucial role in organizing and executing rendering operations efficiently. They provide a flexible and explicit way to define how rendering tasks should be structured and how the output should be presented to the screen or surface. In this section, we will explore the concepts of rendering passes and framebuffers in Vulkan and how they contribute to the rendering pipeline.

1. Rendering Passes

A rendering pass in Vulkan defines a series of subpasses that specify the sequence of rendering operations. Each subpass can read the output of previous subpasses and write its own output. This allows for various rendering techniques like deferred rendering and post-processing effects.

Here's an example of defining a simple rendering pass:

```
VkAttachmentDescription colorAttachment{};
```

```cpp
colorAttachment.format = swapChainImageFormat;

colorAttachment.samples = VK_SAMPLE_COUNT_1_BIT;

colorAttachment.loadOp = VK_ATTACHMENT_LOAD_OP_CLEAR; // Clear the attachment at the start

colorAttachment.storeOp = VK_ATTACHMENT_STORE_OP_STORE; // Store the attachment for later reading

colorAttachment.stencilLoadOp = VK_ATTACHMENT_LOAD_OP_DONT_CARE;

colorAttachment.stencilStoreOp = VK_ATTACHMENT_STORE_OP_DONT_CARE;

colorAttachment.initialLayout = VK_IMAGE_LAYOUT_UNDEFINED;

colorAttachment.finalLayout = VK_IMAGE_LAYOUT_PRESENT_SRC_KHR; // Transition to present layout

VkAttachmentReference colorAttachmentRef{};

colorAttachmentRef.attachment = 0;

colorAttachmentRef.layout = VK_IMAGE_LAYOUT_COLOR_ATTACHMENT_OPTIMAL; // Optimal layout for color attachment

VkSubpassDescription subpass{};

subpass.pipelineBindPoint = VK_PIPELINE_BIND_POINT_GRAPHICS;
```

```cpp
subpass.colorAttachmentCount = 1;

subpass.pColorAttachments = &colorAttachmentRef; // Reference
to the color attachment

VkRenderPassCreateInfo renderPassInfo{};

renderPassInfo.sType                                        =
VK_STRUCTURE_TYPE_RENDER_PASS_CREATE_INFO;

renderPassInfo.attachmentCount = 1;

renderPassInfo.pAttachments = &colorAttachment;

renderPassInfo.subpassCount = 1;

renderPassInfo.pSubpasses = &subpass;

VkRenderPass renderPass;

if (vkCreateRenderPass(device, &renderPassInfo, nullptr,
&renderPass) != VK_SUCCESS) {

// Handle render pass creation failure

}
```

In the code above, we define a rendering pass with a single color attachment. We specify the format, load and store operations, initial and final layouts, and a subpass that references the color attachment.

2. Framebuffers

Framebuffers in Vulkan represent the actual images or surfaces that rendering operations will target within a rendering pass. A framebuffer consists of one or more attachments, typically corresponding to the output of each subpass in the render pass.

Here's how you can create a framebuffer for use with a rendering pass:

```cpp
VkFramebufferCreateInfo framebufferInfo{};

framebufferInfo.sType = VK_STRUCTURE_TYPE_FRAMEBUFFER_CREATE_INFO;

framebufferInfo.renderPass = renderPass; // Reference to the render pass

framebufferInfo.attachmentCount = 1;

framebufferInfo.pAttachments = &swapChainImageView; // Attachment (image view)

framebufferInfo.width = swapChainExtent.width;

framebufferInfo.height = swapChainExtent.height;

framebufferInfo.layers = 1;

VkFramebuffer framebuffer;

if (vkCreateFramebuffer(device, &framebufferInfo, nullptr, &framebuffer) != VK_SUCCESS) {

// Handle framebuffer creation failure

}
```

In this code, we create a framebuffer associated with the previously defined rendering pass. We specify the attachment (in this case, the image view of the swap chain image), width, height, and layers.

3. Render Passes and Framebuffers in Rendering

Once you have created a rendering pass and a framebuffer, you can use them in your rendering pipeline. When recording command buffers for rendering, you will begin a render pass, specify the framebuffer to use, and execute rendering commands within subpasses.

Here's a simplified example of how rendering commands can be recorded within a render pass:

```
VkRenderPassBeginInfo renderPassInfo{};

renderPassInfo.sType = VK_STRUCTURE_TYPE_RENDER_PASS_BEGIN_INFO;

renderPassInfo.renderPass = renderPass;

renderPassInfo.framebuffer = framebuffer;

renderPassInfo.renderArea.offset = {0, 0};

renderPassInfo.renderArea.extent = swapChainExtent;

VkClearValue clearColor = {0.0f, 0.0f, 0.0f, 1.0f};

renderPassInfo.clearValueCount = 1;

renderPassInfo.pClearValues = &clearColor;

vkCmdBeginRenderPass(commandBuffer, &renderPassInfo, VK_SUBPASS_CONTENTS_INLINE);

// Execute rendering commands (draw calls, shaders, etc.)

vkCmdEndRenderPass(commandBuffer);
```

In this code, we begin the render pass and specify the framebuffer, render area, and clear values. We then record rendering commands within the render pass, and finally, we end the render pass.

Rendering passes and framebuffers provide a powerful way to structure rendering operations in Vulkan. By defining how data flows between subpasses and managing the actual images used for rendering, you can efficiently achieve complex rendering techniques and produce visually appealing graphics.

4.5 Drawing Your First Triangle

Drawing a triangle is often the "Hello, World!" equivalent in graphics programming. In Vulkan, this process involves several steps, including setting up a graphics pipeline, defining vertices, creating buffers, and issuing draw commands. In this section, we'll walk through the process of drawing a simple triangle using Vulkan.

1. Vertex Input and Shaders

To draw a triangle, you need to define its vertices and shaders. First, let's define the vertices of the triangle:

```
struct Vertex {

glm::vec2 pos;

glm::vec3 color;

};

const std::vector<Vertex> vertices = {

{{0.0f, -0.5f}, {1.0f, 0.0f, 0.0f}},

{{0.5f, 0.5f}, {0.0f, 1.0f, 0.0f}},
```

```
{{-0.5f, 0.5f}, {0.0f, 0.0f, 1.0f}}
};
```

In this code, we define a Vertex structure with position and color attributes. We then create a vector of vertices representing the triangle.

Next, you'll need vertex and fragment shaders to process this vertex data and render the triangle. Vulkan shaders are typically written in languages like GLSL (OpenGL Shading Language) and are compiled into SPIR-V bytecode. These shaders define how vertices are transformed and how colors are interpolated.

2. Shader Modules and Pipelines

You'll need to load and create shader modules for your vertex and fragment shaders:

```
VkShaderModule vertShaderModule = createShaderModule(device, "path/to/vertex_shader.spv");

VkShaderModule fragShaderModule = createShaderModule(device, "path/to/fragment_shader.spv");
```

The createShaderModule function reads the SPIR-V bytecode and creates Vulkan shader modules.

Now, let's create a graphics pipeline to use these shaders:

```
VkPipelineShaderStageCreateInfo vertShaderStageInfo{};

vertShaderStageInfo.sType = VK_STRUCTURE_TYPE_PIPELINE_SHADER_STAGE_CREAT

vertShaderStageInfo.stage = VK_SHADER_STAGE_VERTEX_BIT;
```

```cpp
vertShaderStageInfo.module = vertShaderModule;

vertShaderStageInfo.pName = "main";

VkPipelineShaderStageCreateInfo fragShaderStageInfo{};

fragShaderStageInfo.sType                                       =
VK_STRUCTURE_TYPE_PIPELINE_SHADER_STAGE_CREATE_

fragShaderStageInfo.stage                                       =
VK_SHADER_STAGE_FRAGMENT_BIT;

fragShaderStageInfo.module = fragShaderModule;

fragShaderStageInfo.pName = "main";

VkPipelineShaderStageCreateInfo         shaderStages[]         =
{vertShaderStageInfo, fragShaderStageInfo};

VkPipelineVertexInputStateCreateInfo vertexInputInfo{};

// Define vertex input format and binding here

VkPipelineInputAssemblyStateCreateInfo inputAssembly{};

// Define assembly topology and other settings here

VkPipelineViewportStateCreateInfo viewportState{};

// Define viewport and scissor rectangle here

VkPipelineRasterizationStateCreateInfo rasterizer{};

// Define rasterization settings here

VkPipelineMultisampleStateCreateInfo multisampling{};

// Define multisampling settings here
```

```cpp
VkPipelineColorBlendAttachmentState colorBlendAttachment{};

// Define color blending settings here

VkPipelineColorBlendStateCreateInfo colorBlending{};

// Define color blending settings for all attachments here

VkPipelineLayout pipelineLayout;

// Create pipeline layout (descriptor sets, push constants, etc.)

VkPipeline graphicsPipeline;

VkGraphicsPipelineCreateInfo pipelineInfo{};

pipelineInfo.sType                          =
VK_STRUCTURE_TYPE_GRAPHICS_PIPELINE_CREATE_INFO

pipelineInfo.stageCount = 2;

pipelineInfo.pStages = shaderStages;

pipelineInfo.pVertexInputState = &vertexInputInfo;

pipelineInfo.pInputAssemblyState = &inputAssembly;

pipelineInfo.pViewportState = &viewportState;

pipelineInfo.pRasterizationState = &rasterizer;

pipelineInfo.pMultisampleState = &multisampling;

pipelineInfo.pColorBlendState = &colorBlending;

pipelineInfo.layout = pipelineLayout;

pipelineInfo.renderPass = renderPass; // Reference to the render pass

pipelineInfo.subpass = 0;
```

```
if (vkCreateGraphicsPipelines(device, VK_NULL_HANDLE, 1,
&pipelineInfo, nullptr, &graphicsPipeline) != VK_SUCCESS) {

// Handle pipeline creation failure

}
```

In this code, we create a graphics pipeline by specifying various configuration options such as shader stages, vertex input format, assembly topology, rasterization settings, and more. The createShaderModule function is used to load and create shader modules.

3. Vertex Buffer and Command Buffer

To pass vertex data to the graphics pipeline, you'll need a vertex buffer. Create a buffer and allocate memory for it:

```
VkBuffer vertexBuffer;

VkDeviceMemory vertexBufferMemory;

createVertexBuffer(vertices, vertexBuffer, vertexBufferMemory);
```

The createVertexBuffer function should handle buffer creation and memory allocation based on the vertex data.

Now, you'll need to record the drawing commands in a command buffer:

```
VkCommandBufferBeginInfo beginInfo{};

beginInfo.sType                                    =
VK_STRUCTURE_TYPE_COMMAND_BUFFER_BEGIN_INFO;

beginInfo.flags = 0; // Optional
```

```cpp
beginInfo.pInheritanceInfo = nullptr; // Optional

if (vkBeginCommandBuffer(commandBuffer, &beginInfo) != VK_SUCCESS) {

// Handle command buffer begin failure

}

VkRenderPassBeginInfo renderPassInfo{};

// Configure render pass info (as shown in previous sections)

vkCmdBeginRenderPass(commandBuffer, &renderPassInfo, VK_SUBPASS_CONTENTS_INLINE);

vkCmdBindPipeline(commandBuffer, VK_PIPELINE_BIND_POINT_GRAPHICS, graphicsPipeline);

VkBuffer vertexBuffers[] = {vertexBuffer};

VkDeviceSize offsets[] = {0};

vkCmdBindVertexBuffers(commandBuffer, 0, 1, vertexBuffers, offsets);

vkCmdDraw(commandBuffer, static_cast<uint32_t>(vertices.size()), 1, 0, 0);

vkCmdEndRenderPass(commandBuffer);

if (vkEndCommandBuffer(commandBuffer) != VK_SUCCESS) {

// Handle command buffer end failure

}
```

In this code, we begin the command buffer, start a render pass, bind the graphics pipeline, bind the vertex buffer, and issue the draw command. The specifics of rendering setup, including render pass configuration, pipeline binding, and vertex buffer binding, are typically performed within a rendering loop.

4. Presentation and Cleanup

To present the rendered image to the screen or surface, you need to submit the command buffer to the graphics queue and present the image:

```cpp
VkSemaphore imageAvailableSemaphore;

VkSemaphore renderFinishedSemaphore;

VkSemaphoreCreateInfo semaphoreInfo{};

semaphoreInfo.sType = VK_STRUCTURE_TYPE_SEMAPHORE_CREATE_INFO;

if (vkCreateSemaphore(device, &semaphoreInfo, nullptr, &imageAvailableSemaphore) != VK_SUCCESS ||

vkCreateSemaphore(device, &semaphoreInfo, nullptr, &renderFinishedSemaphore) != VK_SUCCESS) {

// Handle semaphore creation failure

}

// Inside rendering loop:

{

uint32_t imageIndex;
```

```cpp
vkAcquireNextImageKHR(device, swapChain, UINT64_MAX,
imageAvailableSemaphore, VK_NULL_HANDLE,
&imageIndex);

VkSubmitInfo submitInfo{};

// Configure command buffer submission (as shown in previous
sections)

if (vkQueueSubmit(graphicsQueue, 1, &submitInfo,
VK_NULL_HANDLE) != VK_SUCCESS) {

//
```

##

Chapter 5: Advanced Rendering Techniques

5.1 Textures and Image Loading

Textures play a vital role in computer graphics, enhancing the realism **and** detail of rendered scenes. In Vulkan, loading **and using** textures involves several steps, including image loading, texture mapping, **and** shader integration. In **this** section, we will explore how to work with textures in Vulkan **and** load images **for** use in rendering.

1. Image Loading

Before you can use images as textures in Vulkan, you need to load them from files **or** memory. There are various libraries available **for** image loading, such as **stb_image**, which is a lightweight **and** widely used choice.

Here's **an example of loading an image using **stb_image**:**

```cpp
```

```cpp
#define STB_IMAGE_IMPLEMENTATION

#include <stb_image.h>

// Load image

int texWidth, texHeight, texChannels;

stbi_uc* pixels = stbi_load("path/to/texture.jpg", &texWidth,
&texHeight, &texChannels, STBI_rgb_alpha);

if (!pixels) {

// Handle image loading failure

}

// Create Vulkan image and allocate memory

VkImage textureImage;

VkDeviceMemory textureImageMemory;

createImage(texWidth,                              texHeight,
VK_FORMAT_R8G8B8A8_SRGB,
VK_IMAGE_TILING_OPTIMAL,
VK_IMAGE_USAGE_TRANSFER_DST_BIT                          |
VK_IMAGE_USAGE_SAMPLED_BIT,
VK_MEMORY_PROPERTY_DEVICE_LOCAL_BIT,
textureImage, textureImageMemory);

// Copy image data to Vulkan image

transitionImageLayout(textureImage,
VK_FORMAT_R8G8B8A8_SRGB,
VK_IMAGE_LAYOUT_UNDEFINED,
VK_IMAGE_LAYOUT_TRANSFER_DST_OPTIMAL);
```

```
copyBufferToImage(pixels, static_cast<uint32_t>(texWidth),
static_cast<uint32_t>(texHeight), textureImage);

transitionImageLayout(textureImage,
VK_FORMAT_R8G8B8A8_SRGB,
VK_IMAGE_LAYOUT_TRANSFER_DST_OPTIMAL,
VK_IMAGE_LAYOUT_SHADER_READ_ONLY_OPTIMAL);

// Free the loaded image data

stbi_image_free(pixels);
```

In this code, we use **stb_image** to load an image from a file and obtain its width, height, and channels. We then create a Vulkan image and allocate memory for it. After copying the image data to the Vulkan image, we transition its layout to make it ready for shader access.

2. Texture Mapping

To apply a loaded texture to an object, you need to map it to the object's vertices. This process involves specifying texture coordinates for each vertex, which are used to sample the texture in shaders.

Here's an example of defining texture coordinates for a triangle's vertices:

```
struct Vertex {

glm::vec2 pos;

glm::vec3 color;

glm::vec2 texCoord;

};
```

```
const std::vector<Vertex> vertices = {

{{0.0f, -0.5f}, {1.0f, 0.0f, 0.0f}, {0.5f, 1.0f}},

{{0.5f, 0.5f}, {0.0f, 1.0f, 0.0f}, {1.0f, 0.0f}},

{{-0.5f, 0.5f}, {0.0f, 0.0f, 1.0f}, {0.0f, 0.0f}}

};
```

In this code, we extend the Vertex structure to include texture coordinates (texCoord) in addition to position and color attributes.

3. Shader Integration

To use the loaded texture in shaders, you need to pass it as a uniform or sampler to the fragment shader. Here's an example of binding a texture to a sampler in Vulkan:

```
VkImageView textureImageView;

VkSampler textureSampler;

createImageView(textureImage,
VK_FORMAT_R8G8B8A8_SRGB,
VK_IMAGE_ASPECT_COLOR_BIT, textureImageView);

createTextureSampler(device, textureSampler);

// In the fragment shader

layout(binding = 0) uniform sampler2D textureSampler;

layout(location = 0) in vec2 fragTexCoord;

layout(location = 0) out vec4 fragColor;

void main() {
```

fragColor = texture(textureSampler, fragTexCoord);

}

In this code, we create a texture image view and sampler, then bind the sampler to the fragment shader. In the shader, we sample the texture using the texture function and the provided texture coordinates.

Working with textures is an essential part of advanced rendering techniques in Vulkan. Loading images, mapping textures to vertices, and integrating them into shaders allows you to create visually appealing and realistic graphics in your Vulkan applications.

5.2 Lighting Models in Vulkan

Lighting is a fundamental aspect of computer graphics that simulates how objects interact with light sources in a scene. Vulkan provides the flexibility to implement various lighting models to achieve realistic rendering. In this section, we'll explore common lighting models used in Vulkan applications.

1. Phong Lighting Model

The Phong lighting model is a widely used model for simulating lighting in computer graphics. It consists of three components: ambient, diffuse, and specular lighting.

- **Ambient Lighting**: Represents the overall ambient illumination in a scene, which affects all objects uniformly. It's typically a constant color.

- **Diffuse Lighting**: Models the direct illumination of a surface by a light source. It depends on the angle between the surface normal and the light direction, resulting in brighter areas where the surface is facing the light.

- **Specular Lighting**: Simulates the reflection of light off shiny surfaces. It produces highlights on surfaces and depends on the viewer's position and the angle of reflection.

Here's a simplified example of Phong lighting in a Vulkan fragment shader:

vec3 ambientLight = vec3(0.2, 0.2, 0.2); *// Ambient light color*

vec3 lightColor = vec3(1.0, 1.0, 1.0); *// Diffuse and specular light color*

vec3 lightDir = normalize(lightPosition - fragPos); *// Direction from fragment to light*

vec3 normal = normalize(fragNormal); *// Normalized surface normal*

vec3 viewDir = normalize(viewPosition - fragPos); *// Direction from fragment to viewer*

// Diffuse reflection

float diff = max(dot(normal, lightDir), 0.0);

vec3 diffuse = diff * lightColor;

// Specular reflection

float spec = pow(max(dot(reflect(-lightDir, normal), viewDir), 0.0), shininess);

vec3 specular = spec * lightColor;

vec3 result = (ambientLight + diffuse + specular) * objectColor;

In this code, we calculate ambient, diffuse, and specular components of the lighting equation. fragPos represents the fragment position, fragNormal is the fragment's surface normal, and viewPosition is the viewer's position.

2. Blinn-Phong Lighting Model

The Blinn-Phong lighting model is an improvement over the Phong model. It replaces the reflection vector in the specular term calculation with the halfway vector between the light direction and view direction. This results in smoother highlights and is more computationally efficient.

Here's a simplified example of the Blinn-Phong lighting model in Vulkan:

vec3 halfwayDir = normalize(lightDir + viewDir);

// Specular reflection using the Blinn-Phong model

float spec = pow(max(dot(normal, halfwayDir), 0.0), shininess);

vec3 specular = spec * lightColor;

In this code, halfwayDir represents the normalized halfway vector between the light and view directions.

3. Cook-Torrance Lighting Model

The Cook-Torrance lighting model is a more physically accurate model used in advanced rendering techniques. It considers microfacets on the surface and simulates complex interactions between light and materials. It involves terms like the Fresnel equation, geometric attenuation, and microfacet distribution functions.

Implementing the Cook-Torrance model in Vulkan shaders is more involved and requires additional calculations compared to the Phong or Blinn-Phong models. It is often used for materials like metals and produces realistic results with physically accurate specular reflections.

// Implementing the Cook-Torrance model requires additional calculations not shown here.

// It involves the Fresnel-Schlick approximation, microfacet distribution functions, and more.

The choice of lighting model depends on the desired level of realism and computational complexity. While Phong and Blinn-Phong models are suitable for many applications, the Cook-Torrance model is used for high-quality rendering, especially in physically based rendering (PBR) pipelines. Vulkan's flexibility allows you to implement and experiment with different lighting models to achieve the desired visual effects in your graphics applications.

5.3 Shadows and Reflections

Shadows and reflections are essential elements in rendering realistic scenes in Vulkan. They contribute to the perception of depth, lighting accuracy, and overall visual quality. In this section, we will delve into the concepts of shadows and reflections and how they are implemented in Vulkan applications.

1. Shadows

Shadows are the absence of light caused by an object blocking the path of light sources. In computer graphics, simulating shadows is crucial for creating depth and realism. Vulkan provides techniques to implement shadows, and one commonly used method is shadow mapping.

Shadow Mapping

Shadow mapping is a technique that involves rendering the scene from the perspective of a light source and storing depth information in a texture called the "shadow map." This shadow map is then used to determine whether a pixel is in shadow when rendering from the camera's perspective.

Here's an overview of the shadow mapping process in Vulkan:

1. **Render the Scene from the Light's Perspective**: The scene is rendered from the viewpoint of the light source. Depth information is stored in a shadow map texture.
2. **Render the Scene from the Camera's Perspective**: The scene is rendered from the camera's perspective. For each pixel, a depth comparison is made with the values in the shadow map to determine if it's in shadow or not.
3. **Applying Shadows in Shaders**: In fragment shaders, shadows are applied by comparing the depth of the current fragment with the depth stored in the shadow map.

```
// In the fragment shader

float        shadow      =        calculateShadowFactor(shadowMap,
fragPosLightSpace);

vec3 finalColor = objectColor * (1.0 - shadow);
```

Implementing shadow mapping in Vulkan involves setting up the shadow map, rendering the scene twice (once from the light's perspective and once from the camera's perspective), and performing the depth comparison in shaders.

2. Reflections

Reflections simulate the interaction of light with reflective surfaces, such as mirrors or water. Vulkan provides techniques for implementing reflections, and one common method is environment mapping.

Environment Mapping

Environment mapping involves using a cube map or a spherical map to simulate reflections on reflective surfaces. Cube maps are often used for simulating reflections on objects in 3D scenes.

Here's an overview of the environment mapping process in Vulkan:

1. **Create a Cube Map**: A cube map texture is generated from multiple viewpoints (usually from a reflective object's location) to capture the surrounding environment.
2. **Render Reflections**: When rendering the scene, the cube map is used to sample the reflected environment for each pixel on reflective surfaces.

// In the fragment shader for reflective objects

vec3 reflectedColor = texture(cubeMap, reflectDirection).rgb;

Implementing environment mapping in Vulkan involves creating and updating the cube map, sampling it in shaders, and applying the reflections to reflective objects.

Both shadows and reflections significantly enhance the realism of rendered scenes. Vulkan's flexibility allows developers to implement these effects efficiently, making it possible to create visually stunning graphics in Vulkan applications.

5.4 Post-Processing Effects

Post-processing effects are a powerful tool in computer graphics for enhancing the visual quality of rendered scenes. These effects are applied after the initial rendering pass and can simulate various real-world phenomena, improve image quality, and add artistic flair to Vulkan applications. In this section, we will explore some common post-processing effects and how they can be implemented in Vulkan.

1. Bloom

Bloom is a post-processing effect that simulates the scattering of light in a camera lens. It creates a halo or glow around bright objects, adding a sense of realism and visual appeal. To implement bloom in Vulkan, you can follow these steps:

1. **Render the Scene**: Render the scene to a framebuffer as usual.
2. **Extract Bright Areas**: Apply a fragment shader to extract the bright areas from the rendered image. This shader typically uses a threshold to identify pixels that are considered "bright."
3. **Blur the Bright Areas**: Apply a blur filter to the extracted bright areas. You can use a separable Gaussian blur or other blur techniques to create a smooth, blooming effect.
4. **Combine with Original Image**: Combine the blurred bright areas with the original scene. This can be done using additive blending or other blending modes to achieve the desired bloom effect.

2. Depth of Field (DOF)

Depth of field is an effect that simulates the focal properties of a camera lens. It allows you to control the sharpness of objects at different depths within the scene, creating a realistic sense of depth. To implement depth of field in Vulkan, consider these steps:

1. **Render Depth Map**: Along with the color image, render a depth map that represents the distance of objects from the camera.
2. **Apply DOF Effect**: In a post-processing pass, apply a fragment shader that calculates the depth of field effect. This typically involves performing a convolution on the depth values to determine the blur amount for each pixel.
3. **Combine with Original Image**: Combine the depth of field effect with the original scene, keeping the focused objects sharp while blurring objects at different depths.

3. Screen Space Ambient Occlusion (SSAO)

Screen Space Ambient Occlusion is an effect that simulates the occlusion of ambient light by nearby objects. It adds depth and realism to scenes by darkening areas where objects are close together. Implementing SSAO in Vulkan involves these steps:

1. **Render Normals and Depth**: In addition to the color image, render a normal map and a depth map representing the scene geometry.
2. **Generate Ambient Occlusion**: Apply a fragment shader that calculates the ambient occlusion factor for each pixel based on the surrounding normals and depths. This typically involves sampling neighboring pixels in screen space.
3. **Combine with Original Image**: Combine the ambient

occlusion effect with the original scene to add shadows and darken areas where occlusion occurs.

4. Motion Blur

Motion blur simulates the blurring effect that occurs when objects move rapidly within a scene. It adds realism to dynamic scenes and can be implemented in Vulkan as follows:

1. **Render Motion Vectors**: Along with the color image, render motion vectors that represent the movement of objects between frames.
2. **Apply Motion Blur Effect**: In a post-processing pass, apply a fragment shader that uses the motion vectors to calculate the motion blur effect. This typically involves performing a convolution on the image based on the motion vectors.
3. **Combine with Original Image**: Combine the motion blur effect with the original scene to simulate object motion.

These are just a few examples of post-processing effects that can be implemented in Vulkan. Post-processing allows for creative and realistic enhancements to rendered scenes, and Vulkan's flexibility and performance capabilities make it a suitable choice for implementing these effects in graphics applications.

5.5 Debugging and Profiling Your Rendering

Debugging and profiling are essential aspects of developing Vulkan applications, especially when dealing with complex rendering pipelines and advanced graphics techniques. In this section, we will discuss strategies and tools for debugging and profiling Vulkan applications to optimize performance and identify issues.

1. Validation Layers

Validation layers are a crucial tool for identifying errors and potential issues in Vulkan applications during development. These layers provide detailed error messages and warnings that can help you catch issues early in the development process. To enable validation layers, you should:

- Set up Vulkan with validation layers enabled in your development environment.

- Create a validation callback function that handles validation messages and errors, providing insights into what went wrong.

- Use tools like VK_LAYER_KHRONOS_validation to enable validation layers for your Vulkan instance.

```
VkDebugUtilsMessengerCreateInfoEXT createInfo = {};

createInfo.sType                                    =
VK_STRUCTURE_TYPE_DEBUG_UTILS_MESSENGER_CREATI

createInfo.messageSeverity                          =
VK_DEBUG_UTILS_MESSAGE_SEVERITY_VERBOSE_BIT_EXT
|

VK_DEBUG_UTILS_MESSAGE_SEVERITY_WARNING_BIT_EXT
|

VK_DEBUG_UTILS_MESSAGE_SEVERITY_ERROR_BIT_EXT;
```

createInfo.messageType   =
VK_DEBUG_UTILS_MESSAGE_TYPE_GENERAL_BIT_EXT
|

VK_DEBUG_UTILS_MESSAGE_TYPE_VALIDATION_BIT_EXT
|

VK_DEBUG_UTILS_MESSAGE_TYPE_PERFORMANCE_BIT_E:

createInfo.pfnUserCallback = debugCallback;

VkDebugUtilsMessengerEXT debugMessenger;

VkResult   result   =   CreateDebugUtilsMessengerEXT(instance,
&createInfo, **nullptr**, &debugMessenger);

With validation layers enabled, Vulkan will report issues, such as invalid usage of Vulkan functions or incorrect pipeline configurations, making it easier to debug your code.

2. Vulkan Validation Layers

The Vulkan SDK includes valuable tools for debugging and profiling Vulkan applications:

- **Vulkan Validation Layers**: These layers provide detailed feedback on the correctness of Vulkan API usage. They can be enabled during Vulkan instance creation, and they catch issues like memory leaks and API misuse.

- **RenderDoc**: RenderDoc is a popular open-source frame-capture debugger that allows you to inspect the graphics API calls made during a frame. It supports Vulkan and offers various debugging and profiling capabilities, including frame capture and analysis.

- **APITrace**: APITrace is another tool that allows you to capture and replay Vulkan API calls. It can help diagnose rendering issues and performance bottlenecks.

- **NVIDIA Nsight Graphics and AMD Radeon GPU Profiler**: These GPU vendor-specific tools provide in-depth performance analysis and debugging capabilities for Vulkan applications on NVIDIA and AMD GPUs, respectively.

3. Profiling Vulkan Applications

Profiling Vulkan applications is essential for optimizing performance. Profiling tools help you identify performance bottlenecks, such as inefficient shaders or resource usage. Here are some strategies for profiling Vulkan applications:

- **Timestamp Queries**: Use Vulkan's timestamp queries to measure the time taken by specific rendering stages or GPU operations. This allows you to pinpoint performance hotspots.

- **GPU Vendor Tools**: NVIDIA's Nsight Graphics and AMD's Radeon GPU Profiler provide detailed GPU performance metrics and analysis. These tools can help you understand GPU bottlenecks and optimize your rendering pipeline accordingly.

- **CPU Profiling**: Profiling the CPU side of your application is also crucial. Tools like Visual Studio's CPU Profiling, Intel VTune, and AMD CodeXL can help identify CPU-bound bottlenecks in your Vulkan code.

- **Shader Profiling**: Analyze the performance of your shaders using shader profiling tools. These tools can highlight inefficient code in your shaders and suggest optimizations.

- **Resource Usage Analysis**: Profiling tools can help you monitor resource usage, such as memory allocations and descriptor set updates, to identify inefficient resource management.

- **Frame Analysis**: Analyze the entire frame's rendering process to understand the sequence of rendering commands and GPU utilization throughout the frame.

Profiling Vulkan applications can be a complex task, but it is essential for achieving optimal performance and identifying areas for improvement. Combining the insights gained from validation layers and profiling tools will help you create high-performance Vulkan applications with fewer bugs and better efficiency.

Chapter 6: Introduction to Machine Learning

6.1 What Is Machine Learning?

Machine learning (ML) is a subfield of artificial intelligence (AI) that focuses on the development of algorithms and statistical models that enable computer systems to improve their performance on a specific task through learning from data. In this section, we will explore the fundamental concepts of machine learning, its applications, and its relevance to Vulkan graphics programming.

1. Machine Learning Basics

At its core, machine learning is about building predictive models from data. These models can make decisions, classify objects, or make predictions based on patterns and information contained in the data they are trained on. Machine learning models can be broadly categorized into three types:

- **Supervised Learning**: In supervised learning, the model is trained on a labeled dataset, where each data point is associated with a target or label. The goal is to learn a mapping from input data to the correct output. Common supervised learning tasks include image classification, speech recognition, and regression.

- **Unsupervised Learning**: Unsupervised learning deals with unlabeled data. The model's objective is to find patterns, clusters, or representations in the data without explicit guidance. Clustering, dimensionality reduction, and generative modeling are examples of unsupervised learning tasks.

- **Reinforcement Learning**: In reinforcement learning, an agent learns to make a sequence of decisions to maximize a cumulative reward signal. This type of learning is commonly used in game playing, robotics, and autonomous systems.

2. Machine Learning in Graphics

Machine learning has found numerous applications in the field of computer graphics and game development. Some of the key areas where machine learning intersects with graphics include:

- **Image and Video Processing**: ML techniques can enhance image and video processing tasks, such as denoising, super-resolution, and style transfer. These techniques can improve the visual quality of graphics applications.

- **Procedural Content Generation**: ML models can generate game content, including textures, levels, and character animations. This allows for the automatic creation of diverse and engaging game worlds.

- **Character Animation**: ML-driven character animation can make game characters more lifelike by enabling them to respond intelligently to their environment and interact with players.

- **Physics Simulation**: Reinforcement learning can be used to optimize physics simulations, leading to more realistic and efficient simulations of natural phenomena.

- **Rendering Optimization**: ML algorithms can optimize rendering processes by predicting which parts of a scene are most important and allocating computational resources accordingly.

3. Machine Learning Frameworks

To work with machine learning, developers often rely on specialized frameworks and libraries that provide tools for building, training, and deploying ML models. Some of the popular machine learning frameworks include:

- **TensorFlow**: Developed by Google, TensorFlow is an open-source machine learning framework known for its flexibility and scalability. It supports a wide range of ML tasks and is often used for deep learning.

- **PyTorch**: PyTorch is another popular open-source machine learning framework known for its dynamic computation graph and user-friendly interface. It is widely used for research and prototyping ML models.

- **Scikit-learn**: Scikit-learn is a Python library that provides simple and efficient tools for data mining and data analysis. It's a great choice for traditional machine learning tasks.

- **Keras**: Keras is an API that runs on top of TensorFlow and other frameworks, providing a user-friendly interface for building and training neural networks.

- **Caffe**: Caffe is a deep learning framework developed by Berkeley Vision and Learning Center. It is known for its speed and scalability in the context of deep neural networks.

Machine learning frameworks like TensorFlow and PyTorch are particularly relevant to Vulkan developers as they provide tools for integrating machine learning into graphics applications. These frameworks allow developers to create AI-driven graphics enhancements and optimizations.

In the following sections of this chapter, we will delve deeper into various aspects of machine learning and explore how it can be integrated with Vulkan to create intelligent graphics applications.

6.2 Types of Machine Learning

Machine learning encompasses various approaches and techniques, each suited to different types of problems and data. In this section, we will explore the major categories of machine learning, providing an overview of their characteristics and typical use cases.

1. Supervised Learning

Supervised learning is one of the most common and well-understood forms of machine learning. In this paradigm, the algorithm is trained on a labeled dataset, where each data point is paired with the correct output or label. The goal of supervised learning is to learn a mapping from input data to the correct output.

Typical use cases for supervised learning include:

- **Classification**: This involves assigning input data points to predefined categories or classes. For example, image classification can categorize images of animals into different species.

• **Regression**: In regression tasks, the goal is to predict a continuous value based on input data. Predicting house prices based on features like square footage, number of bedrooms, and location is a common regression problem.

• **Natural Language Processing (NLP)**: Supervised learning is used in NLP tasks like sentiment analysis, where text data is classified as positive or negative.

2. Unsupervised Learning

Unsupervised learning deals with unlabeled data, where the algorithm doesn't have access to explicit output labels. Instead, it aims to discover patterns, relationships, or structures within the data.

Key types of unsupervised learning include:

• **Clustering**: Clustering algorithms group similar data points together based on their intrinsic properties. This is used in customer segmentation, image segmentation, and more.

• **Dimensionality Reduction**: Dimensionality reduction techniques aim to reduce the complexity of high-dimensional data while preserving essential information. Principal Component Analysis (PCA) is a well-known method for dimensionality reduction.

• **Generative Modeling**: Generative models aim to learn the underlying data distribution and can be used to generate new data samples. Variational Autoencoders (VAEs) and Generative Adversarial Networks (GANs) are examples of generative models.

3. Reinforcement Learning

Reinforcement learning (RL) is a different paradigm where an agent interacts with an environment and learns to make sequences of decisions to maximize a cumulative reward signal. The agent learns through trial and error, receiving feedback in the form of rewards or punishments based on its actions.

RL is widely used in applications such as:

- **Game Playing**: RL has been used to train agents to play complex games like chess, Go, and video games. These agents learn strategies and tactics through gameplay.

- **Robotics**: RL is applied to robotic control, where robots learn to perform tasks like grasping objects, walking, and flying by optimizing their actions.

- **Autonomous Systems**: Autonomous vehicles and drones use RL to make decisions based on sensor data to navigate and complete missions.

4. Semi-supervised Learning and Self-supervised Learning

In addition to the main categories, there are variations of machine learning, such as semi-supervised learning and self-supervised learning.

- **Semi-supervised Learning**: Semi-supervised learning combines elements of both supervised and unsupervised learning. It uses a small amount of labeled data and a large amount of unlabeled data to train models.

- **Self-supervised Learning**: Self-supervised learning is a technique where models generate their labels from unlabeled data. For example, a model can be trained to predict missing parts of an image, effectively creating its own labels.

Each type of machine learning has its strengths and weaknesses, making it suitable for different types of problems. In graphics programming with Vulkan, these machine learning paradigms can be integrated to enhance rendering, optimize resource usage, and improve the overall user experience. In subsequent sections of this chapter, we will explore how Vulkan can be used in conjunction with various machine learning techniques to create intelligent and efficient graphics applications.

6.3 Machine Learning Frameworks

Machine learning frameworks are essential tools for developers and researchers working with machine learning models. These frameworks provide a structured environment for building, training, and deploying machine learning models efficiently. In this section, we'll explore some of the popular machine learning frameworks that can be used in conjunction with Vulkan to create intelligent graphics applications.

1. TensorFlow

TensorFlow is an open-source machine learning framework developed by Google. It has gained widespread popularity in the machine learning community due to its flexibility, scalability, and extensive ecosystem of libraries and tools. TensorFlow supports various machine learning tasks, including deep learning, and is known for its ability to train large neural networks efficiently.

Key features of TensorFlow include:

- **TensorFlow Keras**: TensorFlow includes the Keras API as part of its core, making it easy to define and train neural networks. Keras provides a user-friendly and high-level interface for building models.

- **TensorFlow Lite**: TensorFlow Lite is a framework for deploying machine learning models on mobile and edge devices. This is particularly useful for Vulkan applications on mobile platforms.

- **TensorBoard**: TensorFlow comes with TensorBoard, a visualization tool that helps in monitoring and debugging machine learning models during training.

- **Distributed Training**: TensorFlow supports distributed training across multiple GPUs and even multiple machines, allowing for faster training of large models.

- **TensorFlow Serving**: This component enables the deployment of machine learning models in production environments, making it suitable for real-time Vulkan applications.

2. PyTorch

PyTorch is another popular open-source machine learning framework, known for its dynamic computation graph and intuitive Pythonic API. It has gained a strong following among researchers and is widely used for both research and production machine learning tasks.

Key features of PyTorch include:

- **Dynamic Computation Graph**: PyTorch's dynamic computation graph allows for more flexibility in model design and debugging. This makes it a preferred choice for researchers who need to experiment with different model architectures.

- **TorchScript**: TorchScript allows you to compile PyTorch models into a serialized representation that can be executed independently. This is useful for deploying models in production Vulkan applications.

- **LibTorch**: LibTorch is a C++ library that provides PyTorch functionality. It is suitable for integrating PyTorch into C++ Vulkan applications.

- **Strong Community**: PyTorch has a strong and active community, which means access to a wealth of tutorials, libraries, and pre-trained models.

3. Scikit-learn

Scikit-learn is a Python library that focuses on classical machine learning techniques, making it suitable for traditional machine learning tasks. While it may not be as specialized for deep learning as TensorFlow and PyTorch, it excels in areas like data preprocessing, feature engineering, and traditional machine learning algorithms.

Key features of scikit-learn include:

- **Simple and Consistent API**: Scikit-learn provides a consistent and easy-to-use API for various machine learning tasks.

- **Wide Range of Algorithms**: It includes a wide variety of machine learning algorithms for classification, regression, clustering, dimensionality reduction, and more.

- **Data Preprocessing**: Scikit-learn offers robust tools for data preprocessing, including scaling, encoding categorical features, and handling missing values.

- **Model Selection**: It provides utilities for model selection, hyperparameter tuning, and cross-validation.

- **Integration with Other Libraries**: Scikit-learn can be seamlessly integrated with other Python libraries, making it suitable for use in Vulkan applications.

4. ONNX (Open Neural Network Exchange)

ONNX is an open-source format for representing machine learning models. While not a machine learning framework itself, it serves as an intermediate format that allows models trained in one framework to be converted and used in another. This interoperability can be valuable when integrating machine learning with Vulkan.

Key features of ONNX include:

- **Model Interoperability**: ONNX allows you to convert models trained in popular frameworks like TensorFlow, PyTorch, and scikit-learn into a common format that can be used in Vulkan applications.

- **Cross-Platform Compatibility**: ONNX models can be deployed across various platforms, including mobile and edge devices.

- **Ecosystem Support**: Many machine learning frameworks and tools support ONNX, making it a versatile choice for model deployment.

When working with Vulkan and machine learning, the choice of framework depends on your specific requirements, the nature of your machine learning tasks, and the platforms you intend to deploy on. TensorFlow and PyTorch are often preferred for deep learning tasks, while scikit-learn can be valuable for traditional machine learning tasks. ONNX can serve as a bridge between different frameworks, allowing you to choose the best tool for each component of your Vulkan AI application.

6.4 Data Preprocessing and Feature Engineering

Data preprocessing and feature engineering are crucial steps in machine learning that can significantly impact the performance and effectiveness of your models. In this section, we will explore the importance of data preparation and feature engineering when integrating machine learning with Vulkan graphics programming.

1. Data Preprocessing

Data preprocessing involves cleaning, transforming, and organizing raw data into a suitable format for machine learning. Vulkan applications often generate or consume data that may require preprocessing before it can be used effectively in machine learning models.

Common data preprocessing tasks include:

- **Data Cleaning**: This involves handling missing values, outliers, and noisy data points. In Vulkan applications, data from sensors or simulations may have missing or erroneous data that needs to be addressed.

• **Data Scaling and Normalization**: Scaling features to a standard range (e.g., between 0 and 1) or normalizing them (e.g., to have a mean of 0 and a standard deviation of 1) can help models converge faster and perform better.

• **Feature Encoding**: Categorical data, such as object types in a Vulkan scene, may need to be one-hot encoded or transformed into numerical values.

• **Feature Selection**: Choosing relevant features and eliminating irrelevant ones can reduce the dimensionality of the data and improve model efficiency.

• **Data Splitting**: Data is typically split into training, validation, and test sets to evaluate and validate models.

Data preprocessing code can vary greatly depending on the nature of the data and the machine learning framework being used. Below is a simplified example of data preprocessing in Python using scikit-learn:

```python
from sklearn.preprocessing import StandardScaler, OneHotEncoder

from sklearn.compose import ColumnTransformer

from sklearn.pipeline import Pipeline

# Define preprocessing steps for numerical and categorical features
numeric_features = ['feature1', 'feature2']

categorical_features = ['category']
```

```
numeric_transformer = Pipeline(steps=[

('scaler', StandardScaler())])

categorical_transformer = Pipeline(steps=[

('onehot', OneHotEncoder())])

# Combine preprocessing for both types of features

preprocessor = ColumnTransformer(

transformers=[

('num', numeric_transformer, numeric_features),

('cat', categorical_transformer, categorical_features)])

# Transform the data

X_train = preprocessor.fit_transform(X_train)

X_test = preprocessor.transform(X_test)
```

2. Feature Engineering

Feature engineering involves creating new features or modifying existing ones to better represent the underlying patterns in the data. In Vulkan applications, feature engineering can involve extracting meaningful information from graphical data, sensor readings, or other sources.

Feature engineering is a creative process and may require domain knowledge. Some techniques for feature engineering in Vulkan applications include:

- **Texture Analysis**: Extracting texture features from images or textures used in Vulkan scenes can provide valuable information for machine learning models.

- **Geometry Analysis**: Analyzing the geometry of 3D models or scenes can lead to the creation of features related to object shapes, sizes, or spatial relationships.

- **Temporal Features**: For time-series data in Vulkan applications, temporal features such as trends, seasonality, or moving averages can be engineered.

- **Custom Shaders**: In some cases, custom Vulkan shaders can be used to preprocess data on the GPU before it's sent to machine learning models.

Feature engineering code can be highly specialized and depend on the specifics of the Vulkan application and the machine learning task. It often involves creating custom functions or shaders tailored to the data and task at hand.

Effective data preprocessing and feature engineering are critical for achieving good machine learning results in Vulkan applications. These steps ensure that your models can learn meaningful patterns from the data and make accurate predictions or decisions. The choice of preprocessing techniques and feature engineering methods should align with the goals of your Vulkan AI application and the characteristics of the data you're working with.

6.5 Supervised Learning vs. Unsupervised Learning

In the realm of machine learning, two fundamental categories of learning algorithms stand out: supervised learning and unsupervised learning. Each of these approaches has its own unique characteristics and use cases. In this section, we will explore the differences between supervised and unsupervised learning and discuss scenarios where each is relevant when integrated with Vulkan graphics programming.

1. Supervised Learning

Supervised learning is the most prevalent form of machine learning. In this paradigm, the algorithm is provided with a labeled dataset, which means each data point in the training data is associated with a corresponding target or label. The algorithm's goal is to learn a mapping from input data to the correct output.

Key characteristics of supervised learning include:

- **Training with Labeled Data**: Supervised learning models are trained using data where the correct answers are known. This facilitates the learning process as the algorithm can compare its predictions to the ground truth during training.

- **Types of Tasks**: Supervised learning can be applied to both classification tasks (where the goal is to assign data points to predefined categories or classes) and regression tasks (where the goal is to predict continuous values).

- **Examples**: Image classification (assigning images to categories), sentiment analysis (classifying text as positive or negative), and object detection (detecting and classifying objects within an image) are common applications of supervised learning in Vulkan.

Here is a simplified example of supervised learning code using Python and scikit-learn:

```python
from sklearn.model_selection import train_test_split

from sklearn.ensemble import RandomForestClassifier

# Split the data into training and testing sets

X_train, X_test, y_train, y_test = train_test_split(features, labels, test_size=0.2)

# Create a supervised learning model (Random Forest classifier)

clf = RandomForestClassifier()

# Train the model on the training data

clf.fit(X_train, y_train)

# Make predictions on the test data

predictions = clf.predict(X_test)
```

2. Unsupervised Learning

Unsupervised learning, on the other hand, deals with unlabeled data, meaning the algorithm does not have access to explicit output labels during training. Instead, it focuses on discovering patterns, structures, or relationships within the data.

Key characteristics of unsupervised learning include:

- **No Labeled Data Required**: Unsupervised learning does not rely on labeled data, making it applicable to scenarios where labeled data is scarce or unavailable.

- **Types of Tasks**: Common unsupervised learning tasks include clustering (grouping similar data points together), dimensionality reduction (reducing the number of features while preserving information), and generative modeling (learning the underlying data distribution).

- **Examples**: Unsupervised learning can be used in Vulkan for tasks like texture clustering (grouping similar textures in a scene), dimensionality reduction of high-dimensional feature data, and generative modeling for procedural content generation.

Here's a simplified example of unsupervised learning code using Python and scikit-learn:

```python
from sklearn.cluster import KMeans

# Create an unsupervised learning model (K-Means clustering)

kmeans = KMeans(n_clusters=3)

# Fit the model to the data

kmeans.fit(data)

# Get cluster assignments for each data point

cluster_labels = kmeans.labels_
```

3. Combining Supervised and Unsupervised Learning

In many real-world scenarios, a combination of supervised and unsupervised learning can be beneficial. For example, unsupervised learning can be used for initial data exploration and feature extraction, followed by supervised learning to build predictive models using the derived features.

In Vulkan graphics programming, this combination can be leveraged for tasks such as optimizing rendering pipelines (unsupervised clustering of scene data) and then using supervised learning to predict optimal rendering settings based on the identified clusters.

The choice between supervised and unsupervised learning, or a combination of both, depends on the specific goals of your Vulkan AI application and the nature of the data you are working with. Careful consideration of these approaches can lead to more effective and efficient graphics applications that leverage machine learning.

Chapter 7: Integrating AI with Vulkan

7.1 Machine Learning in Graphics

Machine learning has found numerous applications in the field of computer graphics, including Vulkan-based graphics programming. This section explores the role of machine learning in graphics and how it can be integrated with Vulkan to enhance rendering, optimize performance, and enable new capabilities.

1. Enhancing Graphics Quality

Machine learning can be employed to enhance graphics quality in Vulkan applications. One common use case is image upscaling or super-resolution. Machine learning models, such as convolutional neural networks (CNNs), can be trained to upscale low-resolution images or textures to higher resolutions while preserving details. This technique can lead to crisper and more detailed visuals in real-time graphics.

```python
# Example code for using a pre-trained super-resolution model

import tensorflow as tf

# Load a pre-trained super-resolution model

super_res_model = tf.keras.applications.EfficientSR()

# Upscale a low-resolution image

upscaled_image = super_res_model.upscale(low_res_image)
```

2. Real-time Object Detection

Machine learning models for object detection, such as YOLO (You Only Look Once) or Faster R-CNN, can be integrated with Vulkan applications to enable real-time object detection within the rendered scene. This can have applications in augmented reality (AR) and virtual reality (VR) scenarios where detecting and interacting with objects in the environment is crucial.

```python
# Example code for real-time object detection using YOLO

import cv2

# Load YOLO model

yolo_model = cv2.dnn.readNet("yolov3.weights", "yolov3.cfg")

# Perform object detection on a frame

blob = cv2.dnn.blobFromImage(frame, 1 / 255.0, (416, 416), swapRB=True, crop=False)

yolo_model.setInput(blob)

detection_results = yolo_model.forward()
```

3. AI-driven Graphics Enhancement

Machine learning can be used to dynamically adjust graphics settings in Vulkan applications based on factors like hardware capabilities, scene complexity, and user preferences. This can result in smoother performance and improved visual quality. Reinforcement learning algorithms, for example, can adapt rendering settings in real-time to maintain a target frame rate while maximizing visual fidelity.

```python
# Example code for reinforcement learning-based graphics adjustment
```

```python
import gym

import stable_baselines3

# Define an environment for graphics adjustment

env = gym.make("VulkanGraphics-v0")

# Train a reinforcement learning agent to optimize graphics settings

model = stable_baselines3.PPO("MlpPolicy", env)

model.learn(total_timesteps=10000)
```

4. Procedural Content Generation

Machine learning can assist in generating procedural content for Vulkan applications. Generative adversarial networks (GANs) and recurrent neural networks (RNNs) can be used to create textures, models, and even entire scenes procedurally. This can be especially useful in game development to reduce manual content creation efforts.

```python
# Example code for procedural texture generation using a GAN

import tensorflow as tf

# Load a pre-trained GAN model for texture generation

gan_model = tf.keras.models.load_model("texture_gan.h5")

# Generate a new texture

generated_texture = gan_model.generate_texture()
```

5. Performance Optimization

Machine learning can aid in optimizing the performance of Vulkan applications by predicting rendering bottlenecks, suggesting rendering settings, and dynamically adjusting rendering techniques based on real-time performance metrics. This can lead to smoother and more responsive graphics applications.

```python
# Example code for using machine learning to predict rendering bottlenecks

import sklearn

# Load a machine learning model for bottleneck prediction

bottleneck_model = sklearn.load_model("bottleneck_prediction_model")

# Predict rendering bottlenecks based on scene data

bottleneck = bottleneck_model.predict(scene_data)
```

Integrating machine learning with Vulkan graphics programming opens up exciting possibilities for enhancing graphics quality, enabling real-time interactions, and optimizing performance. However, it also introduces challenges related to data preprocessing, model deployment, and real-time inference. Careful consideration of the specific requirements and goals of your Vulkan AI application is essential for successful integration.

7.2 Using TensorFlow with Vulkan

TensorFlow is one of the most popular machine learning frameworks, and it can be seamlessly integrated with Vulkan graphics programming to leverage the power of deep learning. In this section, we will explore how to use TensorFlow with Vulkan and discuss scenarios where this integration can be beneficial.

1. TensorFlow and Vulkan Interoperability

TensorFlow provides TensorFlow Lite (TFLite) and TensorFlow Serving as tools for deploying machine learning models on various platforms, including Vulkan-supported environments. TFLite allows you to convert trained TensorFlow models into a format suitable for mobile and embedded devices, making it a natural choice for Vulkan applications on platforms like Android and iOS.

To get started with TensorFlow and Vulkan integration, you can follow these steps:

1. **Train or obtain a TensorFlow model**: First, you need a trained machine learning model. This could be a model for image classification, object detection, super-resolution, or any other task relevant to your Vulkan application.
2. **Convert the model to TensorFlow Lite format**: Use TensorFlow tools to convert your trained model to TFLite format. This format is optimized for deployment on resource-constrained devices, making it suitable for Vulkan applications.
3. **Integrate TFLite with Vulkan**: In your Vulkan application code, load the TFLite model and integrate it into your rendering pipeline. You can use Vulkan compute shaders to perform inference with the model.

Here's a simplified example of how you can load a TFLite model and perform inference within a Vulkan application:

// Load the TFLite model

```cpp
std::unique_ptr<tflite::FlatBufferModel>        model        =
tflite::FlatBufferModel::BuildFromFile("model.tflite");

// Create a TensorFlow interpreter

tflite::ops::builtin::BuiltinOpResolver resolver;

tflite::InterpreterBuilder builder(*model, resolver);

std::unique_ptr<tflite::Interpreter> interpreter;

builder(&interpreter);

// Allocate input and output tensors

interpreter->AllocateTensors();

// Load input data into the input tensor

float* input_data = interpreter->typed_input_tensor<float>(0);

// Populate input_data with your input data

// Run inference

interpreter->Invoke();

// Get the output tensor data

float* output_data = interpreter->typed_output_tensor<float>(0);

// Process the output data within your Vulkan application
```

2. Vulkan and Deep Learning

Vulkan's parallel computing capabilities, especially through compute shaders, align well with the requirements of deep learning inference. You can utilize Vulkan's GPU-accelerated compute capabilities to speed up inference tasks, making real-time AI-driven graphics more feasible.

Some scenarios where you can leverage TensorFlow with Vulkan include:

- **Image Processing**: You can integrate TensorFlow models for image processing tasks, such as style transfer or image-to-image translation, into your Vulkan rendering pipeline. This allows you to apply artistic styles to rendered scenes or dynamically modify textures.

- **Dynamic Content Generation**: TensorFlow can be used to generate dynamic content based on real-time inputs. For example, you can generate procedural terrain textures or adapt game levels based on player behavior using machine learning models.

- **AI-driven Interactions**: Incorporate machine learning models trained for gesture recognition or voice commands into your Vulkan-based AR or VR applications. This enables more natural and interactive experiences.

- **Performance Optimization**: TensorFlow models can predict rendering bottlenecks and recommend optimizations based on scene data. Vulkan can then dynamically adjust rendering settings to improve performance while maintaining visual quality.

- **Real-time Object Detection**: Utilize TensorFlow models for object detection within your Vulkan application, allowing you to interact with and manipulate objects in the rendered environment.

3. Challenges and Considerations

Integrating TensorFlow with Vulkan comes with certain challenges and considerations:

- **Performance**: Real-time machine learning inference on the GPU can be computationally intensive. Careful optimization and workload management are essential to avoid performance bottlenecks.

- **Data Transfer**: Efficient data transfer between Vulkan and TensorFlow is crucial. You may need to implement data preprocessing and synchronization mechanisms to ensure smooth communication.

- **Model Size**: Consider the size of the TensorFlow model, especially for mobile and embedded platforms. Larger models may require additional storage and memory resources.

- **Latency**: Minimizing inference latency is crucial for interactive applications. Optimizing model size, using hardware acceleration, and managing resource allocation can help reduce latency.

- **Deployment**: Ensure that you can easily deploy and update your Vulkan application with integrated TensorFlow models on target platforms.

Integrating TensorFlow with Vulkan provides exciting opportunities for AI-powered graphics applications. With the ability to perform deep learning inference directly on the GPU, you can create immersive and intelligent graphics experiences that respond to real-time inputs and adapt to user interactions.

7.3 Training and Inference Pipelines

Incorporating machine learning into Vulkan applications often involves two key phases: training and inference. Training is the process of creating and optimizing machine learning models using labeled data, while inference is the process of using these trained models to make predictions or decisions in real-time. This section explores how training and inference pipelines can be set up and managed in the context of Vulkan and AI integration.

1. Training Machine Learning Models

Training machine learning models typically occurs offline, often on powerful workstations or cloud infrastructure. This phase involves:

- **Data Collection and Preprocessing**: Gathering and preparing labeled data for training. This includes data cleaning, augmentation, and splitting into training and validation sets.

- **Model Design and Architecture**: Defining the architecture of the machine learning model, including layers, activation functions, and loss functions.

- **Training Process**: Iteratively optimizing the model's parameters (weights and biases) using optimization algorithms like stochastic gradient descent (SGD). This process involves feeding batches of training data through the model and updating the parameters to minimize the loss function.

- **Validation and Hyperparameter Tuning**: Evaluating the model's performance on a separate validation dataset and adjusting hyperparameters (e.g., learning rate, batch size) to improve performance.

- **Exporting Trained Models**: Saving the trained model in a format suitable for inference, such as TensorFlow SavedModel or TensorFlow Lite (TFLite) format.

Here is an example code snippet illustrating the training process of a simple machine learning model using TensorFlow:

```python
import tensorflow as tf

# Load and preprocess your training data

train_data = load_and_preprocess_data()

# Define the model architecture

model = tf.keras.Sequential([

tf.keras.layers.Dense(128,                          activation='relu',
input_shape=(input_shape,)),

tf.keras.layers.Dense(64, activation='relu'),

tf.keras.layers.Dense(output_classes, activation='softmax')

])

# Compile the model with appropriate loss and optimizer

model.compile(loss='categorical_crossentropy',    optimizer='adam',
metrics=['accuracy'])

# Train the model

model.fit(train_data, epochs=num_epochs, batch_size=batch_size)
```

 # Save the trained model

model.save('trained_model.h5')

2. Inference in Vulkan Applications

Once the machine learning model is trained and saved, it can be integrated into Vulkan applications for real-time inference. Inference pipelines within Vulkan applications involve the following steps:

- **Model Loading**: Loading the pre-trained machine learning model, which was saved during the training phase. TensorFlow Lite (TFLite) models are commonly used for Vulkan inference due to their lightweight nature.

- **Vulkan Integration**: Integrating the model within the Vulkan rendering pipeline. This often requires the use of Vulkan compute shaders to perform inference tasks on the GPU.

- **Input Data Preparation**: Preparing input data for the model. This data could be generated from the rendered scene or obtained from external sensors (e.g., camera feeds in AR applications).

- **Inference Execution**: Running inference on the GPU using Vulkan compute shaders or other GPU-accelerated techniques. The output of the inference can be used to make real-time decisions or modify the rendering pipeline.

Here is a simplified example of how you can perform inference using a TensorFlow Lite model within a Vulkan application:

// Load the TensorFlow Lite model

```
tflite::Interpreter interpreter;

interpreter->AllocateTensors();

interpreter->SetInputTensor(input_tensor_index, input_data);

interpreter->Invoke();

// Get the output tensor data

float*                         output_data                         =
interpreter->typed_output_tensor<float>(output_tensor_index);

// Process the output data within your Vulkan application

// (e.g., adjust rendering parameters or interact with objects based on
the inference results)
```

3. Synchronization and Performance

Efficient synchronization between the Vulkan rendering pipeline and the machine learning inference pipeline is crucial for real-time applications. Vulkan provides mechanisms for inter-pipeline synchronization, such as pipeline barriers and semaphores. Careful management of synchronization points ensures that inference results are available when needed for rendering.

Performance optimization in the inference phase is also essential. This includes leveraging GPU acceleration, batch processing, and optimizing memory usage to minimize latency and maximize frame rates.

Integrating training and inference pipelines in Vulkan applications allows for intelligent, adaptive, and interactive graphics experiences. Machine learning models trained offline can be used to make real-time decisions, enhancing graphics quality, enabling dynamic content generation, and facilitating AI-driven interactions in AR, VR, and gaming applications.

7.4 Real-time Object Detection

Real-time object detection is a crucial application of machine learning in Vulkan graphics programming. It involves identifying and localizing objects within a scene in real-time, enabling a wide range of interactive and intelligent graphics experiences. In this section, we explore the integration of real-time object detection using machine learning models within Vulkan applications.

1. Object Detection Models

Real-time object detection relies on machine learning models specifically designed for this task. Two popular types of models used for object detection are:

- **Single Shot MultiBox Detector (SSD)**: SSD is a real-time object detection model that combines object localization and classification in a single pass through the network. It is known for its speed and accuracy and is suitable for interactive applications.

- **YOLO (You Only Look Once)**: YOLO is another real-time object detection model that offers a good balance between accuracy and speed. YOLO divides the image into a grid and predicts bounding boxes and class probabilities for each grid cell.

These models are typically trained on large datasets containing labeled images with object annotations.

2. Integration with Vulkan

Integrating real-time object detection with Vulkan applications involves several steps:

- **Model Loading**: Load a pre-trained object detection model. TensorFlow models in TensorFlow Lite (TFLite) format are commonly used due to their lightweight nature.

- **Input Data Preparation**: Prepare input data for the model, which usually involves capturing the scene from the camera or rendering the scene and providing it as input to the model.

- **Inference**: Run the object detection model's inference on the input data using Vulkan compute shaders or other GPU-accelerated techniques. The output provides information about detected objects' bounding boxes and class probabilities.

- **Rendering with Object Detection**: Use the object detection results to modify the rendering pipeline. For example, you can highlight or interact with detected objects in the rendered scene, adjust lighting or shadows based on object positions, or trigger specific events in response to detected objects.

Here's a simplified example of how you can perform real-time object detection within a Vulkan application:

// Load the TensorFlow Lite object detection model

tflite::Interpreter interpreter;

```
interpreter->AllocateTensors();

interpreter->SetInputTensor(input_tensor_index,
input_image_data);

interpreter->Invoke();

// Get the output tensor data containing detected objects' bounding
boxes and class probabilities

float*                     output_data                     =
interpreter->typed_output_tensor<float>(output_tensor_index);

// Process the output data within your Vulkan application

// (e.g., highlight or interact with detected objects in the rendered scene)
```

3. Applications of Real-time Object Detection

Real-time object detection opens up a wide range of possibilities for interactive graphics applications:

- **AR and VR Interactions**: In augmented reality (AR) and virtual reality (VR) applications, real-time object detection can be used to recognize physical objects or user gestures, enabling more immersive and interactive experiences.

- **Gaming**: Game developers can use object detection to enhance gameplay, such as detecting and reacting to player movements or recognizing in-game objects for interactions.

- **Simulations**: In training simulations and serious games, object detection can identify and track objects relevant to the training scenario, providing real-time feedback and analysis.

• **Visual Effects**: Object detection can be employed in film and visual effects production to track and modify scenes in real-time, making it easier to composite digital elements into live-action footage.

• **Robotics**: Object detection is a crucial component of robotics applications, enabling robots to perceive and interact with their environment in real-time.

4. Performance Considerations

Efficient integration of real-time object detection with Vulkan applications requires careful consideration of performance:

• **Latency**: Minimizing inference latency is essential, especially in interactive applications. Optimizations like batching and GPU acceleration can help reduce latency.

• **Model Size**: The size of the object detection model can impact memory usage. Efficient model architectures and compression techniques can help manage memory resources.

• **Synchronization**: Ensuring proper synchronization between the object detection pipeline and the rendering pipeline is critical to achieving smooth and responsive interactions.

• **Hardware Acceleration**: Leveraging GPU acceleration for object detection tasks can significantly improve performance, especially on platforms with capable GPUs.

Integrating real-time object detection into Vulkan applications enhances the capabilities of graphics programming by enabling intelligent, context-aware interactions. Whether in gaming, AR/VR, simulations, or other interactive graphics contexts, object detection adds a new layer of interactivity and realism to the user experience.

7.5 AI-driven Graphics Enhancement

AI-driven graphics enhancement is a transformative application of machine learning in Vulkan programming. It involves using machine learning models to improve the quality, realism, and performance of graphics rendering in real-time. In this section, we explore how AI-driven graphics enhancement can be integrated into Vulkan applications.

1. Enhancing Graphics Quality

One of the primary applications of AI-driven graphics enhancement is improving the visual quality of rendered scenes. This can be achieved through techniques such as:

- **Super-Resolution**: Using deep learning models to upscale lower-resolution textures, images, or rendered frames to higher resolutions. Super-resolution techniques enhance details and reduce pixelation.

- **Anti-Aliasing**: Machine learning models can be employed to reduce jagged edges and aliasing artifacts commonly seen in real-time rendering. MLAA (Machine Learning Anti-Aliasing) is an example of such a technique.

- **Texture Enhancement**: Enhancing the quality of textures by upscaling, denoising, or generating high-quality textures from lower-quality sources. This improves the realism of materials and surfaces in the rendered scene.

2. Realistic Lighting and Shadows

AI-driven graphics enhancement can also enhance lighting and shadows in real-time rendering. This includes:

- **Global Illumination**: Simulating global illumination effects in real-time, such as indirect lighting, ambient occlusion, and radiosity, to create more realistic and immersive scenes.

- **Dynamic Lighting**: Adjusting the intensity, color, and direction of dynamic lights based on scene content and user interactions, allowing for more dynamic and responsive lighting.

- **Shadow Generation**: Generating high-quality and realistic shadows using machine learning models. This includes soft shadows, penumbra effects, and accurate self-shadowing.

3. Performance Optimization

AI-driven graphics enhancement can also play a role in optimizing performance:

- **Adaptive Rendering**: Adjusting rendering quality and detail based on scene complexity and hardware capabilities. Machine learning models can help make real-time decisions on which rendering techniques to apply.

• **Predictive Rendering**: Predicting user actions or camera movements and pre-rendering or optimizing parts of the scene in anticipation, reducing latency and improving responsiveness.

4. Integration with Vulkan

Integrating AI-driven graphics enhancement within Vulkan applications involves several steps:

• **Model Loading**: Load pre-trained machine learning models that perform the desired graphics enhancement tasks. These models are often based on deep learning architectures.

• **Input Data Preparation**: Prepare the scene data or rendered frames as input to the AI-driven models. This could involve capturing the scene, rendering a frame, or processing textures.

• **Inference**: Run the AI-driven models' inference on the input data using Vulkan compute shaders or other GPU-accelerated techniques. The output from the models contains enhanced graphics data.

• **Rendering with Enhanced Graphics**: Integrate the enhanced graphics data into the rendering pipeline to achieve higher-quality visuals and more realistic lighting and shadows.

Here's a simplified example of how you can perform AI-driven graphics enhancement within a Vulkan application:

```
// Load the pre-trained AI-driven graphics enhancement model

tflite::Interpreter interpreter;

interpreter->AllocateTensors();

interpreter->SetInputTensor(input_tensor_index,
input_scene_data);

interpreter->Invoke();

// Get the output tensor data containing enhanced graphics information

float*                         output_data                         =
interpreter->typed_output_tensor<float>(output_tensor_index);

// Use the enhanced graphics data in your Vulkan rendering pipeline

// (e.g., apply super-resolution, anti-aliasing, or improved lighting)
```

5. Performance and Realism Balance

When integrating AI-driven graphics enhancement, striking a balance between performance and realism is crucial. AI-driven techniques can be computationally intensive, and it's essential to ensure that the enhanced graphics do not lead to significant performance drops, especially in real-time applications.

Performance optimization techniques, such as using optimized model architectures, hardware acceleration, and efficient memory management, can help achieve a balance that meets the application's requirements.

AI-driven graphics enhancement has the potential to revolutionize the gaming, entertainment, and design industries by offering unprecedented levels of realism and interactivity in real-time graphics. These enhancements can lead to more immersive gaming experiences, more realistic virtual environments in AR/VR, and better visualization in fields such as architecture, engineering, and film production.

Chapter 8: GPU Accelerated Machine Learning

8.1 GPU Computing and CUDA

In this section, we delve into the realm of GPU-accelerated machine learning in Vulkan programming. GPU (Graphics Processing Unit) acceleration is a powerful technique that leverages the parallel processing capabilities of GPUs to perform machine learning tasks efficiently. We'll start by exploring GPU computing and its integration with Vulkan applications, with a particular focus on CUDA (Compute Unified Device Architecture), NVIDIA's parallel computing platform and API.

1. Understanding GPU Computing

GPU computing is the process of using GPUs to perform general-purpose computing tasks beyond traditional graphics rendering. GPUs consist of thousands of small cores capable of executing tasks concurrently, making them well-suited for parallelizable workloads like machine learning.

2. Why GPU Acceleration?

GPU acceleration offers several advantages for machine learning tasks in Vulkan:

- **Parallelism**: GPUs excel at parallel processing, enabling them to handle massive amounts of data and computations simultaneously, which is crucial for training and inference in deep learning models.

- **Performance**: GPUs can significantly accelerate machine learning workloads, reducing training and inference times from hours to minutes or even seconds, depending on the complexity of the task.

- **Scalability**: GPUs can be easily scaled by using multiple GPUs in a single system, further boosting performance and enabling the training of larger models and datasets.

- **Energy Efficiency**: GPUs provide better performance per watt compared to CPUs, making them more energy-efficient for intensive machine learning tasks.

3. Introduction to CUDA

CUDA is a parallel computing platform and API developed by NVIDIA for GPU programming. It provides a comprehensive ecosystem for GPU-accelerated computing, including:

- **CUDA Toolkit**: A software development kit that includes libraries, tools, and compilers for CUDA development.

- **cuDNN**: The CUDA Deep Neural Network library, which provides GPU-accelerated primitives for deep neural networks.

- **cuBLAS**: The CUDA Basic Linear Algebra Subprograms library, which offers GPU-accelerated linear algebra routines.

- **cuSPARSE**: The CUDA sparse matrix library, useful for sparse matrix operations.

4. Integrating CUDA with Vulkan

Integrating CUDA with Vulkan allows Vulkan applications to harness the power of GPUs for machine learning tasks. This integration involves several steps:

- **CUDA Initialization**: Initialize the CUDA runtime in your Vulkan application to access GPU resources.

- **Memory Management**: Allocate and manage GPU memory for machine learning data and models.

- **Data Transfer**: Transfer data between the Vulkan and CUDA contexts efficiently, ensuring minimal overhead.

- **Kernel Execution**: Launch CUDA kernels to perform machine learning computations on the GPU.

- **Synchronization**: Ensure proper synchronization between Vulkan and CUDA operations to avoid data race conditions.

Here's a simplified example of how you can use CUDA within a Vulkan application:

```
// Initialize CUDA

cudaSetDevice(0); // Select the GPU device

cudaMalloc((void**)&d_data, data_size); // Allocate GPU memory

cudaMemcpy(d_data, h_data, data_size, cudaMemcpyHostToDevice); // Transfer data to GPU

myCUDAKernel<<<gridSize, blockSize>>>(d_data); // Launch a CUDA kernel
```

cudaMemcpy(h_result,   d_result,   result_size,
cudaMemcpyDeviceToHost); *// Transfer result back to CPU*

5. Performance Considerations

When integrating CUDA with Vulkan, it's essential to consider performance optimization:

- **Data Transfer**: Minimize data transfer between the CPU and GPU, as it can be a performance bottleneck. Use shared memory or peer-to-peer communication if available.

- **Kernel Optimization**: Optimize CUDA kernels for better GPU utilization and parallelism. Profiling tools like NVIDIA Nsight can help identify performance bottlenecks.

- **Multi-GPU Scaling**: If your system has multiple GPUs, explore techniques like data parallelism or model parallelism to leverage all available GPU resources.

- **Memory Management**: Efficient GPU memory management is critical. Avoid unnecessary memory allocations and deallocate GPU memory when no longer needed.

- **Synchronization**: Proper synchronization between Vulkan and CUDA operations is vital to ensure data consistency and avoid race conditions.

GPU-accelerated machine learning with CUDA and Vulkan offers the potential for significant performance improvements in a wide range of applications, from real-time object detection to training complex neural networks. Understanding the principles of GPU computing and effectively integrating CUDA into Vulkan programming can unlock the full potential of modern graphics hardware for machine learning tasks.

8.2 Vulkan Compute Shaders

Vulkan Compute Shaders are a fundamental component of GPU-accelerated machine learning in Vulkan. Compute shaders are specialized shaders that can perform highly parallelized computations on GPU data. In this section, we'll explore the role of compute shaders in GPU-accelerated machine learning and how to use them effectively in Vulkan.

1. Compute Shader Basics

A compute shader is a type of shader in Vulkan that is designed specifically for general-purpose computing tasks rather than rendering. It operates on data in parallel and is ideal for tasks like matrix operations, data manipulation, and machine learning computations.

2. Parallelism in Compute Shaders

Compute shaders leverage the massively parallel architecture of GPUs. They execute many threads, known as workgroups or thread groups, in parallel. Each thread in a workgroup can perform a specific computation, and communication between threads within a workgroup is efficient.

3. Using Compute Shaders for Machine Learning

Compute shaders are a powerful tool for implementing machine learning algorithms on the GPU. Here's how they can be applied:

- **Matrix Operations**: Machine learning often involves matrix operations like matrix multiplication, which can be efficiently parallelized using compute shaders.

- **Neural Network Layers**: Compute shaders can be used to implement layers of neural networks, such as fully connected layers and convolutional layers.

- **Data Preprocessing**: Compute shaders can preprocess data, including normalization, augmentation, and data loading, to prepare it for machine learning tasks.

4. HLSL and SPIR-V

Compute shaders in Vulkan can be written in HLSL (High-Level Shading Language) or SPIR-V (Standard Portable Intermediate Representation). HLSL is a high-level language developed by Microsoft, while SPIR-V is an intermediate representation that Vulkan understands.

Here's an example of a simple compute shader in HLSL that adds two arrays element-wise:

```
[numthreads(256, 1, 1)]

void main(uint3 DTid : SV_DispatchThreadID) {

output[DTid.x] = input1[DTid.x] + input2[DTid.x];

}
```

This shader adds elements of input1 and input2 arrays in parallel.

5. Dispatching Compute Shaders

To execute a compute shader in Vulkan, you need to dispatch it using Vulkan API calls. Here's a simplified example:

```
// Create a Vulkan command buffer

VkCommandBuffer commandBuffer;

// Bind the compute shader pipeline

vkCmdBindPipeline(commandBuffer,
VK_PIPELINE_BIND_POINT_COMPUTE,
computePipeline);

// Bind descriptor sets (if required)

vkCmdBindDescriptorSets(commandBuffer,
VK_PIPELINE_BIND_POINT_COMPUTE, pipelineLayout, 0,
1, &descriptorSet, 0, nullptr);

// Dispatch the compute shader with appropriate workgroup
dimensions

vkCmdDispatch(commandBuffer,                numWorkgroupsX,
numWorkgroupsY, numWorkgroupsZ);
```

In this example, computePipeline represents the Vulkan pipeline containing the compute shader, and descriptorSet represents descriptor sets if any are required for the shader.

6. Performance Considerations

When using compute shaders for machine learning in Vulkan, consider these performance optimization techniques:

- **Workgroup Size**: Choose an appropriate workgroup size that maximizes GPU utilization without causing excessive thread synchronization.

- **Data Layout**: Optimize data layout in GPU memory to minimize memory access times.

- **Resource Management**: Manage GPU resources efficiently, including memory allocation and deallocation.

- **Synchronization**: Use Vulkan's synchronization mechanisms carefully to avoid race conditions and ensure proper data flow between compute shaders and other parts of your application.

Vulkan compute shaders provide a powerful and efficient way to accelerate machine learning workloads on the GPU. By leveraging parallelism and optimizing shader code, you can harness the full potential of modern graphics hardware for machine learning tasks.

8.3 GPU-accelerated Machine Learning Libraries

In the world of GPU-accelerated machine learning in Vulkan, leveraging specialized libraries can significantly simplify the development process and enhance performance. Several GPU-accelerated machine learning libraries are available, each catering to specific use cases and hardware. In this section, we'll explore some of these libraries and how they can be integrated into Vulkan applications.

1. cuDNN (CUDA Deep Neural Network Library)

cuDNN, developed by NVIDIA, is a GPU-accelerated library specifically designed for deep neural networks (DNNs). It provides a collection of highly optimized routines for common DNN operations such as convolution, pooling, and activation functions. cuDNN is widely used in machine learning frameworks like TensorFlow and PyTorch for GPU acceleration.

To integrate cuDNN into a Vulkan application, you'll typically follow these steps:

- Initialize CUDA for GPU access.

- Allocate GPU memory for data and model parameters.

- Use cuDNN functions to perform DNN operations.

- Ensure synchronization between Vulkan and CUDA operations.

Here's a simplified example of using cuDNN for convolution in a Vulkan application:

```
// Initialize CUDA

cudaSetDevice(0);

// Initialize cuDNN

cudnnHandle_t cudnn;

cudnnCreate(&cudnn);

// Allocate GPU memory for data and model

float* d_input_data, *d_output_data;
```

```
cudaMalloc((void**)&d_input_data, input_size);

cudaMalloc((void**)&d_output_data, output_size);

// Create cuDNN convolution descriptor and convolution parameters

cudnnConvolutionDescriptor_t convDesc;

cudnnCreateConvolutionDescriptor(&convDesc);

// Set convolution parameters (e.g., padding, stride, dilation)

// Perform convolution using cuDNN

cudnnConvolutionForward(cudnn, &alpha, inputTensorDesc,
d_input_data, filterDesc, d_filter_data, convDesc, algo,
d_workspace, workspaceSize, &beta, outputTensorDesc,
d_output_data);

// Release resources

cudnnDestroyConvolutionDescriptor(convDesc);

cudaFree(d_input_data);

cudaFree(d_output_data);

// Destroy cuDNN

cudnnDestroy(cudnn);
```

2. ROCm and MIOpen

ROCm (Radeon Open Compute) is an open-source platform developed by AMD for GPU computing. It includes MIOpen (Machine Intelligence Open), a GPU-accelerated machine learning library similar to cuDNN but designed for AMD GPUs. MIOpen provides optimized routines for deep learning tasks and is compatible with popular deep learning frameworks.

To integrate MIOpen into a Vulkan application with AMD GPUs, you'd follow similar steps to the cuDNN example but tailored to ROCm and MIOpen libraries.

3. TensorFlow GPU Support

TensorFlow, one of the most popular deep learning frameworks, offers GPU support for both NVIDIA and AMD GPUs. TensorFlow automatically leverages GPU acceleration when available, making it easier for Vulkan applications that use TensorFlow for machine learning tasks to benefit from GPU acceleration.

To use TensorFlow GPU support within Vulkan applications, ensure that TensorFlow is compiled with GPU support and that the appropriate GPU drivers are installed on your system. TensorFlow will then handle GPU integration transparently.

4. PyTorch GPU Support

PyTorch, another popular deep learning framework, provides GPU support for both NVIDIA and AMD GPUs. Similar to TensorFlow, PyTorch allows Vulkan applications to benefit from GPU acceleration without significant code changes.

To utilize PyTorch GPU support, ensure PyTorch is installed with GPU support, and your system has the necessary GPU drivers.

5. Vulkan Interoperability

To efficiently use GPU-accelerated machine learning libraries within Vulkan applications, it's essential to establish efficient interoperability between Vulkan and the GPU libraries. This includes managing GPU memory, data transfers between Vulkan and library contexts, and synchronization to ensure data consistency.

6. Performance Considerations

When integrating GPU-accelerated machine learning libraries into Vulkan applications, consider the following performance optimization strategies:

- **Memory Management**: Efficiently manage GPU memory to minimize allocation and deallocation overhead.

- **Data Transfer**: Minimize data transfers between Vulkan and GPU libraries to reduce latency.

- **Workload Balancing**: Distribute workloads efficiently between Vulkan compute shaders and library functions to utilize GPU resources effectively.

- **Synchronization**: Ensure proper synchronization between Vulkan and library operations to prevent data race conditions.

Integrating GPU-accelerated machine learning libraries with Vulkan applications can unlock substantial performance gains in machine learning workloads. Careful consideration of library selection, memory management, and synchronization is key to achieving optimal results.

8.4 Parallelism and Performance Optimization

In the realm of GPU-accelerated machine learning with Vulkan, optimizing performance is crucial to harness the full potential of modern graphics hardware. This section delves into the concepts of parallelism and performance optimization techniques to make the most of Vulkan's capabilities.

1. Parallelism in Machine Learning

Parallelism is at the heart of GPU-accelerated machine learning. Modern GPUs are designed with thousands of cores capable of executing parallel tasks simultaneously. Here's how parallelism can be exploited:

- **Data Parallelism**: Divide large datasets into smaller chunks and process them concurrently on different GPU cores. This is common in training deep neural networks.

- **Model Parallelism**: Split a deep neural network model across multiple GPUs, allowing each GPU to focus on a portion of the model. This is useful for very large models that don't fit in the memory of a single GPU.

- **Task Parallelism**: Perform different tasks concurrently, such as data preprocessing, inference, and model training, to fully utilize GPU resources.

2. Thread and Workgroup Organization

In Vulkan, compute shaders are organized into threads and workgroups (thread groups). Understanding how to structure these is vital for optimizing performance:

- **Threads**: Individual threads within a workgroup. They can communicate efficiently but are limited in number by the GPU's compute unit.

- **Workgroups**: Groups of threads that execute independently. Workgroups are larger in number than threads and can run concurrently.

3. Load Balancing

Efficient load balancing ensures that work is evenly distributed among threads and workgroups. Load imbalance can lead to underutilization of GPU resources. Techniques such as dynamic load balancing can help distribute tasks effectively.

4. Memory Optimization

Memory access patterns significantly impact performance. Techniques to optimize memory usage include:

- **Data Layout**: Arrange data in memory for efficient access. For example, use coalesced memory access patterns to minimize memory stalls.

- **Shared Memory**: Utilize shared memory (also known as local memory) for communication between threads within a workgroup. Shared memory is faster than global memory.

5. Asynchronous Execution

Vulkan allows for asynchronous execution of compute shaders and graphics tasks. Taking advantage of asynchronous execution can reduce idle time and improve overall throughput.

Here's an example of asynchronously dispatching compute shaders in Vulkan:

// Submit a graphics command buffer (assumes Vulkan setup)

vkQueueSubmit(graphicsQueue, 1, &graphicsCommandBuffer, fence);

// Submit a compute command buffer asynchronously

vkQueueSubmit(computeQueue, 1, &computeCommandBuffer, fence);

// Wait for both command buffers to complete

vkWaitForFences(device, 1, &fence, VK_TRUE, UINT64_MAX);

6. Pipeline Barriers

Vulkan provides pipeline barriers to control memory dependencies and synchronization between command buffers. Properly using pipeline barriers ensures that memory reads and writes are synchronized correctly.

7. Profiling and Benchmarking

Profiling tools help identify performance bottlenecks in Vulkan applications. Tools like Vulkan's built-in validation layers, GPU vendor-specific profilers, and external profilers can provide insights into application performance.

8. Performance Considerations for Machine Learning

When optimizing machine learning workloads in Vulkan, consider these additional performance tips:

- **Batching**: Process data in batches to minimize memory access overhead.

- **Reduced Precision**: Use reduced precision (e.g., 16-bit floating-point) when precision isn't critical. This can speed up computations.

- **Quantization**: Convert high-precision model weights to lower precision (e.g., int8) for inference tasks.

- **Kernel Fusion**: Combine multiple operations into a single compute shader to reduce synchronization overhead.

Optimizing performance in GPU-accelerated machine learning with Vulkan is an iterative process that involves profiling, benchmarking, and fine-tuning. By effectively utilizing parallelism, optimizing memory usage, and applying performance techniques, you can achieve significant speedups in your machine learning workloads.

8.5 Implementing Neural Networks in Vulkan

Implementing neural networks in Vulkan involves designing and executing compute shaders that perform forward and backward propagation, enabling training and inference of machine learning models. This section explores the process of building neural networks within the Vulkan framework.

1. Forward and Backward Propagation

In neural network training, forward propagation computes the model's predictions given the input data, while backward propagation calculates gradients and updates model weights during training. Both of these operations can be implemented as Vulkan compute shaders.

Here's a simplified example of a Vulkan compute shader for forward propagation in a fully connected layer:

```glsl
#version 450

layout(set = 0, binding = 0) buffer InputData {

float data[];

};

layout(set = 0, binding = 1) buffer OutputData {

float data[];

};

layout(set = 0, binding = 2) buffer Weights {

float weights[];

};

layout(set = 0, binding = 3) buffer Biases {

float biases[];

};

layout(set = 0, binding = 4) buffer LayerInfo {

uint inputSize;
uint outputSize;

};
```

```glsl
void main() {

uint idx = gl_GlobalInvocationID.x;

uint inputSize = gl_WorkGroupSize.x;

uint outputSize = gl_WorkGroupSize.y;

float result = 0.0;

for (uint i = 0; i < inputSize; ++i) {

result += data[i] * weights[idx * inputSize + i];

}

result += biases[idx];

data[idx] = result;

}
```

Implementing backward propagation and gradient computation follows a similar pattern but involves additional complexity for gradient descent optimization.

2. Network Architecture

Building neural networks in Vulkan allows for flexibility in designing custom architectures. You can create complex models with multiple layers, including fully connected, convolutional, and recurrent layers. Each layer can be implemented as a separate Vulkan compute shader, and data can be efficiently passed between them.

3. Training and Inference Pipelines

Vulkan pipelines can be designed for both training and inference of neural networks. During training, forward and backward passes are executed repeatedly with data updates and weight adjustments. In contrast, inference pipelines focus on prediction using pre-trained models without weight updates.

4. Model Serialization and Deserialization

To save and load trained neural network models, you need mechanisms for model serialization and deserialization. You can implement custom formats or use popular formats like TensorFlow's SavedModel format or PyTorch's TorchScript.

5. Integration with GPU-accelerated Libraries

As mentioned in previous sections, integrating Vulkan with GPU-accelerated machine learning libraries like cuDNN or MIOpen can simplify the implementation of neural network layers. These libraries provide highly optimized routines for common neural network operations.

6. Vulkan Compute Shader Limitations

While Vulkan compute shaders are powerful for implementing neural networks, they come with some limitations:

- Limited debugging and error reporting: Debugging compute shaders can be challenging compared to CPU-based implementations.

- Complexity: Implementing complex neural network layers from scratch in compute shaders can be time-consuming.

- Precision: Vulkan shaders typically operate on floating-point numbers, which may have limited precision compared to CPU implementations. This can impact model training and inference accuracy.

• Memory management: Managing GPU memory for model weights, activations, and gradients requires careful consideration to avoid memory leaks.

7. Performance Optimization

Optimizing neural network implementations in Vulkan involves techniques discussed in the previous section, such as parallelism, memory optimization, and pipeline barriers. Profiling and benchmarking are essential for identifying performance bottlenecks.

Implementing neural networks in Vulkan offers the advantage of GPU acceleration, making it suitable for training and inference tasks that require high computational power. However, it requires expertise in both Vulkan and machine learning to achieve efficient and accurate results.

Chapter 9: Cross-Platform Development

Cross-platform development in the context of Vulkan involves the challenges and strategies for creating applications that run seamlessly on multiple operating systems and platforms. This chapter explores the considerations, tools, and techniques necessary for achieving cross-platform compatibility with Vulkan-based applications.

9.1 Challenges in Cross-Platform Development

Cross-platform development offers the advantage of reaching a broader audience with your Vulkan applications. However, it also presents unique challenges that developers must address to ensure consistent performance and user experience across different platforms. Here are some of the key challenges:

1. OS and API Variations

Different operating systems (e.g., Windows, Linux, macOS) have their APIs and system-specific nuances. Vulkan, while cross-platform by design, may still require platform-specific code to handle differences in window management, input handling, and system integration.

2. Hardware Diversity

Vulkan supports a wide range of hardware, each with varying capabilities and performance characteristics. Ensuring your application runs smoothly on different GPUs, CPUs, and memory configurations can be a complex task.

3. Input Handling

User input methods vary across platforms, including keyboard and mouse on desktops, touchscreens on mobile devices, and game controllers on gaming consoles. Implementing consistent and intuitive input handling across platforms is essential for a positive user experience.

4. Window Management

Managing application windows and rendering contexts can differ significantly between platforms. You may need to adapt your window management code to create and handle Vulkan surfaces appropriately on each platform.

5. File System and Permissions

File system access and permissions may vary between platforms. Applications that rely on file I/O must account for differences in file paths, file access rights, and storage locations.

6. Performance Optimization

Each platform may have its performance characteristics and bottlenecks. Optimizing your Vulkan application for each target platform may require platform-specific tweaks and profiling.

7. API Abstraction

To simplify cross-platform development, developers often use API abstraction layers and frameworks like SDL, GLFW, or Qt. These libraries provide a consistent interface for window management, input, and other platform-specific tasks.

8. Testing and Debugging

Thorough testing on each target platform is crucial to identify and resolve platform-specific issues. Debugging tools and techniques must also be adapted for different platforms.

9.1 Strategies for Cross-Platform Development

Addressing the challenges of cross-platform development with Vulkan requires careful planning and the following strategies:

1. Platform Abstraction

Use platform abstraction libraries and frameworks to encapsulate platform-specific code. These libraries provide a unified interface for common tasks like window creation, input handling, and file I/O.

2. Conditional Compilation

Utilize conditional compilation and preprocessor directives to include or exclude platform-specific code sections based on the target platform. This allows you to maintain a single codebase while accommodating platform differences.

3. Hardware Profiling

Profile your application's performance on different hardware configurations to identify bottlenecks and optimize resource usage for each platform.

4. User Interface Adaptation

Adapt your user interface (UI) to the conventions and design guidelines of each platform. A consistent and platform-specific UI improves user acceptance.

5. Thorough Testing

Perform extensive testing on each target platform to catch platform-specific bugs and ensure a consistent user experience. Emulators and virtual machines can help simulate different platforms during development.

6. Community and Documentation

Leverage developer communities, forums, and platform-specific documentation to seek guidance and solutions for platform-related challenges.

Cross-platform development with Vulkan can be demanding but is essential for reaching a wider user base. By addressing the challenges and employing the right strategies, you can create Vulkan applications that perform reliably and consistently across diverse platforms.

9.2 Vulkan on Windows, Linux, and macOS

Vulkan's cross-platform nature makes it possible to develop applications that run on Windows, Linux, and macOS. However, each of these operating systems has its nuances and requirements when it comes to Vulkan development. In this section, we will explore the considerations and steps needed to work with Vulkan on these three major platforms.

Windows

1. Vulkan SDK Installation

To start Vulkan development on Windows, you need to install the Vulkan SDK, which includes the necessary libraries, headers, and tools. You can download the SDK from the official LunarG website or use package managers like vcpkg.

2. Development Environment

Windows developers often use Visual Studio for Vulkan development due to its robust integration with the Windows platform. You can set up a Visual Studio project and use the Vulkan SDK's libraries and headers.

3. Window Management

For window management on Windows, you can use the Windows API or libraries like GLFW or SDL, which simplify window creation and input handling. Vulkan surfaces need to be created using platform-specific extensions.

4. Debugging and Profiling

Visual Studio provides debugging tools for Vulkan applications. You can also use external profilers like RenderDoc or NVIDIA Nsight for performance analysis and debugging.

5. Deployment

When deploying Vulkan applications on Windows, you need to ensure that the target system has the necessary Vulkan runtime libraries installed. Consider using installer packages or deployment scripts for distribution.

Linux

1. Vulkan SDK Installation

On Linux, you can install the Vulkan SDK using package managers like apt or dnf. This includes Vulkan libraries, headers, and development tools.

2. Development Environment

Linux developers typically use IDEs like Visual Studio Code or command-line tools for Vulkan development. Ensure that you link against the Vulkan loader and libraries during compilation.

3. Window Management

Linux desktop environments often use X11 or Wayland for window management. Libraries like GLFW and SDL provide cross-platform window and input handling, making it easier to create Vulkan surfaces.

4. Debugging and Profiling

Linux offers a range of debugging and profiling tools, including GDB for debugging and tools like RenderDoc and VK_EXT_debug_utils for Vulkan-specific debugging.

5. Deployment

When distributing Vulkan applications on Linux, consider packaging your application for popular package managers like APT or creating AppImage or Flatpak packages for broader compatibility.

macOS

1. Vulkan SDK Installation

While Vulkan is not natively supported on macOS, you can use MoltenVK, an open-source implementation of Vulkan on top of Apple's Metal API. Install MoltenVK to access Vulkan functionality on macOS.

2. Development Environment

For macOS Vulkan development, Xcode is a common choice. You'll need to set up a project that links against MoltenVK and use Objective-C or Swift for macOS-specific integration.

3. Window Management

Window management on macOS is different from Windows and Linux. You'll need to use macOS-specific APIs for window creation and input handling.

4. Debugging and Profiling

Debugging Vulkan applications on macOS can be challenging due to the limited native support. You can use MoltenVK-specific debugging tools and consider using external profilers.

5. Deployment

When deploying Vulkan applications on macOS, you'll need to bundle the MoltenVK framework with your application to ensure Vulkan functionality is available.

In summary, Vulkan development on Windows, Linux, and macOS requires platform-specific considerations for SDK installation, development environments, window management, debugging, and deployment. Understanding these platform nuances is crucial for successful cross-platform Vulkan development.

9.3 Mobile Platforms and Vulkan

Mobile platforms, including Android and iOS, have gained prominence in the world of Vulkan development. Bringing Vulkan to mobile devices allows developers to harness the power of modern graphics APIs for immersive mobile gaming and applications. In this section, we'll explore the considerations and steps for developing Vulkan applications on mobile platforms.

Android

1. Vulkan Support

Vulkan is well-supported on Android devices. Most Android smartphones and tablets come with Vulkan-compatible GPUs, making it a viable choice for mobile graphics development.

2. Vulkan SDK Installation

To develop Vulkan applications for Android, you need to install the Android NDK (Native Development Kit), which includes the necessary Vulkan headers and libraries. Android Studio is the recommended IDE for Android development.

3. Native Activity or Game Engines

Android provides Native Activity, which allows you to create Vulkan applications without using the Java-based Android framework. Alternatively, you can leverage popular game engines like Unity or Unreal Engine, which offer Vulkan support for mobile platforms.

4. Vulkan Layers

Android supports Vulkan validation layers for debugging and validation. These layers help identify and resolve issues in your Vulkan code. You can enable them during development and disable them for release builds.

5. Deployment

When deploying Vulkan applications on Android, you need to package your application as an APK (Android Package). Ensure that you include the Vulkan loader and any necessary Vulkan extensions in your APK.

iOS

1. MoltenVK

Vulkan is not natively supported on iOS, but you can use MoltenVK, as mentioned earlier for macOS. MoltenVK translates Vulkan calls into Metal API calls, allowing you to run Vulkan applications on iOS devices.

2. Development Environment

For iOS Vulkan development, you can use Xcode, Apple's integrated development environment. You'll need to set up your project to link against MoltenVK and use Objective-C or Swift for iOS-specific integration.

3. Debugging and Profiling

Debugging Vulkan applications on iOS can be challenging due to the use of MoltenVK. Utilize MoltenVK-specific debugging tools and consider using external profilers for performance analysis.

4. Deployment

When deploying Vulkan applications on iOS, ensure that you bundle the MoltenVK framework with your application to enable Vulkan functionality on iOS devices. You'll distribute your application through the Apple App Store.

Cross-Platform Development

To target both Android and iOS with a single codebase, you can explore cross-platform development frameworks like Unity, Unreal Engine, or multi-platform Vulkan libraries. These tools help streamline development and deployment to multiple mobile platforms.

In summary, Vulkan development on mobile platforms offers exciting opportunities for creating high-performance graphics applications. Understanding the platform-specific nuances of Android and iOS, as well as leveraging tools like MoltenVK, can enable you to harness the full potential of Vulkan on mobile devices.

9.4 API Abstraction Layers

Developing graphics applications that target multiple platforms often involves dealing with the nuances of each platform's graphics API, such as Vulkan, DirectX, or Metal. To simplify cross-platform development and ensure your application runs smoothly on various devices, API abstraction layers or frameworks can be immensely helpful. In this section, we'll explore the concept of API abstraction layers and how they can streamline the development process.

What Are API Abstraction Layers?

API abstraction layers are software libraries or frameworks that provide a higher-level interface for graphics programming. They sit between your application code and the platform-specific graphics APIs, abstracting away the platform-specific details. This abstraction allows developers to write code that is more portable and platform-agnostic.

Benefits of Using API Abstraction Layers

1. **Cross-Platform Compatibility:** API abstraction layers enable developers to write code once and run it on multiple platforms without significant modifications. This reduces development time and effort.
2. **Simplified Development:** These layers provide a more straightforward and consistent API that abstracts the complexities of different graphics APIs. Developers can focus on application logic rather than dealing with low-level graphics intricacies.
3. **Reduced Maintenance:** When platform-specific changes or updates occur, the abstraction layer can be updated to accommodate them, sparing developers from making extensive changes to their codebase.
4. **Access to Advanced Features:** Abstraction layers often expose features and capabilities that are not available in all underlying graphics APIs. This allows developers to take advantage of the latest graphics technologies.
5. **Community and Support:** Popular API abstraction layers often have active communities and support forums, making it easier to find solutions to common issues and share knowledge with other developers.

Common API Abstraction Layers

1. **OpenGL:** Although considered a lower-level API, OpenGL serves as an abstraction layer for platform-specific graphics APIs like DirectX and Metal. Libraries like GLFW and SDL provide additional abstraction and simplify window management.
2. **Vulkan-Hpp:** This is a C++ wrapper for the Vulkan API, which makes Vulkan development more accessible to C++ developers. It provides a higher-level, object-oriented interface while maintaining the low-level control that Vulkan offers.
3. **MoltenVK:** As mentioned earlier, MoltenVK allows Vulkan applications to run on iOS and macOS by translating Vulkan calls into Metal API calls. It's a powerful abstraction layer for Apple platforms.
4. **Unity and Unreal Engine:** These game engines provide extensive abstraction layers for graphics programming. They offer cross-platform support, including Vulkan, DirectX, and Metal, making it easy to develop and deploy games on various devices.

Choosing the Right Abstraction Layer

The choice of an API abstraction layer depends on your project's requirements and target platforms. Consider factors like platform support, performance, community support, and ease of use when selecting an abstraction layer. Additionally, evaluate whether the layer aligns with your team's skills and development workflow.

In conclusion, API abstraction layers simplify the development of graphics applications for multiple platforms, offering benefits such as cross-platform compatibility, simplified development, reduced maintenance, and access to advanced features. Understanding these layers and choosing the right one for your project can greatly enhance your development process and help you reach a broader audience with your graphics applications.

9.5 Testing and Compatibility Issues

Testing is a critical aspect of Vulkan development, especially when targeting multiple platforms and devices. Ensuring that your Vulkan application works correctly and efficiently across a range of hardware and software configurations is essential for a successful deployment. In this section, we'll explore testing and compatibility issues specific to Vulkan development.

Device Compatibility

One of the primary challenges in Vulkan development is dealing with a diverse range of GPU architectures and driver versions. To address this, consider the following:

- **Device Selection:** Vulkan allows you to query available devices and select one that meets your application's requirements. Carefully choose devices based on capabilities, performance, and Vulkan API support.

- **Driver Updates:** Keep track of driver updates from GPU manufacturers. New drivers may offer performance improvements or bug fixes, which can significantly impact your application.

Validation Layers

Validation layers in Vulkan are crucial for debugging and identifying issues in your application. However, different validation layers may behave differently on various platforms. Here are some considerations:

- **Platform-Specific Validation:** Some validation layers may have platform-specific behaviors or issues. Be aware of these platform nuances and test your application on each target platform.

- **Validation Layer Versions:** Ensure that you are using the latest version of Vulkan validation layers. Older versions may not support newer Vulkan features or report issues accurately.

Windowing and Surface Management

Vulkan applications often rely on windowing systems to create surfaces for rendering. Compatibility with different windowing systems is crucial:

- **Platform-Specific Surface Creation:** Be aware that surface creation may differ between platforms. Ensure that you properly create surfaces using platform-specific code.

- **Window Resizing:** Handle window resizing gracefully. Vulkan applications need to recreate swap chains and associated resources when the window size changes.

Cross-Platform Development

When developing Vulkan applications for multiple platforms, cross-platform libraries and tools become invaluable:

- **Testing on All Platforms:** Test your application on all target platforms regularly. Use platform-specific testing environments or devices to ensure compatibility.

- **Continuous Integration:** Implement a continuous integration (CI) pipeline that builds and tests your application on various platforms automatically. This helps catch issues early in development.

- **Platform-Specific Code:** Use conditional compilation or platform-specific code paths when necessary. Implement platform-specific features or optimizations as needed.

Performance Profiling

Performance testing is crucial for Vulkan applications, as performance can vary significantly between devices and configurations:

- **Profiling Tools:** Utilize Vulkan-specific profiling tools and external profilers to identify performance bottlenecks. Optimize your code for various GPU architectures.

- **Performance Metrics:** Collect and analyze performance metrics on different platforms to ensure your application runs smoothly and efficiently.

User Feedback

Engaging with your user base and collecting feedback is essential for resolving compatibility issues:

- **Feedback Channels:** Provide clear channels for users to report compatibility problems. Act on user feedback promptly to address issues in future updates.

- **Beta Testing:** Conduct beta testing on a diverse range of hardware and software configurations. Beta testers can help identify compatibility issues early.

In conclusion, testing and ensuring compatibility are vital aspects of Vulkan development, especially when targeting multiple platforms. Consider device compatibility, validation layers, windowing and surface management, cross-platform development practices, performance profiling, and user feedback to create Vulkan applications that work seamlessly across a wide range of hardware and software configurations. Testing rigorously and addressing compatibility issues proactively will lead to a more robust and successful Vulkan application deployment.

Chapter 10: Performance Optimization

10.1 Profiling Your Application

Profiling is a crucial step in the development of Vulkan applications, especially when aiming for optimal performance. Profiling involves analyzing the runtime behavior of your application to identify bottlenecks and areas where optimization can be applied. In this section, we will explore the importance of profiling in Vulkan development and discuss various profiling tools and techniques.

Why Profiling Matters

Profiling your Vulkan application serves several essential purposes:

1. **Identifying Performance Bottlenecks:** Profiling helps pinpoint areas of your code that consume the most CPU or GPU resources. This allows you to focus your optimization efforts where they will have the most significant impact.

2. **Optimization Opportunities:** Profiling provides data that can guide your optimization efforts. By understanding which parts of your application are performance-critical, you can prioritize optimization tasks effectively.

3. **Validating Assumptions:** Profiling can reveal whether your assumptions about performance are accurate. It helps ensure that your application meets performance goals and runs smoothly on target hardware.

4. **Avoiding Over-Optimization:** Profiling prevents over-optimization, where you spend time optimizing code that doesn't significantly impact performance. This can lead to wasted development effort.

Profiling Tools and Techniques

Several profiling tools and techniques are available for Vulkan applications:

1. Vulkan-Specific Profilers

- **RenderDoc:** RenderDoc is a popular graphics debugger and profiler that supports Vulkan. It allows you to capture frames, inspect API calls, and analyze GPU performance.

- **AMD Radeon GPU Profiler (RGP):** AMD's RGP tool provides detailed insights into GPU performance. It's particularly useful for AMD GPU users.

- **NVIDIA Nsight Graphics:** If you're developing for NVIDIA GPUs, Nsight Graphics offers a suite of profiling and debugging tools tailored for Vulkan and other APIs.

2. CPU Profilers

- **Intel VTune Profiler:** VTune Profiler is a powerful CPU profiler that can help you identify CPU bottlenecks in your Vulkan application.

- **Linux Perf:** On Linux, the perf tool provides various profiling capabilities, including CPU and memory profiling. It can be useful for identifying CPU-related bottlenecks.

3. GPU Performance Counters

Many modern GPUs offer performance counters that can be accessed through Vulkan extensions. These counters provide detailed information about GPU activity, such as shader occupancy, memory bandwidth, and pipeline statistics.

4. Timing Queries

Vulkan allows you to insert timing queries into your command buffers, which can measure the time taken to execute specific GPU operations. Timing queries are valuable for understanding how long various rendering tasks take.

Profiling Workflow

Here's a general workflow for profiling your Vulkan application:

1. **Instrument Your Code:** Introduce timing queries and markers into your Vulkan commands to gather performance data.
2. **Capture Frames:** Use a profiling tool like RenderDoc or an integrated GPU profiler to capture frames of your application in action.
3. **Analyze the Data:** Examine the captured frames to identify performance bottlenecks, CPU/GPU usage, and problematic rendering passes.
4. **Optimize:** Once you've identified bottlenecks, focus on optimizing the relevant parts of your code. This might involve optimizing shaders, reducing draw calls, or minimizing data transfers between the CPU and GPU.
5. **Repeat:** Profiling is an iterative process. Capture frames, analyze data, optimize, and repeat until your application

meets its performance goals.

Best Practices

- **Profile on Target Hardware:** Whenever possible, perform profiling on the same hardware and configurations as your target audience. This ensures that you are optimizing for the correct platform.

- **Profile Across Different Scenes:** Profiling should cover a variety of scenes and scenarios that your application will encounter. Don't focus solely on a single scene; instead, consider the typical use cases of your application.

- **Keep Profiling Overheads in Mind:** Profiling tools themselves can introduce some overhead. Be aware of this and consider it when interpreting the profiling data.

- **Regular Profiling:** Profiling should be a routine part of your development process, not just a one-time activity. Regular profiling helps catch performance issues early and ensures ongoing optimization.

In conclusion, profiling is a critical step in optimizing the performance of your Vulkan application. It helps identify bottlenecks, guides optimization efforts, and ensures that your application runs smoothly on target hardware. By using Vulkan-specific profiling tools and techniques, you can gain valuable insights into both CPU and GPU performance, leading to a more efficient and responsive application.

10.2 Bottleneck Analysis

Bottleneck analysis is a crucial part of performance optimization in Vulkan applications. Identifying and addressing bottlenecks can lead to significant improvements in your application's frame rate and overall performance. In this section, we will delve into the process of bottleneck analysis, the common types of bottlenecks in Vulkan, and strategies to resolve them.

What Is a Bottleneck?

A bottleneck, in the context of computer graphics and Vulkan, refers to a part of your application that limits its overall performance. Bottlenecks can occur in various areas, such as CPU, GPU, memory, or the interaction between these components. Understanding where bottlenecks occur is the first step in optimizing your application effectively.

Common Types of Bottlenecks

1. **CPU Bound:** If your application spends a significant amount of time on the CPU processing tasks like updating game logic, preparing command buffers, or managing resources, it's considered CPU-bound. CPU bottlenecks can lead to longer frame times and reduced frame rates.

2. **GPU Bound:** When the GPU is the limiting factor, your application is GPU-bound. This happens when the GPU takes a long time to execute rendering commands, shaders, or other GPU-intensive tasks. GPU bottlenecks can result in frame rate drops and stuttering.

3. **Memory Bound:** Memory-bound scenarios occur when your application frequently accesses memory, causing stalls or cache misses. This can happen due to inefficient memory

management or high memory consumption.

4. **Synchronization:** Synchronization bottlenecks occur when multiple threads or GPU compute units need to coordinate their actions. Excessive synchronization can lead to stalls and performance degradation.

5. **Draw Call Overhead:** High draw call counts can overwhelm the CPU, causing it to spend more time preparing and submitting commands to the GPU. Reducing draw call overhead is a common optimization target.

6. **Shader Performance:** Inefficient shaders or complex shader programs can slow down the GPU. Optimizing shaders and reducing unnecessary calculations can help mitigate this bottleneck.

Strategies for Bottleneck Analysis

To identify and address bottlenecks in your Vulkan application, follow these strategies:

1. **Profiling:** Use profiling tools like RenderDoc, GPU profilers, and CPU profilers to gather data on frame times, CPU and GPU utilization, and memory usage. Profiling helps pinpoint performance bottlenecks.

2. **Frame Analysis:** Analyze captured frames to identify areas where frame times are excessively high. Look for spikes in frame time or consistently long frame times.

3. **GPU Timings:** Use Vulkan's timing queries to measure the GPU time spent on different rendering tasks, such as drawing, rendering passes, and memory transfers. This helps identify GPU-bound bottlenecks.

4. **CPU Timing:** Measure CPU times for various tasks, including command buffer generation, resource

management, and game logic. Identify CPU-bound areas that need optimization.

5. **Memory Analysis:** Monitor memory usage and analyze memory allocation patterns. Optimize memory management to reduce memory-bound bottlenecks.

6. **Multithreading:** Utilize Vulkan's multithreading capabilities to parallelize CPU tasks and reduce CPU-bound bottlenecks. Be cautious with synchronization to avoid introducing new bottlenecks.

7. **Shader Optimization:** Profile and optimize shaders to reduce GPU bottlenecks. Eliminate unnecessary calculations and use shader-specific profiling tools.

8. **Draw Call Reduction:** Minimize the number of draw calls by using techniques like batching, instancing, and culling. Reducing draw call overhead can alleviate CPU bottlenecks.

9. **Resource Management:** Optimize resource loading and management to minimize stalls caused by memory access. Use techniques like resource streaming and resource pooling.

10. **Pipeline Barriers:** Use Vulkan pipeline barriers efficiently to synchronize GPU operations. Avoid unnecessary barriers that can introduce synchronization bottlenecks.

Bottleneck analysis is an iterative process that requires continuous monitoring, profiling, and optimization. By addressing bottlenecks in your Vulkan application, you can achieve smoother and more responsive graphics performance, enhancing the overall user experience.

10.3 Multi-threading and Parallelism

Multi-threading and parallelism are essential techniques for achieving high performance in Vulkan applications. By effectively utilizing multiple CPU cores and parallelizing tasks, you can optimize your application's performance and make the most of modern hardware. In this section, we'll explore the concepts of multi-threading and parallelism in the context of Vulkan.

Why Multi-threading?

Modern CPUs come with multiple cores, allowing them to execute multiple threads in parallel. To fully harness the power of these CPUs, Vulkan applications can distribute tasks across multiple threads, making better use of available resources. Multi-threading offers several advantages:

1. **Improved CPU Utilization:** Multi-threading allows you to utilize all available CPU cores, reducing CPU bottlenecks and increasing overall performance.
2. **Parallel Task Execution:** Certain tasks in a Vulkan application, such as command buffer generation, resource loading, and game logic, can be executed concurrently on different threads.
3. **Responsiveness:** Multi-threading can improve the responsiveness of your application by offloading CPU-intensive tasks to separate threads, ensuring the user interface remains smooth.
4. **Load Balancing:** Effective multi-threading ensures that the workload is evenly distributed across CPU cores, preventing core imbalances.

Vulkan and Multi-threading

Vulkan is designed to support multi-threading, allowing you to create and manage resources, generate command buffers, and submit rendering commands from multiple threads. Here are key points to consider:

1. Vulkan Device and Instance

- Vulkan instances and physical devices can be created and managed independently by different threads. However, be cautious when accessing Vulkan objects simultaneously to avoid synchronization issues.

2. Command Buffer Generation

- Command buffer generation, a CPU-bound task, can be parallelized. You can create multiple threads to generate command buffers concurrently, improving performance.

```
// Pseudocode for parallel command buffer generation

std::vector<std::thread> threads;

for (int i = 0; i < numThreads; ++i) {

threads.emplace_back([&device, &commandBuffers, i]() {

// Each thread generates command buffers for a subset of the frame.

GenerateCommandBuffers(device, commandBuffers, i);

});

}
```

```cpp
for (auto& thread : threads) {

thread.join();

}
```

3. Resource Loading

- Resource loading can also benefit from multi-threading. Load and preprocess assets concurrently to reduce loading times.

```cpp
// Pseudocode for parallel resource loading

std::vector<std::thread> threads;

for (int i = 0; i < numThreads; ++i) {

threads.emplace_back([&resources, i]() {

// Each thread loads a subset of resources.

LoadResources(resources, i);

});

}

for (auto& thread : threads) {

thread.join();

}
```

4. Synchronization

- When using multiple threads in Vulkan, ensure proper synchronization using Vulkan synchronization primitives like semaphores, fences, and pipeline barriers.

5. Thread Safety

- Take precautions to make Vulkan objects thread-safe. For example, Vulkan queues can be used from multiple threads, but access to Vulkan objects like command buffers should be synchronized.

Thread Pools

Creating and managing threads can introduce overhead. Consider using thread pools, which maintain a pool of worker threads, to manage tasks efficiently. Libraries like C++17's <thread> library and thread pool libraries can simplify multi-threading implementation.

Conclusion

Multi-threading and parallelism are powerful techniques for optimizing Vulkan applications. By distributing tasks across multiple threads and cores, you can achieve better CPU utilization and improved overall performance. However, it's essential to implement multi-threading carefully to avoid synchronization issues and race conditions. With effective multi-threading, you can create Vulkan applications that take full advantage of modern hardware capabilities.

10.4 Memory Management and Resource Pools

Efficient memory management is crucial in Vulkan to ensure optimal performance and resource utilization. In this section, we'll delve into memory management techniques and the use of resource pools to streamline Vulkan applications.

Vulkan Memory Management Overview

Vulkan provides explicit control over memory allocation and management. Unlike some other graphics APIs, Vulkan doesn't abstract memory management, giving developers fine-grained control. Key concepts in Vulkan memory management include:

1. Memory Heaps and Memory Types

- Vulkan devices offer multiple memory heaps, each with specific properties (e.g., device-local, host-visible, coherent, etc.). Memory types are derived from these heaps and represent specific combinations of memory properties.

2. Memory Allocation

- To allocate memory, you need to create a Vulkan memory object and bind it to a Vulkan resource, such as a buffer or an image.

// Pseudocode for memory allocation

```
VkMemoryAllocateInfo allocateInfo = {};
```

```
allocateInfo.sType                                    =
VK_STRUCTURE_TYPE_MEMORY_ALLOCATE_INFO;
```

```
allocateInfo.allocationSize = memorySize;
```

allocateInfo.memoryTypeIndex = memoryTypeIndex; // *Derived from memory properties*

```
VkDeviceMemory memory;
```

```
vkAllocateMemory(device, &allocateInfo, nullptr, &memory);
```

```
vkBindBufferMemory(device, buffer, memory, 0);
```

3. *Memory Pools*

- Vulkan allows you to create memory pools, which are useful for efficiently managing memory allocations for resources like command buffers. Memory pools reduce the overhead of individual memory allocations.

// *Pseudocode for memory pool creation*

```
VkCommandPoolCreateInfo poolInfo = {};
```

```
poolInfo.sType                                    =
VK_STRUCTURE_TYPE_COMMAND_POOL_CREATE_INFO;
```

```
poolInfo.queueFamilyIndex = queueFamilyIndex;
```

```
VkCommandPool commandPool;
```

```
vkCreateCommandPool(device, &poolInfo, nullptr, &commandPool);
```

Resource Pools

Resource pools are a valuable technique in Vulkan for managing resources efficiently. These pools allocate and manage a predefined number of resources (e.g., command buffers, descriptor sets) in advance. Resource pools offer several advantages:

1. Reduced Allocation Overhead

- Resource pools allocate resources in bulk, reducing the overhead of individual resource creation and destruction during runtime.

2. Improved Memory Fragmentation

- By allocating resources in predefined batches, resource pools can help mitigate memory fragmentation issues that can arise from frequent resource creation and destruction.

3. Better Resource Utilization

- Resource pools ensure that a fixed number of resources are available at all times, optimizing resource utilization.

Implementing a Command Buffer Pool

One common use case for resource pools is managing command buffers. Here's a simplified example of implementing a command buffer pool:

```cpp
class CommandBufferPool {

public:
```

```cpp
CommandBufferPool(VkDevice device, VkCommandPool commandPool, uint32_t bufferCount)

:        device(device),        commandPool(commandPool), bufferCount(bufferCount) {

// Create and allocate command buffers

commandBuffers.resize(bufferCount);

VkCommandBufferAllocateInfo allocInfo = {};

allocInfo.sType = VK_STRUCTURE_TYPE_COMMAND_BUFFER_ALLOCATE_INF

allocInfo.commandPool = commandPool;

allocInfo.level = VK_COMMAND_BUFFER_LEVEL_PRIMARY;

allocInfo.commandBufferCount = bufferCount;

vkAllocateCommandBuffers(device, &allocInfo, commandBuffers.data());

}

// Get a command buffer from the pool

VkCommandBuffer GetCommandBuffer() {

if (currentIndex >= bufferCount) {

currentIndex = 0; // Reset index if we run out of buffers

}

return commandBuffers[currentIndex++];
```

```
}

private:

VkDevice device;

VkCommandPool commandPool;

uint32_t bufferCount;

uint32_t currentIndex = 0;

std::vector<VkCommandBuffer> commandBuffers;

};
```

In this example, the CommandBufferPool class manages a pool of command buffers. When you request a command buffer, it returns one from the pool, ensuring efficient usage of command buffers.

Conclusion

Efficient memory management is vital for Vulkan applications, and resource pools are a valuable tool to achieve this. By carefully managing memory allocation and using resource pools for frequently used resources like command buffers, you can optimize your Vulkan application's performance and memory utilization. Remember to release resources and manage memory properly to avoid memory leaks and resource exhaustion.

10.5 GPU Debugging Tools

Debugging is an essential part of the development process, and when working with Vulkan, understanding the available GPU debugging tools can greatly simplify the task of identifying and resolving issues.

In this section, we'll explore some of the tools and techniques for debugging Vulkan applications.

Validation Layers

Validation layers are an integral part of Vulkan's debugging infrastructure. They help catch common mistakes and errors in Vulkan applications, such as incorrect API usage or invalid memory accesses. While validation layers are essential during development, it's important to note that they may introduce some overhead, so they are typically disabled in release builds.

To enable validation layers, you must set up your Vulkan instance to use them during initialization. Here's a simplified example:

```cpp
// Enable validation layers during instance creation

VkInstanceCreateInfo createInfo = {};

createInfo.sType                                    = VK_STRUCTURE_TYPE_INSTANCE_CREATE_INFO;

// Specify validation layers to enable

const char* enabledLayers[] = { "VK_LAYER_KHRONOS_validation" };

createInfo.enabledLayerCount = 1;

createInfo.ppEnabledLayerNames = enabledLayers;

// Create the Vulkan instance

VkInstance instance;

vkCreateInstance(&createInfo, nullptr, &instance);
```

Vulkan Debug Utils Extension

The Vulkan Debug Utils Extension is an extension to Vulkan that provides more fine-grained control over debugging and validation. It allows you to define custom debug callback functions that can capture and handle debug messages generated by the Vulkan runtime.

Here's an example of how to set up a debug callback using the Vulkan Debug Utils Extension:

```
// Define a callback function to handle debug messages

VKAPI_ATTR VkBool32 VKAPI_CALL DebugCallback(

VkDebugUtilsMessageSeverityFlagBitsEXT messageSeverity,

VkDebugUtilsMessageTypeFlagsEXT messageType,

const VkDebugUtilsMessengerCallbackDataEXT* pCallbackData,

void* pUserData) {

// Print or handle the debug message as needed

// ...

return VK_FALSE; // Return VK_TRUE to stop the application

}

// Create a debug messenger

VkDebugUtilsMessengerCreateInfoEXT createInfo = {};

createInfo.sType                                      =
VK_STRUCTURE_TYPE_DEBUG_UTILS_MESSENGER_CREAT
```

```
createInfo.messageSeverity                                    =
VK_DEBUG_UTILS_MESSAGE_SEVERITY_WARNING_BIT_EXT
|

VK_DEBUG_UTILS_MESSAGE_SEVERITY_ERROR_BIT_EXT;

createInfo.messageType                                        =
VK_DEBUG_UTILS_MESSAGE_TYPE_GENERAL_BIT_EXT
|

VK_DEBUG_UTILS_MESSAGE_TYPE_VALIDATION_BIT_EXT
|

VK_DEBUG_UTILS_MESSAGE_TYPE_PERFORMANCE_BIT_EX

createInfo.pfnUserCallback = DebugCallback;

VkDebugUtilsMessengerEXT messenger;

vkCreateDebugUtilsMessengerEXT(instance, &createInfo, nullptr,
&messenger);
```

With the debug callback in place, you can customize how your application handles different types and severity levels of debug messages, making it easier to diagnose and fix issues.

RenderDoc

RenderDoc is a popular third-party debugging tool for graphics applications, including Vulkan. It allows you to capture and inspect the state of the GPU at various points in your application's execution. RenderDoc provides a visual interface for analyzing rendering frames, examining draw calls, and identifying rendering errors.

To use RenderDoc with your Vulkan application, you'll need to integrate the RenderDoc SDK into your project and capture frames during execution. Refer to the RenderDoc documentation for specific integration details.

GPU Vendor-Specific Tools

GPU manufacturers like NVIDIA, AMD, and Intel provide vendor-specific tools and profilers for debugging and optimizing GPU-bound workloads. These tools offer insights into GPU performance, memory usage, and shader debugging. For example:

- NVIDIA Nsight Graphics: A powerful tool for analyzing and debugging GPU workloads on NVIDIA GPUs.

- AMD Radeon Developer Tools: Includes tools like Radeon GPU Profiler (RGP) for AMD GPUs, which helps optimize GPU performance.

- Intel Graphics Performance Analyzers (Intel GPA): Offers a suite of tools for profiling and optimizing Intel integrated GPUs.

Depending on your target GPU, these vendor-specific tools can provide valuable insights into your Vulkan application's performance and behavior.

Conclusion

Debugging Vulkan applications can be challenging, but understanding the available debugging tools and techniques can simplify the process. Validation layers, the Vulkan Debug Utils Extension, third-party tools like RenderDoc, and vendor-specific

GPU tools all play a crucial role in identifying and resolving issues in Vulkan applications. By utilizing these tools effectively, you can streamline your debugging workflow and create more reliable and performant Vulkan applications.

Chapter 11: Ray Tracing and Vulkan

Section 11.1: Introduction to Ray Tracing

Ray tracing is a rendering technique that simulates the way light interacts with objects in a virtual environment to produce realistic images. Unlike traditional rasterization, which focuses on rendering individual polygons, ray tracing models the behavior of light rays as they travel through a scene. This approach enables the simulation of complex lighting effects, including global illumination, shadows, reflections, and refractions. In this section, we will explore the fundamentals of ray tracing and its integration with Vulkan.

Ray Tracing Principles

At its core, ray tracing follows a simple principle: for each pixel on the screen, trace one or more rays of light into the scene and calculate their interactions with objects. These rays may bounce off surfaces, refract through materials, or be absorbed, depending on the properties of the objects they encounter. By tracing rays backward from the camera's viewpoint, we can determine the color of each pixel based on the contributions of these rays.

Realism and Visual Fidelity

Ray tracing is renowned for its ability to achieve high levels of visual fidelity and realism. It accurately simulates how light behaves in the real world, leading to photorealistic graphics. This is especially valuable in applications like video games, architectural visualization, and film production, where visual quality is crucial.

Ray Tracing in Vulkan

Vulkan, as a modern and versatile graphics API, provides support for ray tracing through extensions. These extensions introduce new shaders, structures, and pipeline stages that are essential for ray tracing. Vulkan's support for ray tracing enables developers to harness the power of hardware-accelerated ray tracing on compatible GPUs.

Ray Tracing Extensions

To use ray tracing in Vulkan, developers must make use of the VK_KHR_ray_tracing extension. This extension introduces ray tracing pipelines, ray tracing shaders, and acceleration structures. Ray tracing pipelines are created and configured similarly to graphics pipelines, allowing developers to define how rays are traced through the scene.

Real-Time Ray Tracing

One of the most exciting aspects of Vulkan's ray tracing support is its potential for real-time ray tracing. With the right hardware and optimizations, it is possible to achieve interactive frame rates even in complex ray-traced scenes. This opens up new possibilities for gaming and interactive applications.

Conclusion

Ray tracing is a groundbreaking rendering technique that has the potential to revolutionize computer graphics. In this section, we have introduced the basic principles of ray tracing and highlighted its integration with Vulkan. In the following sections of this chapter, we will delve deeper into Vulkan's ray tracing capabilities and explore how to build ray tracing applications with Vulkan.

Section 11.2: Vulkan Ray Tracing Extensions

Vulkan's ray tracing capabilities are made possible through the use of extensions, primarily the VK_KHR_ray_tracing extension. In this section, we will explore the key components and features of this extension, which enable developers to implement ray tracing in Vulkan applications.

VK_KHR_ray_tracing Extension Overview

The VK_KHR_ray_tracing extension introduces several new features and structures to Vulkan, which are essential for ray tracing:

1. **Ray Tracing Pipelines:** Ray tracing pipelines in Vulkan are similar in concept to graphics and compute pipelines. They define the shader stages, shaders, and resources used for ray tracing. Developers can create and configure these pipelines to specify how rays are traced through the scene.

2. **Ray Tracing Shaders:** Vulkan's ray tracing extension introduces new shader stages specifically designed for ray tracing. These shaders include the closest-hit, any-hit, and miss shaders, each serving a distinct purpose in the ray tracing process.

3. **Acceleration Structures:** Ray tracing relies on acceleration structures, which are data structures used to optimize ray-object intersection tests. Vulkan introduces the concept of bottom-level and top-level acceleration structures, allowing developers to efficiently organize and traverse scene geometry.

4. **Ray Tracing Descriptors:** To interact with resources in ray tracing shaders, Vulkan introduces ray tracing descriptor sets and binding tables. These enable shaders to access textures, buffers, and other data required for ray

tracing calculations.

5. **Ray Tracing Pipeline Creation:** Developers can create ray tracing pipelines that define the shader stages and their interactions. These pipelines include configuration options for ray tracing, such as enabling or disabling specific shader stages and specifying recursion depths.

Key Concepts in Ray Tracing Pipelines

Ray tracing pipelines in Vulkan consist of several stages and shaders:

- **Ray Generation Stage:** This stage defines the primary rays and is responsible for launching rays into the scene. The ray generation shader specifies the camera's behavior and initial ray directions.

- **Miss and Hit Shaders:** Miss shaders are executed when a ray misses all objects in the scene, allowing developers to specify background colors or environment maps. Hit shaders, on the other hand, are invoked when a ray intersects an object. They handle shading, material properties, and any secondary ray generation.

- **Any-Hit Shaders:** Any-hit shaders are executed when a ray hits an object but before it determines the closest intersection. These shaders are useful for effects like transparency and procedural materials.

Building Ray Tracing Applications

To build ray tracing applications in Vulkan, developers need to follow these general steps:

1. **Initialization:** Initialize Vulkan and enable the

VK_KHR_ray_tracing extension. Create the Vulkan device with ray tracing capabilities.

2. **Shader Compilation:** Write and compile ray tracing shaders for the ray generation, miss, and hit stages. Specify the shader code and its entry points when creating ray tracing pipelines.

3. **Acceleration Structures:** Build acceleration structures for scene geometry. Populate bottom-level and top-level acceleration structures with vertex and index data.

4. **Descriptor Sets:** Create descriptor sets and binding tables to provide ray tracing shaders with access to resources like textures and buffers.

5. **Ray Tracing Pipeline Creation:** Configure and create ray tracing pipelines that define how rays are traced through the scene.

6. **Ray Tracing Dispatch:** Dispatch ray tracing workloads by invoking the ray generation shader and tracing rays through the scene.

7. **Shading and Rendering:** Implement shading in hit shaders to determine pixel colors based on ray-object intersections. Accumulate results for each pixel.

8. **Framebuffer Presentation:** Present the rendered image to the screen or output it to a suitable destination.

Vulkan's ray tracing extensions provide the flexibility and performance required for implementing ray tracing in real-time applications. Developers can leverage these extensions to create stunning visual effects and realistic graphics in their Vulkan projects. In the following sections, we will explore the practical aspects of building ray tracing applications with Vulkan in more detail.

Section 11.3: Building a Ray Tracing

Application

In this section, we will delve into the practical aspects of building a ray tracing application using Vulkan and its ray tracing extensions. Building a ray tracing application involves several crucial steps, from setting up the Vulkan environment to implementing ray tracing shaders and dispatching rays through the scene.

Setting Up the Vulkan Environment

Before you can begin developing a ray tracing application, you must set up your Vulkan environment. This includes initializing the Vulkan instance, creating a logical device with ray tracing capabilities, and configuring the swap chain for rendering.

Here's a high-level overview of the Vulkan initialization process:

// Create a Vulkan instance

VkInstance instance;

VkApplicationInfo appInfo = {}; *// Fill in application info*

VkInstanceCreateInfo createInfo = {}; *// Fill in instance creation info*

vkCreateInstance(&createInfo, nullptr, &instance);

// Enumerate and select a suitable physical device

VkPhysicalDevice physicalDevice;

uint32_t deviceCount;

vkEnumeratePhysicalDevices(instance, &deviceCount, nullptr);

std::vector<VkPhysicalDevice> devices(deviceCount);

```cpp
vkEnumeratePhysicalDevices(instance,           &deviceCount,
devices.data());

for (const auto& device : devices) {

// Check for ray tracing support

if (IsDeviceSuitable(device)) {

physicalDevice = device;

break;

}

}

// Create a logical device with ray tracing support

VkDevice device;

VkDeviceCreateInfo deviceInfo = {}; // Fill in device creation info

vkCreateDevice(physicalDevice, &deviceInfo, nullptr, &device);

// Create a swap chain and rendering resources

CreateSwapChain(device);
```

Ray Tracing Shaders

Ray tracing in Vulkan involves writing specialized shaders, including the ray generation, miss, and hit shaders. These shaders are written in the SPIR-V intermediate representation and loaded into Vulkan.

Here's an example of a simple ray generation shader in GLSL-like syntax:

```glsl
#version 460
```

```glsl
#extension GL_EXT_ray_tracing : require

layout(binding = 0, set = 0) buffer OutputImage {

rgba8un image[];

};

void main() {

// Calculate ray direction based on screen coordinates

vec3 rayDirection = ...;

// Trace a ray into the scene

traceRayEXT(rayDirection, 0.0, 1.0, 0, 0, 0);

}
```

Building Acceleration Structures

Acceleration structures are essential for efficient ray tracing. You'll need to build bottom-level acceleration structures (BLAS) and top-level acceleration structures (TLAS) to organize scene geometry.

```glsl
// Create and populate BLAS for scene geometry

VkAccelerationStructureKHR blas = CreateBottomLevelAS(device, ...);

// Create and populate TLAS for instances in the scene

VkAccelerationStructureKHR tlas = CreateTopLevelAS(device, blas, ...);
```

Dispatching Ray Tracing Workloads

Dispatching ray tracing workloads involves invoking the ray generation shader and tracing rays through the scene. Vulkan provides the vkCmdTraceRaysEXT command for this purpose.

```
// Begin a command buffer

vkBeginCommandBuffer(commandBuffer, ...);

// Bind the ray tracing pipeline

vkCmdBindPipeline(commandBuffer,
VK_PIPELINE_BIND_POINT_RAY_TRACING_KHR,
rayTracingPipeline);

// Set ray tracing shader groups

vkCmdTraceRaysEXT(commandBuffer,
&raygenShaderBindingTable, ...);

// End the command buffer and submit it

vkEndCommandBuffer(commandBuffer);

vkQueueSubmit(queue, ...);
```

Shading and Rendering

In hit shaders, you perform shading calculations based on ray-object intersections. You can implement various shading models, such as Phong or physically-based rendering, to determine the final color of pixels.

```
#version 460

#extension GL_EXT_ray_tracing : require
```

```
layout(location = 0) rayPayloadEXT vec4 payload;

void main() {

// Calculate shading based on material properties and lighting

payload = vec4(...); // Set the pixel color in the payload

}
```

Framebuffer Presentation

Finally, after ray tracing and shading, you present the rendered image to the screen or save it to a file using Vulkan's presentation capabilities.

Building a complete ray tracing application with Vulkan is a complex task that involves many details. This section provides an overview of the key steps involved, but the actual implementation requires in-depth knowledge of Vulkan and its ray tracing extensions. In the following sections, we will explore advanced ray tracing techniques and optimizations to create visually stunning graphics.

Section 11.4: Real-time Ray Traced Graphics

Real-time ray tracing is a groundbreaking technology that enables highly realistic rendering in interactive applications. In this section, we'll explore the concepts and techniques involved in achieving real-time ray traced graphics using Vulkan's ray tracing extensions.

Ray Tracing Pipeline

To enable real-time ray tracing in Vulkan, you need to create a dedicated ray tracing pipeline. This pipeline consists of multiple stages, including ray generation, intersection, and closest hit shaders, which are executed for each ray traced.

Here's an overview of the ray tracing pipeline setup in Vulkan:

VkPipeline CreateRayTracingPipeline(VkDevice device, ... /* *shader code and descriptions* */) {

// *Create ray tracing shader modules*

VkShaderModule raygenModule = CreateShaderModule(device, raygenShaderCode);

VkShaderModule missModule = CreateShaderModule(device, missShaderCode);

VkShaderModule hitModule = CreateShaderModule(device, hitShaderCode);

// *Create shader stages*

VkPipelineShaderStageCreateInfo raygenStage = CreateShaderStage(raygenModule,
VK_SHADER_STAGE_RAYGEN_BIT_KHR, "main");

VkPipelineShaderStageCreateInfo missStage = CreateShaderStage(missModule,
VK_SHADER_STAGE_MISS_BIT_KHR, "main");

VkPipelineShaderStageCreateInfo hitStage = CreateShaderStage(hitModule,
VK_SHADER_STAGE_CLOSEST_HIT_BIT_KHR, "main");

// *Create ray tracing pipeline layout*

VkPipelineLayoutCreateInfo pipelineLayoutInfo = CreatePipelineLayoutInfo(... /* *descriptor set layout* */);

```
VkPipelineLayout pipelineLayout;

vkCreatePipelineLayout(device, &pipelineLayoutInfo, nullptr, &pipelineLayout);
```

// Create ray tracing pipeline

```
VkRayTracingPipelineCreateInfoKHR pipelineInfo = CreateRayTracingPipelineInfo(... /* shader stages */, pipelineLayout);

VkPipeline rayTracingPipeline;

vkCreateRayTracingPipelinesKHR(device, VK_NULL_HANDLE, VK_NULL_HANDLE, 1, &pipelineInfo, nullptr, &rayTracingPipeline);

return rayTracingPipeline;

}
```

Ray Tracing in the Main Loop

To achieve real-time ray traced graphics, ray tracing must be integrated into the main rendering loop of your application. In each frame, you'll dispatch rays, trace them through the scene, and accumulate the results into a final image.

Here's a simplified example of the main loop:

```
while (!window.ShouldClose()) {
```

// Start a new frame

```
vkAcquireNextImageKHR(... /* acquire swap chain image */, imageAvailableSemaphore);
```

// Build the command buffer for ray tracing

```
BuildRayTracingCommandBuffer(commandBuffer);

// Submit ray tracing command buffer

vkQueueSubmit(...        /*    submit    command    buffer    */,
renderFinishedSemaphore);

// Present the frame

vkQueuePresentKHR(...        /*        present    image    */,
renderFinishedSemaphore);

// Wait for GPU to finish rendering

vkQueueWaitIdle(... /* wait for queue to become idle */);

}
```

Ray Tracing Optimization Techniques

Real-time ray tracing can be computationally intensive, so optimization is crucial. Techniques such as denoising, spatial acceleration structures, and level of detail (LOD) management are commonly used to improve performance.

Denoising

Denoising algorithms can be applied to ray traced images to reduce noise and improve visual quality. NVIDIA's OptiX AI denoiser is a popular choice.

BVH Hierarchies

Bounding Volume Hierarchies (BVH) are acceleration structures that help reduce the number of ray-object intersections to be tested.

LOD Management

Varying the level of detail of ray traced objects based on their distance from the camera can significantly improve performance without sacrificing quality.

Realistic Materials and Lighting

To achieve realistic graphics, ray tracing allows for advanced materials and lighting models. You can implement physically-based rendering (PBR), global illumination, and reflections with ray tracing.

Hardware Requirements

Real-time ray tracing demands powerful GPU hardware. Ensure that your target platforms support ray tracing, such as NVIDIA's RTX series or AMD's RDNA 2 architecture.

Real-time ray tracing is a rapidly evolving field with immense potential for creating visually stunning graphics in games and simulations. By mastering the techniques mentioned above and staying up-to-date with the latest developments in ray tracing hardware and software, you can harness the full capabilities of this technology in your Vulkan applications.

Section 11.5: Hybrid Rendering Techniques

Hybrid rendering techniques represent a convergence of traditional rasterization-based rendering and real-time ray tracing. These techniques leverage the strengths of both approaches to deliver visually impressive and performant graphics in Vulkan applications.

The Need for Hybrid Rendering

While real-time ray tracing can achieve stunning visual fidelity, it can be computationally expensive, especially for complex scenes with numerous objects and light sources. Rasterization, on the other hand, is highly efficient but may struggle to produce certain effects like accurate global illumination and reflections. Hybrid rendering aims to strike a balance by using ray tracing for specific tasks and rasterization for others.

Ray Traced Shadows

One common use of ray tracing in hybrid rendering is for rendering shadows. Ray tracing can produce soft and accurate shadows by tracing rays from each point on a surface to the light source. This is particularly useful for achieving realistic penumbra effects in shadows.

Here's a simplified code snippet for implementing ray traced shadows in Vulkan:

// Ray generation shader

void RayGenMain() {

// Ray generation logic

Ray ray = ComputeRayForPixel(); *// Compute ray for the current pixel*

Color shadowColor = TraceShadowRay(ray); *// Trace ray for shadow testing*

// Combine shadowColor with other contributions (e.g., direct lighting)

// Write final color to the output image

```
}
```

Reflections and Ambient Occlusion

Another area where ray tracing excels is in handling reflections and ambient occlusion. By tracing rays to simulate reflection rays or to calculate ambient occlusion, you can enhance the visual quality of your scenes.

Here's an example of how to implement ray traced reflections in a hybrid renderer:

```
// Ray generation shader

void RayGenMain() {

// Ray generation logic

Ray ray = ComputeReflectionRay(); // Compute reflection ray for the current pixel

Color reflectionColor = TraceReflectionRay(ray); // Trace ray for reflections

// Combine reflectionColor with other contributions (e.g., direct lighting)

// Write final color to the output image

}
```

Performance Considerations

While hybrid rendering can deliver stunning results, it's essential to consider performance. To avoid excessive ray tracing, you can implement techniques such as screen-space reflections (SSR) for some reflective surfaces and use ray tracing selectively for high-quality reflections on specific objects.

Integration into the Rendering Pipeline

To implement hybrid rendering in Vulkan, you'll need to create a pipeline that combines both rasterization and ray tracing techniques. This pipeline will use ray generation shaders for ray tracing and traditional shaders for rasterization-based rendering.

```
VkPipeline              HybridRenderingPipeline              =
CreateHybridRenderingPipeline(...);
```

Future of Hybrid Rendering

Hybrid rendering techniques are continually evolving as hardware and software capabilities improve. Future Vulkan updates and advancements in GPU architecture may further enhance the feasibility and performance of hybrid rendering, making it even more accessible to developers.

In conclusion, hybrid rendering techniques in Vulkan offer a powerful approach to balance visual quality and performance in graphics applications. By intelligently combining ray tracing and rasterization, developers can achieve remarkable results while catering to various hardware capabilities and performance constraints.

Chapter 12: AI for Game Development

Section 12.1: AI in Game Design

Artificial Intelligence (AI) plays a crucial role in modern game development, enriching player experiences by creating dynamic, responsive, and challenging virtual worlds. In this section, we'll explore the various aspects of AI in game design, from character behavior to strategic decision-making.

The Role of AI in Games

AI in games encompasses a wide range of functionalities, including character movement, decision-making, pathfinding, and even procedural content generation. These AI systems contribute to the realism and immersion of games, making non-player characters (NPCs) and adversaries act intelligently and adapt to changing conditions.

Character Behavior

One of the primary applications of AI in games is character behavior. NPCs in open-world games, for example, can be programmed to simulate lifelike behavior patterns. They can roam cities, engage in conversations, follow schedules, and react to in-game events.

```
// Pseudocode for NPC behavior

if (playerIsNear) {

if (playerIsFriendly) {

TalkToPlayer();
```

```
} else {

AttackPlayer();

}

} else {

WanderAround();

}
```

Pathfinding

Pathfinding algorithms are essential for NPCs and game entities to navigate the game world efficiently. A* (A-star) and Dijkstra's algorithms are commonly used to find the shortest path from one point to another, considering obstacles and terrain.

```
# Pseudocode for pathfinding

path = findShortestPath(startPosition, endPosition)

followPath(path)
```

Decision-Making

AI-controlled opponents in strategy and simulation games rely on decision-making algorithms. These algorithms assess various factors like player actions, resources, and game objectives to make intelligent choices.

```
// Pseudocode for enemy decision-making

if (playerHasMoreResources) {
```

```
BuildStrongDefenses();

} else {

LaunchCounterattack();

}
```

Procedural Content Generation

AI-driven procedural content generation creates game content dynamically, such as levels, maps, and quests. This approach ensures that no two playthroughs are identical, increasing replayability.

—Pseudocode for procedural map generation

```
function generateMap(seed) {

initializeRandom(seed)

createTerrain()

placeResources()

generateDungeons()

}
```

Challenges in Game AI

Developing AI for games poses several challenges. AI systems must be efficient, responsive, and capable of handling complex scenarios. Balancing AI difficulty to make games challenging yet enjoyable for players is also a significant challenge.

Moreover, game AI must run in real-time, often with limited computational resources. This constraint requires optimization techniques to ensure smooth gameplay.

Future Trends in Game AI

The future of AI in game development looks promising. Machine learning and deep reinforcement learning are increasingly used to create adaptive AI that can learn from player behavior. This enables AI opponents to become more challenging over time and adapt to players' strategies.

As AI technologies continue to advance, we can expect even more realistic and immersive game experiences. AI-driven procedural content generation and character behavior will likely become more sophisticated, further blurring the line between virtual and real worlds in gaming.

In summary, AI is a cornerstone of modern game development, enhancing gameplay, creating immersive environments, and challenging players. As technology continues to evolve, game AI will continue to push the boundaries of what's possible in interactive entertainment.

Section 12.2: Behavior Trees and Decision Making

In game development, achieving believable and dynamic character behaviors is essential for creating immersive experiences. One popular approach to modeling character behaviors is by using Behavior Trees (BTs). In this section, we will explore the concept of Behavior Trees and their role in decision-making for game characters.

Understanding Behavior Trees

A Behavior Tree is a hierarchical model used to represent character behaviors. It consists of nodes that define actions, conditions, and control flow. Behavior Trees are well-suited for modeling complex, decision-based behaviors in games.

Node Types

1. **Action Nodes:** These nodes represent specific actions that a character can perform, such as moving, attacking, or interacting with objects.

<Sequence>

<MoveToPosition />

<AttackEnemy />

</Sequence>

1. **Condition Nodes:** Condition nodes check if a certain condition is met. If the condition is true, the tree proceeds down one branch; otherwise, it goes down another.

<Selector>

<Condition1 />

<Condition2 />

</Selector>

1. **Composite Nodes:** Composite nodes define the structure of the tree. Examples include sequences (all children must succeed) and selectors (at least one child must succeed).

Control Flow

Behavior Trees follow a specific control flow. Starting from the root node, the tree traverses nodes based on their type and the outcomes of their evaluations. This traversal continues until an action node is reached, and the corresponding action is executed.

Implementing Behavior Trees

Let's look at a simplified example of implementing a Behavior Tree in Python for an NPC character in a game:

```python
class BehaviorTree:

def __init__(self):

self.root = None

def execute(self):

if self.root:

return self.root.execute()

return None

class SequenceNode:

def __init__(self, children):

self.children = children

def execute(self):

for child in self.children:

result = child.execute()
```

```python
if result == "FAILURE":

return "FAILURE"

return "SUCCESS"

class ActionNode:

def __init__(self, action):

self.action = action

def execute(self):

# Perform the action here

return "SUCCESS"

# Creating a simple Behavior Tree

bt = BehaviorTree()

bt.root = SequenceNode([

ActionNode("Move to Player"),

ActionNode("Attack Player")

])

# Executing the Behavior Tree

result = bt.execute()

if result == "SUCCESS":

print("Character successfully executed the behavior.")
```

In this example, the Behavior Tree defines a sequence of actions: first, "Move to Player," and then "Attack Player." If all actions succeed, the tree returns "SUCCESS."

Advantages of Behavior Trees

Behavior Trees offer several advantages for game AI development:

- **Modularity:** Behavior Trees are modular and can be easily extended or modified by adding or changing nodes.

- **Hierarchical Structure:** They allow for complex behaviors to be built hierarchically, making it easier to manage and understand character AI.

- **Dynamic Decision-Making:** Behavior Trees can adapt to changing conditions, allowing characters to make real-time decisions based on game events.

In summary, Behavior Trees are a powerful tool for designing character behaviors in games. They provide a clear and structured way to define decision-making processes, making it possible to create dynamic and engaging gameplay experiences.

Section 12.3: Pathfinding and Navigation

In game development, character movement is a crucial aspect of creating immersive and realistic gameplay. Pathfinding and navigation systems play a pivotal role in guiding game characters through complex environments. In this section, we will delve into the concepts and techniques behind pathfinding and navigation in games.

Pathfinding Algorithms

Pathfinding is the process of finding the optimal path from a starting point to a destination while avoiding obstacles. Several pathfinding algorithms are commonly used in games, each with its own strengths and weaknesses. Here are a few notable ones:

1. **A* (A Star):** A* is a popular and versatile pathfinding algorithm that combines the benefits of both Dijkstra's algorithm and greedy search. It efficiently finds the shortest path while considering the cost of reaching each node.

2. **Dijkstra's Algorithm:** Dijkstra's algorithm finds the shortest path in a weighted graph but may not be the most efficient choice for games due to its high computational cost.

3. **Breadth-First Search (BFS):** BFS explores all nodes at the current depth level before moving deeper. While it guarantees the shortest path, it can be slower than A*.

4. **Depth-First Search (DFS):** DFS explores as far as possible along each branch before backtracking. It's less suitable for pathfinding in games due to its tendency to get stuck in infinite loops.

Navigation Meshes

In complex game environments, manually defining every obstacle and path can be impractical. Navigation meshes, often referred to as nav meshes, provide an efficient solution. A navigation mesh is a simplified representation of the game world that divides it into walkable and non-walkable areas. Characters can navigate through the walkable areas without colliding with obstacles.

NavMesh Components

- **Polygons:** The nav mesh is composed of polygons that define walkable regions. These polygons are connected to form a network.

- **Nodes:** Nodes represent key points within polygons, aiding in smoother character movement.

- **Links:** Links connect nodes across polygons, allowing characters to transition between them.

- **Obstacle Avoidance:** Nav meshes also incorporate algorithms for avoiding dynamic obstacles encountered during movement.

Implementing Pathfinding

Let's explore a simple Python example of implementing A* pathfinding:

```python
import heapq

class Node:

def __init__(self, position):

self.position = position

self.g = 0 # Cost from start to current node

self.h = 0 # Heuristic (estimated) cost from current node to goal

self.parent = None

def astar(start, goal):
```

```python
open_list = []

closed_set = set()

heapq.heappush(open_list, (0, start))

while open_list:

    _, current_node = heapq.heappop(open_list)

    if current_node == goal:

        path = []

        while current_node:

            path.append(current_node.position)

            current_node = current_node.parent

        return path[::-1] # Reverse the path

    closed_set.add(current_node)

    for neighbor in get_neighbors(current_node):

        if neighbor in closed_set:

            continue

        tentative_g = current_node.g + distance(current_node, neighbor)

        if neighbor not in open_list or tentative_g < neighbor.g:

            neighbor.parent = current_node

            neighbor.g = tentative_g

            neighbor.h = distance(neighbor, goal)
```

```python
heapq.heappush(open_list, (neighbor.g + neighbor.h, neighbor))

return None

def get_neighbors(node):

# Implement a function to return valid neighboring nodes

pass

def distance(node1, node2):

# Implement a distance metric (e.g., Euclidean distance)

pass

# Example usage

start_node = Node((0, 0))

goal_node = Node((4, 4))

path = astar(start_node, goal_node)

print(path)
```

This code demonstrates a basic A* implementation, which can find the shortest path between a start and goal node while avoiding obstacles.

Conclusion

Pathfinding and navigation are essential components of game development, enabling characters to navigate through complex game worlds. Whether using traditional pathfinding algorithms or navigation meshes, developers must choose the right approach to create a seamless and engaging player experience.

Section 12.4: Dynamic AI with Machine Learning

In the realm of game development, creating dynamic and adaptive non-player characters (NPCs) is a pivotal aspect of enhancing gameplay. Machine learning techniques empower game developers to imbue NPCs with more lifelike behaviors and decision-making abilities. In this section, we will explore how machine learning can be applied to achieve dynamic AI in games.

Traditional AI vs. Dynamic AI

Traditional AI in games often relies on rule-based systems and scripted behaviors. While effective to some extent, these approaches can lead to repetitive and predictable NPC behaviors, limiting the immersion and replayability of the game.

Dynamic AI, on the other hand, leverages machine learning to enable NPCs to adapt and learn from their interactions with the game world and players. This results in NPCs that can exhibit a wider range of behaviors and responses.

Reinforcement Learning for NPCs

Reinforcement learning (RL) is a machine learning paradigm particularly well-suited for creating dynamic NPCs. RL involves training agents (NPCs) to maximize a cumulative reward signal by taking actions in an environment. The agent learns through trial and error, adjusting its actions based on the outcomes and feedback received.

Here's a simplified overview of how RL can be applied to create dynamic NPCs:

1. **State Representation:** Define the state space, which represents the game environment's current conditions, such as the player's position, health, and surroundings.
2. **Action Space:** Specify the possible actions the NPC can take. For example, move left, move right, attack, or defend.
3. **Reward System:** Design a reward function that assigns positive or negative rewards based on the NPC's actions. For example, successfully defeating an enemy might yield a positive reward, while taking damage could result in a negative reward.
4. **Training:** Employ RL algorithms such as Q-learning, Deep Q-Networks (DQN), or Proximal Policy Optimization (PPO) to train the NPC agent. During training, the NPC explores different actions and learns which actions lead to higher rewards.
5. **Inference:** Once trained, the NPC can make decisions in real-time based on the learned policy.

Examples of Dynamic AI in Games

1. **Enemy Behavior:** Dynamic AI can be applied to enemies in combat scenarios. NPCs can learn to adapt to the player's tactics, making battles more challenging and engaging.
2. **NPC Conversations:** In role-playing games, NPCs can engage in conversations with the player. Dynamic AI can be used to generate more contextually relevant dialogues and responses.
3. **Strategic Decision-Making:** In strategy games, AI-controlled factions can employ dynamic AI to make strategic decisions such as resource management, troop deployment, and diplomacy.

Challenges and Considerations

While dynamic AI can greatly enhance gameplay, it also presents challenges:

- **Training Data:** Collecting training data and defining appropriate reward functions can be complex, depending on the game's complexity.

- **Computational Resources:** Training AI models can be resource-intensive, requiring powerful hardware.

- **Balancing Difficulty:** Dynamic NPCs should provide a challenge without becoming too frustrating for players.

Conclusion

Dynamic AI powered by machine learning is revolutionizing the gaming industry by creating more immersive and unpredictable gaming experiences. By incorporating these techniques, game developers can craft games with NPCs that evolve, adapt, and respond to players in ways that were previously unattainable, ultimately elevating the overall gaming experience.

Section 12.5: Adaptive NPCs in Vulkan Games

In modern game development, creating captivating and immersive gaming experiences is essential. One way to achieve this is by implementing adaptive non-player characters (NPCs) that can dynamically adjust their behavior based on player interactions and the game's context. In this section, we'll explore the concept of adaptive NPCs and how Vulkan can be utilized to enhance their capabilities.

The Importance of Adaptive NPCs

Adaptive NPCs are characters within a game that can adapt their actions, behaviors, and decisions in response to changing circumstances. This adaptability adds depth and realism to the game world, making it more engaging for players. Adaptive NPCs can be found in various game genres, including role-playing games (RPGs), open-world games, and simulations.

Implementing Adaptive NPCs

1. Behavior Trees:

Behavior trees are a common tool for implementing adaptive NPC behavior. They consist of nodes that represent actions, conditions, and decisions. The tree structure allows for a hierarchical representation of behaviors, making it easy to create complex and adaptive NPC routines.

```
BehaviorTreeSequenceNode root = new BehaviorTreeSequenceNode();

root.AddChild(new PatrolAction());

root.AddChild(new CheckPlayerDistanceCondition());

root.AddChild(new AttackAction());
```

2. Finite State Machines (FSMs):

FSMs are another technique for modeling NPC behavior. An NPC can transition between different states, such as "idle," "chasing," or "attacking," based on specific conditions. This approach is well-suited for NPCs with distinct behaviors.

```
class NPCStateMachine {

State currentState;

void Update() {

currentState.Execute();

}

void ChangeState(State newState) {

currentState.Exit();

currentState = newState;

currentState.Enter();

}

}
```

3. *Machine Learning:*

Machine learning, as discussed in previous sections, can be used to create adaptive NPCs. NPCs can learn from player interactions and adjust their behavior accordingly. Reinforcement learning techniques can be particularly effective in this context.

Vulkan's Role in Adaptive NPCs

Vulkan, with its high-performance graphics capabilities, can play a significant role in enhancing the visuals and interactions associated with adaptive NPCs:

- **Realistic Rendering:** Vulkan's advanced rendering features can be leveraged to create visually stunning NPCs with lifelike animations, which further immerse players in the game world.

• **AI-Driven Graphics:** Vulkan can be used to implement AI-driven graphics techniques, such as procedural animation, dynamic LOD (Level of Detail), and AI-generated content.

• **Multi-threading:** Vulkan's multi-threading support can be used to offload AI calculations to separate threads, ensuring that NPC behaviors do not impact overall game performance.

• **Interaction Feedback:** Vulkan can provide visual feedback for NPC interactions, such as highlighting interactive objects or displaying emotion through facial expressions and animations.

Challenges and Considerations

Implementing adaptive NPCs comes with challenges:

• **Complexity:** Creating adaptive NPCs can be complex, especially for large and open-world games with numerous NPCs.

• **Balancing:** Striking the right balance between adaptability and predictability is crucial to maintain gameplay enjoyment.

• **Performance:** Ensuring that adaptive NPCs do not cause performance bottlenecks is essential, and Vulkan's optimization features can assist in this regard.

Conclusion

Adaptive NPCs are a vital component of modern gaming, enhancing player immersion and gameplay depth. By combining techniques like behavior trees, finite state machines, and machine learning with the graphics and performance capabilities of Vulkan, game developers can create compelling and dynamic NPC experiences that captivate players and contribute to the overall success of their games.

Chapter 13: Vulkan and Augmented Reality

Section 13.1: AR Fundamentals

Augmented Reality (AR) is a technology that superimposes digital information, such as 3D models, text, or animations, onto the real world, enhancing the user's perception of their surroundings. AR has gained significant popularity in recent years, finding applications in various domains, including gaming, education, healthcare, and more. In this section, we will delve into the fundamentals of AR and how Vulkan can be harnessed to create immersive AR experiences.

Understanding Augmented Reality

AR is often distinguished from Virtual Reality (VR) in that it blends the virtual and real worlds rather than completely replacing reality. AR applications typically run on devices like smartphones, tablets, or specialized AR glasses, using their cameras and sensors to capture the real environment and overlay digital content on top of it.

Types of AR

1. **Marker-Based AR:** This approach uses markers, such as QR codes or image targets, as reference points for AR content placement. When the device's camera detects these markers, it superimposes digital objects or information on them.
2. **Markerless AR:** Markerless AR relies on computer vision and object recognition algorithms to anchor digital content to objects or locations in the real world without the need for markers.

3. **Location-Based AR:** Location-based AR apps use GPS
    and other sensors to deliver content based on the user's
    geographical location. This is often used in navigation or
    location-aware gaming.

AR SDKs and Libraries

To develop AR applications, developers can leverage AR software
development kits (SDKs) and libraries that provide tools, APIs, and
pre-built components for creating AR experiences. Some popular
AR development platforms include:

- **ARCore (for Android):** Developed by Google,
  ARCore enables AR app development on Android
  devices. It provides features like motion tracking,
  environmental understanding, and light estimation.

- **ARKit (for iOS):** Apple's ARKit offers similar
  capabilities but is designed for iOS devices. It supports
  features like world tracking, object recognition, and face
  tracking.

- **Vuforia:** Vuforia is a cross-platform AR development
  kit that supports marker-based and markerless AR. It's
  widely used for creating AR applications in various
  industries.

- **ARToolkit:** ARToolkit is an open-source toolkit for
  marker-based AR development. It offers libraries for
  multiple programming languages.

Vulkan for AR Rendering

Vulkan's capabilities in rendering high-quality 3D graphics make it an ideal choice for AR applications. Here's how Vulkan can enhance AR rendering:

- **Realistic Rendering:** Vulkan's advanced rendering features can create realistic 3D objects and animations that seamlessly blend with the real environment.

- **Low Latency:** AR applications require low latency to ensure that digital objects align accurately with the real world. Vulkan's efficient multi-threading and rendering techniques contribute to reduced latency.

- **High Performance:** Vulkan's low-level access to the GPU and efficient resource management ensure that AR applications can run smoothly even on mobile devices.

- **Multi-Platform Support:** Vulkan is cross-platform, allowing developers to target a wide range of devices, from smartphones to PCs and AR glasses.

- **Custom Shaders:** Vulkan enables developers to create custom shaders to achieve specific visual effects and interactions in AR.

Building AR Experiences with Vulkan

Developing AR applications with Vulkan involves combining AR-specific libraries and Vulkan for rendering. Developers need to:

1. Use an AR SDK or library (e.g., ARCore or ARKit) to handle AR-specific tasks like tracking, object recognition, and camera input.

2. Integrate Vulkan for rendering 3D objects and animations on top of the AR camera feed.
3. Optimize performance by leveraging Vulkan's capabilities for efficient rendering and resource management.

In conclusion, Augmented Reality offers exciting possibilities for creating immersive experiences that blend the real and digital worlds. By combining AR development tools with Vulkan's rendering capabilities, developers can build AR applications that deliver stunning visuals and exceptional performance on a variety of devices.

Section 13.2: AR SDKs and Libraries

When developing Augmented Reality (AR) applications, developers have the option to utilize AR Software Development Kits (SDKs) and libraries. These tools provide a foundation for AR development by offering pre-built components, APIs, and utilities for creating AR experiences. In this section, we will explore some of the popular AR SDKs and libraries that can be used to build AR applications.

ARCore (for Android)

ARCore is an AR platform developed by Google, primarily designed for Android devices. It empowers developers to create AR applications that make use of motion tracking, environmental understanding, and light estimation. ARCore is compatible with a wide range of Android smartphones and tablets, making it a versatile choice for Android AR development.

Key Features of ARCore:

- **Motion Tracking:** ARCore allows devices to understand and track their position and orientation as they move through the environment. This is crucial for anchoring virtual objects in the real world accurately.

• **Environmental Understanding:** The platform can detect horizontal surfaces like floors and tables. This enables developers to place virtual objects realistically on such surfaces.

• **Light Estimation:** ARCore can estimate the lighting conditions in the real world, allowing virtual objects to cast accurate shadows and match the lighting of the surroundings.

ARKit (for iOS)

Apple's ARKit is the counterpart to ARCore, tailored for iOS devices such as iPhones and iPads. ARKit provides a comprehensive set of features for AR development on iOS, including world tracking, object recognition, and face tracking. This SDK has been used to create popular AR apps available on the App Store.

Key Features of ARKit:

• **World Tracking:** ARKit enables devices to track the user's position and orientation, creating a shared understanding of the environment. This is crucial for precise placement of virtual objects.

• **Object Recognition:** ARKit can recognize and track specific objects, making it suitable for applications like augmented shopping or interactive experiences with physical products.

- **Face Tracking:** ARKit supports high-quality face tracking, which is useful for creating AR experiences involving facial expressions and masks.

Vuforia

Vuforia is a cross-platform AR development kit that offers flexibility for developers. It supports both marker-based and markerless AR, making it suitable for a variety of applications. Vuforia has been widely adopted in industries such as education, gaming, and manufacturing.

Key Features of Vuforia:

- **Marker-Based AR:** Vuforia excels in marker-based AR, allowing developers to use image targets as reference points for placing virtual objects.

- **Object Recognition:** Vuforia's object recognition capabilities enable it to identify and track objects in the real world without markers. This is ideal for applications that require interactions with physical objects.

- **Cross-Platform:** Vuforia supports multiple platforms, including iOS, Android, and Unity, making it accessible to a broad audience of developers.

ARToolkit

ARToolkit is an open-source toolkit for AR development. It provides libraries and APIs for multiple programming languages, making it accessible to developers with various coding preferences. ARToolkit is known for its marker-based AR capabilities and has been used in numerous AR projects.

Key Features of ARToolkit:

- **Marker-Based AR:** ARToolkit specializes in marker-based AR tracking, making it a valuable tool for applications that rely on markers for tracking and interaction.

- **Open Source:** Being open-source, ARToolkit is customizable and adaptable to different AR project requirements.

- **Multi-Language Support:** ARToolkit offers libraries and APIs for various programming languages, including C++, Java, and JavaScript, making it accessible to developers from different backgrounds.

These are just a few examples of AR SDKs and libraries available to developers. The choice of which SDK or library to use depends on factors such as the target platform, project requirements, and the developer's familiarity with a particular toolkit. By leveraging these AR development tools, developers can expedite the creation of AR applications and focus on delivering compelling AR experiences to users.

Section 13.3: Vulkan for AR Rendering

Augmented Reality (AR) applications often require efficient rendering of virtual objects onto the real-world environment. Vulkan, with its low-level graphics API capabilities, can be a powerful choice for rendering AR content. In this section, we'll explore how Vulkan can be used for AR rendering and the key considerations for building AR experiences.

Leveraging Vulkan's Performance

Vulkan's low-level nature allows developers to have fine-grained control over rendering operations. This control can be beneficial for AR applications that demand high performance and responsiveness. By directly managing the rendering pipeline and resources, developers can optimize rendering to ensure a smooth AR experience.

In AR, where real-time tracking and rendering are crucial, Vulkan's performance advantages become apparent. It can efficiently handle the rendering of 3D objects, overlays, and visual effects, all while maintaining low latency.

Integration with AR SDKs

When building AR applications with Vulkan, it's common to integrate Vulkan-based rendering with AR SDKs and libraries like ARCore or ARKit. These SDKs provide essential capabilities like motion tracking, environmental understanding, and camera access.

Vulkan can be used to render virtual objects and scenes over the camera feed provided by AR SDKs. This integration allows developers to create AR experiences where virtual objects appear to interact seamlessly with the real world. Vulkan's rendering capabilities make it possible to apply realistic lighting, shadows, and physics to virtual objects, enhancing the overall AR experience.

Shader Development for AR

Shader development plays a critical role in AR rendering. Shaders are responsible for tasks like object tracking, occlusion handling, and rendering realistic materials. Vulkan's shader programming capabilities enable developers to create custom shaders tailored to the requirements of their AR application.

For instance, shaders can be used to implement features like:

- **Realistic Object Occlusion:** Shaders can be employed to calculate how virtual objects should appear when partially or fully occluded by real-world objects. This enhances the illusion of virtual objects interacting with the environment.

- **Environmental Reflections:** Shaders can simulate reflections and lighting conditions, making virtual objects look as though they belong in the real world.

- **Shadow Casting:** Shaders can generate shadows cast by virtual objects onto real surfaces, further enhancing realism.

Optimization for Mobile AR

Many AR applications target mobile devices, which have resource constraints compared to desktop or dedicated AR hardware. Vulkan's ability to optimize resource usage is crucial for delivering AR experiences on these platforms. Techniques like dynamic resource loading, level of detail (LOD) management, and efficient memory usage are essential for mobile AR development.

Additionally, Vulkan's multi-threading capabilities can be utilized to distribute rendering tasks efficiently across multiple CPU cores, improving performance on mobile devices.

Cross-Platform AR Rendering

Vulkan's cross-platform support makes it possible to develop AR applications that run on various devices and operating systems. While ARCore and ARKit primarily target Android and iOS, respectively, Vulkan can be used to build AR experiences that work on both platforms with a unified codebase.

Developers can leverage cross-platform frameworks and engines that support Vulkan, such as Unity or Unreal Engine, to streamline the development process for AR applications that target multiple platforms.

In summary, Vulkan's low-level capabilities, performance optimizations, and cross-platform support make it a valuable choice for rendering content in AR applications. When integrated with AR SDKs and libraries, Vulkan empowers developers to create immersive and high-performance AR experiences that can run on a variety of devices. With careful consideration of shader development, optimization techniques, and cross-platform strategies, developers can leverage Vulkan to unlock the full potential of AR rendering.

Section 13.4: AR Interaction and User Experience

Augmented Reality (AR) applications are known for their ability to blend digital content with the real world, providing users with interactive and engaging experiences. In this section, we'll delve into AR interaction techniques and strategies for enhancing the user experience in AR applications.

Gesture-Based Interaction

One of the primary ways users interact with AR applications is through gestures. AR platforms like ARCore and ARKit provide APIs for recognizing common gestures such as tapping, swiping, and pinching. These gestures can be used to manipulate virtual objects, navigate menus, or trigger actions in the AR environment.

Developers can implement gesture-based interaction by registering gesture recognition handlers and defining how the application responds to specific gestures. For instance, a pinch gesture might be used to resize a virtual object, while a tap gesture could trigger an object's behavior.

 # Example code for registering a tap gesture handler in an AR app

arSession.onTap { tapLocation, hitTestResults **in**

// Handle tap gesture at the specified location

// Perform hit testing to determine the object tapped

// Trigger appropriate actions based on the tapped object

}

Spatial Anchors and Object Persistence

AR applications often involve placing virtual objects in the real world. To ensure a consistent user experience, it's essential to use spatial anchors or markers. Spatial anchors allow virtual objects to persist in specific locations in the real world, even if the user moves away and returns to the same location later.

Spatial anchors are crucial for applications like AR games, where users might leave virtual objects in the environment and expect them to be there when they return. These anchors are also valuable for collaborative AR experiences, where multiple users need to see and interact with the same virtual objects in a shared space.

// Example code for creating a spatial anchor in ARKit

let anchor = ARAnchor(transform: objectTransform)

arSession.add(anchor: anchor)

Realistic Physics and Object Behavior

Enhancing the user experience in AR often involves making virtual objects behave realistically in the real world. This includes implementing physics simulations for objects, enabling them to respond to forces like gravity and collisions.

Physics engines like Unity's PhysX or Apple's RealityKit Physics provide tools for simulating realistic object behavior in AR. Developers can use these engines to create AR games, simulations, or training applications that involve dynamic object interactions.

// Example code for applying physics to an AR object in Unity

```
Rigidbody                     arObjectRigidbody              =
arObject.GetComponent<Rigidbody>();

arObjectRigidbody.AddForce(Vector3.up        *            5.0f,
ForceMode.Impulse);
```

User Interface (UI) in AR

AR applications often require user interfaces to provide information, settings, and controls. Designing UI for AR is a unique challenge since it needs to be integrated seamlessly with the real-world environment. Heads-up displays (HUDs), context-aware menus, and tooltips are common UI elements in AR.

Developers can use AR-specific UI libraries or frameworks to create AR-friendly user interfaces. These UI elements should adapt to changes in the user's perspective and be easy to interact with using gestures or voice commands.

// Example code for creating a HUD element in ARKit

```
let hudNode = HUDNode(text: "Tap to interact")
```

sceneView.overlaySKScene = hudNode

Cross-Platform Considerations

When developing AR applications, it's essential to consider cross-platform compatibility. Different AR platforms may have variations in their gesture recognition systems, tracking accuracy, and device support. To reach a broad audience, developers should test and optimize their AR applications for multiple platforms.

In summary, AR interaction and user experience are critical aspects of creating engaging AR applications. Developers can leverage gesture-based interaction, spatial anchors, realistic physics, AR-specific UI, and cross-platform considerations to enhance the overall user experience. By combining these elements, developers can create AR applications that seamlessly blend the digital and physical worlds, providing users with immersive and interactive AR experiences.

Section 13.5: Building AR Applications with Vulkan

Building Augmented Reality (AR) applications with Vulkan opens up exciting possibilities for creating high-performance and visually stunning AR experiences. In this section, we'll explore the key considerations and techniques for developing AR applications using the Vulkan graphics API.

Vulkan's Role in AR

Vulkan is a low-level graphics API known for its efficiency and flexibility. It provides developers with direct control over the GPU, making it suitable for rendering complex 3D scenes, which are often integral to AR applications. While many AR frameworks and SDKs offer their rendering solutions, integrating Vulkan can be advantageous when aiming for maximum performance and customization.

Scene Rendering and Integration

To create an AR application with Vulkan, you'll need to render the virtual objects seamlessly into the real-world environment captured by the device's camera. Vulkan's rendering capabilities can be harnessed to achieve this integration effectively.

One approach is to use a technique called "passthrough rendering," where the real-world camera feed is rendered as a background texture, and virtual objects are overlaid onto it. Vulkan allows for efficient rendering of both the camera feed and virtual objects, ensuring that they align correctly in the final AR view.

```
// Example code for rendering passthrough camera feed in Vulkan

void renderARFrame(VkCommandBuffer commandBuffer) {

// Bind camera feed texture

vkCmdBindDescriptorSets(commandBuffer, ...);

// Render virtual objects

vkCmdDrawIndexed(commandBuffer, ...);

// Submit command buffer for rendering

vkQueueSubmit(queue, ...);

}
```

Tracking and Pose Estimation

For AR applications to work accurately, they must track the device's position and orientation in real-time. This tracking data is crucial for placing virtual objects precisely within the physical environment. Vulkan itself doesn't handle tracking or pose estimation, but it can be combined with AR tracking libraries or techniques provided by AR SDKs.

Implementing pose estimation involves continuously updating the transformation matrix of the virtual camera or virtual objects based on tracking data. This matrix ensures that the virtual content aligns with the real world as the device moves.

```
// Example code for updating the pose of a virtual object in Vulkan

void updateVirtualObjectPose(glm::mat4 poseMatrix) {

// Apply pose matrix to the object's model matrix

objectModelMatrix = poseMatrix;

}
```

Interaction and User Interface

AR applications often involve user interaction with virtual objects or information overlays. Vulkan provides the graphical foundation for creating responsive and immersive interactions within the AR environment.

User interface elements, such as buttons or information panels, can be rendered using Vulkan. These elements can respond to user input through touch gestures, voice commands, or device motion. Vulkan's low-level control allows for fine-tuning the responsiveness and visual feedback of these interactions.

```
// Example code for rendering interactive UI elements in Vulkan

void renderUI(VkCommandBuffer commandBuffer) {

// Bind UI textures and shaders

vkCmdBindPipeline(commandBuffer, ...);

// Render UI elements

vkCmdDrawIndexed(commandBuffer, ...);

// Submit command buffer for UI rendering

vkQueueSubmit(queue, ...);

}
```

Cross-Platform Considerations

To reach a broader audience, consider the cross-platform compatibility of your AR application. Vulkan is supported on various platforms, including Windows, Linux, and Android, but may not be available on iOS devices. When targeting multiple platforms, it's essential to implement platform-specific code paths and ensure consistent AR experiences across devices.

In conclusion, building AR applications with Vulkan allows developers to create high-performance and customizable AR experiences. By leveraging Vulkan's rendering capabilities, integrating AR tracking, implementing interactions, and considering cross-platform compatibility, developers can craft AR applications that seamlessly blend the digital and physical worlds, providing users with engaging and immersive experiences.

Section 14.1: Computer Vision Basics

Computer vision is a multidisciplinary field that focuses on enabling computers to interpret and understand visual information from the world, much like the human visual system. It plays a vital role in various applications, including image and video analysis, object recognition, tracking, and more. This section provides an introduction to the fundamental concepts and techniques of computer vision.

Understanding Pixels

At the core of computer vision lies the concept of a pixel. A pixel, short for "picture element," is the smallest unit in a digital image. It represents a single point in a rasterized image and contains information about color, brightness, and sometimes transparency. Images consist of a grid of pixels, with each pixel having a specific position defined by its row and column.

In a typical color image, each pixel is composed of three color channels: red, green, and blue (RGB). By combining different intensities of these three channels, we can represent a wide range of colors. For grayscale images, each pixel has only one intensity value, usually ranging from 0 (black) to 255 (white).

Image Processing Operations

Computer vision often involves various image processing operations to enhance, analyze, or transform images. Some common image processing operations include:

1. **Image Filtering:** Filtering operations, such as blurring and sharpening, are used to modify the appearance of an image. Filters are applied to each pixel or a neighborhood

of pixels to achieve effects like noise reduction or edge detection.

2. **Thresholding:** Thresholding is a technique used for image segmentation, where pixels are classified as foreground or background based on a certain threshold value. It's commonly used for object detection.

3. **Morphological Operations:** Morphological operations, including erosion and dilation, are used to process binary images (black and white) by manipulating the shape and structure of objects.

4. **Histogram Equalization:** This operation redistributes the pixel intensities in an image to enhance contrast and improve the overall appearance.

Feature Extraction

In computer vision, features are distinctive patterns or structures within an image that can be used for tasks like object recognition and tracking. Feature extraction involves identifying and describing these relevant parts of an image. Common features include corners, edges, and keypoints.

One widely used technique for feature extraction is the Harris Corner Detector, which identifies key points in an image by looking for significant changes in intensity. These key points can be used as landmarks for matching and tracking objects.

```
# Example code using OpenCV to detect Harris corners

import cv2

# Load an image

image = cv2.imread('image.jpg', cv2.IMREAD_GRAYSCALE)
```

 # Detect Harris corners

corners = cv2.cornerHarris(image, blockSize=2, ksize=3, k=0.04)

 # Draw detected corners on the image

image[corners > 0.01 * corners.max()] = [0, 0, 255] *# Highlight corners in red*

 # Display the result

cv2.imshow('Harris Corners', image)

cv2.waitKey(0)

cv2.destroyAllWindows()

Applications of Computer Vision

Computer vision finds applications in diverse fields, such as:

- **Object Detection:** Identifying and locating objects within an image or video stream, often used in security systems and autonomous vehicles.

- **Facial Recognition:** Recognizing and verifying individuals based on their facial features, used in security and authentication systems.

- **Gesture Recognition:** Interpreting human gestures and movements, used in gaming and human-computer interaction.

- **Medical Imaging:** Analyzing medical images, such as X-rays and MRIs, to aid in diagnosis and treatment planning.

- **Augmented Reality:** Overlapping digital content with the real world, enhancing user experiences.

- **Robotics:** Enabling robots to perceive and interact with their surroundings.

These are just a few examples, and the potential applications of computer vision continue to grow as technology advances.

In summary, computer vision is a fascinating field that empowers computers to understand and interpret visual information. This section provided an overview of fundamental concepts, including pixels, image processing operations, feature extraction, and real-world applications. Computer vision plays a crucial role in many industries and has the potential to transform various aspects of our daily lives.

Section 14.2: Convolutional Neural Networks (CNNs)

Convolutional Neural Networks, commonly known as CNNs or ConvNets, are a class of deep learning models specifically designed for processing grid-like data, such as images and videos. They have revolutionized the field of computer vision and are the foundation for many state-of-the-art image recognition and analysis tasks.

The Need for CNNs

Traditional machine learning approaches, such as support vector machines and decision trees, struggled to efficiently process images due to their high-dimensional nature. Images have a large number of pixels, and each pixel is considered a separate feature. This approach is computationally expensive and lacks the ability to capture spatial relationships in images.

CNNs address these challenges by introducing the following key concepts:

1. Convolutional Layers

CNNs use convolutional layers to automatically learn and extract meaningful features from images. A convolution operation involves sliding a small filter (also known as a kernel) over the input image. The filter's weights are learned during training, enabling the network to detect various patterns, such as edges, textures, and object parts.

2. Pooling Layers

Pooling layers downsample the spatial dimensions of feature maps produced by convolutional layers. This reduces the amount of computation and helps the network focus on the most relevant information. Max pooling and average pooling are common pooling operations.

3. Hierarchical Feature Learning

CNNs are composed of multiple layers, allowing them to learn hierarchical representations of visual information. Lower layers detect simple features, while higher layers learn to combine these features to recognize more complex patterns and objects.

CNN Architecture

A typical CNN architecture consists of the following components:

Input Layer

The input layer receives the raw pixel values of an image.

Convolutional Layers

Multiple convolutional layers are stacked to learn hierarchical features.

Activation Functions

Activation functions, such as ReLU (Rectified Linear Unit), introduce non-linearity to the network.

Pooling Layers

Pooling layers reduce spatial dimensions.

Fully Connected Layers

Fully connected layers are typically used in the final part of the network for classification or regression tasks.

Output Layer

The output layer produces the network's predictions.

Training CNNs

CNNs are trained using labeled datasets through a process called backpropagation. During training, the network learns to adjust its internal parameters (filter weights and biases) to minimize a loss function, which measures the difference between predicted and actual values. Optimizers like stochastic gradient descent (SGD) are commonly used for this purpose.

Transfer Learning

One of the advantages of CNNs is their ability to perform transfer learning. Pretrained CNN models trained on large datasets, such as ImageNet, can be fine-tuned for specific tasks with relatively small datasets. This is particularly useful when you have limited labeled data for your specific application.

Code Example

Here's a simplified code example using Python and TensorFlow/Keras to create a basic CNN for image classification:

```python
import tensorflow as tf

from tensorflow.keras import layers, models

# Create a Sequential model

model = models.Sequential()

# Add a convolutional layer

model.add(layers.Conv2D(32, (3, 3), activation='relu', input_shape=(64, 64, 3)))

# Add a max-pooling layer

model.add(layers.MaxPooling2D((2, 2)))

# Flatten the output for fully connected layers

model.add(layers.Flatten())

# Add fully connected layers

model.add(layers.Dense(128, activation='relu'))
```

model.add(layers.Dense(10, activation='softmax')) # *10 classes for classification*

Compile the model

model.compile(optimizer='adam',

loss='sparse_categorical_crossentropy',

metrics=['accuracy'])

In this example, we've created a simple CNN with one convolutional layer, one max-pooling layer, and two fully connected layers for image classification. This is just a basic illustration, and CNN architectures can become much more complex for real-world tasks.

In summary, Convolutional Neural Networks have had a profound impact on computer vision, enabling machines to understand and interpret visual data. They excel in image recognition tasks and are an essential tool for various applications, from autonomous vehicles to medical imaging. Understanding the architecture and training process of CNNs is fundamental for anyone working in the field of computer vision and deep learning.

Section 14.3: Transfer Learning and Pretrained Models

Transfer learning is a machine learning technique where a model trained on one task is adapted or fine-tuned for a different but related task. In the context of deep learning, transfer learning is widely used, especially for Convolutional Neural Networks (CNNs), to leverage preexisting knowledge and models trained on large datasets. Section 14.3 discusses the concept of transfer learning and the use of pretrained models.

The Motivation for Transfer Learning

Transfer learning addresses several challenges in deep learning:

1. **Data Scarcity:** Collecting and labeling a large dataset for a specific task can be time-consuming and costly. Transfer learning allows us to use pretrained models and adapt them to our tasks with relatively small amounts of data.
2. **Computational Resources:** Training deep neural networks from scratch on large datasets requires significant computational resources. Transfer learning reduces the computational cost because we start with pretrained weights.
3. **Generalization:** Pretrained models have already learned to capture general features from data, which can be beneficial for various related tasks.

Pretrained Models and Datasets

Many deep learning frameworks, such as TensorFlow and PyTorch, provide access to a variety of pretrained models trained on massive datasets like ImageNet. These models have learned to recognize a wide range of features, including edges, textures, shapes, and object classes.

Steps in Transfer Learning

The typical workflow for transfer learning with pretrained models includes the following steps:

1. **Choose a Pretrained Model:** Select a pretrained model that is relevant to your task. Models like VGG, ResNet, and Inception are commonly used for various computer vision tasks.

2. **Modify the Top Layers:** Remove the final layers responsible for the original classification task and replace them with new layers suited to your task. These new layers often include a softmax layer for classification.

3. **Freeze Pretrained Layers:** Optionally, freeze some or all of the pretrained layers to prevent their weights from being updated during training. This can be useful when you have limited data.

4. **Train on Your Data:** Train the modified model on your dataset. This fine-tuning step updates the weights of the added layers while keeping the knowledge learned from the original dataset.

5. **Evaluate and Adjust:** Evaluate the fine-tuned model's performance on your task. You may need to adjust hyperparameters, layers, or the amount of freezing based on the results.

Code Example

Here's a simplified code example in Python using TensorFlow/Keras to perform transfer learning with a pretrained model (ResNet-50) on a custom image classification task:

```python
import tensorflow as tf

from tensorflow.keras.applications import ResNet50

from tensorflow.keras.layers import Dense, GlobalAveragePooling2D

from tensorflow.keras.models import Model

# Load the pretrained ResNet-50 model without the top classification layer
```

```python
base_model = ResNet50(weights='imagenet', include_top=False)

# Add custom classification layers

x = base_model.output

x = GlobalAveragePooling2D()(x)

x = Dense(1024, activation='relu')(x)

predictions = Dense(num_classes, activation='softmax')(x)  # num_classes is the number of classes in your custom dataset

# Create a new model

model = Model(inputs=base_model.input, outputs=predictions)

# Freeze the layers of the base model

for layer in base_model.layers:

layer.trainable = False

# Compile the model

model.compile(optimizer='adam', loss='categorical_crossentropy', metrics=['accuracy'])
```

In this example, we load the ResNet-50 model pretrained on ImageNet and replace its top layers with custom layers for a different classification task. We also freeze the layers of the pretrained model to retain its knowledge during training on the new dataset.

Transfer learning is a powerful technique that significantly speeds up model training and improves performance, especially when you have limited data for your specific task. It has applications not only in computer vision but also in natural language processing and other domains.

Section 14.4: Image Recognition in Vulkan

Image recognition, a subfield of computer vision, involves the task of classifying and identifying objects or patterns within images. It has numerous applications, from identifying objects in photos to assisting self-driving cars in recognizing road signs. In this section, we will explore the concept of image recognition in the context of Vulkan, focusing on how Vulkan can be used for image processing and recognition tasks.

Utilizing Vulkan for Image Recognition

Vulkan, primarily designed as a graphics API, can also be employed for image recognition tasks, although it may not be the most common choice for this purpose. Here's how Vulkan can be used for image recognition:

1. **Image Preprocessing:** Before feeding images into a machine learning model for recognition, it's often necessary to preprocess them. Vulkan can be used to accelerate image preprocessing tasks, such as resizing, cropping, and color space conversion. By utilizing Vulkan's parallelism and efficient memory management, these operations can be performed swiftly.

2. **GPU Accelerated Inference:** Once a neural network model is trained for image recognition, inference (the process of making predictions on new, unseen data) can be accelerated using Vulkan. Vulkan compute shaders can execute the forward pass of a neural network efficiently on GPU, enabling real-time or near-real-time inference.

3. **Integration with Vulkan Applications:** If your application involves rendering graphics alongside image recognition, Vulkan can provide seamless integration. For

instance, in augmented reality (AR) applications, Vulkan can render the augmented scene while concurrently processing and recognizing objects within the camera feed.

GPU-accelerated Libraries

To leverage Vulkan for image recognition, you may choose to use GPU-accelerated libraries and frameworks. These libraries are designed to harness the power of GPUs for deep learning tasks. Some popular options include:

- **TensorFlow with Vulkan:** TensorFlow, a widely used deep learning framework, has experimental support for Vulkan execution backends. This allows you to execute TensorFlow models on Vulkan-compatible GPUs, including image recognition models.

- **Vulkan Compute Shaders:** Writing custom Vulkan compute shaders for image recognition tasks is another option. While this approach offers more flexibility, it requires a good understanding of Vulkan's compute capabilities and shader programming.

Code Example

Here's a simplified code example illustrating how Vulkan can be used for image preprocessing in Python using the Vulkan API through the pyvulkan library:

```python
import pyvulkan as vk

# Initialize Vulkan context and device

# Create a Vulkan image for input data
```

```python
input_image = vk.ImageCreateInfo(

format=vk.FORMAT_R8G8B8A8_UNORM,

extent=vk.Extent3D(width=image_width,   height=image_height,
depth=1),

usage=vk.IMAGE_USAGE_STORAGE_BIT                                    |
vk.IMAGE_USAGE_SAMPLED_BIT,

)

# Create a Vulkan image for output (processed) data

output_image = vk.ImageCreateInfo(

format=vk.FORMAT_R8G8B8A8_UNORM,

extent=vk.Extent3D(width=output_width, height=output_height,
depth=1),

usage=vk.IMAGE_USAGE_STORAGE_BIT                                    |
vk.IMAGE_USAGE_SAMPLED_BIT,

)

# Create Vulkan compute pipeline for image preprocessing

preprocessing_pipeline = create_preprocessing_pipeline()

# Execute the preprocessing pipeline on GPU

execute_preprocessing_pipeline(input_image,        output_image,
preprocessing_pipeline)

# Read the processed image data back from the GPU if necessary

processed_data = read_processed_data(output_image)
```

 # Further processing or inference with the processed image data

In this example, Vulkan is used to create and execute a compute pipeline for image preprocessing. While this code provides an overview, the specific Vulkan setup and shaders for image preprocessing would require more detailed implementation.

In summary, Vulkan can be harnessed for image recognition tasks, primarily for image preprocessing and GPU-accelerated inference. While it may not be the first choice for deep learning, it offers advantages in terms of parallelism and efficient memory management, making it suitable for certain image processing and recognition scenarios, especially when integrated into Vulkan-based applications.

Section 14.5: Object Tracking and Pose Estimation

Object tracking and pose estimation are crucial tasks in computer vision with applications ranging from augmented reality (AR) to robotics. In this section, we will explore these topics in the context of Vulkan and discuss how Vulkan can be utilized for real-time object tracking and pose estimation tasks.

Object Tracking with Vulkan

Object tracking involves locating and following a specific object within a sequence of images or frames. Vulkan, primarily designed as a graphics API, can contribute to object tracking in several ways:

1. **GPU Accelerated Feature Extraction:** Feature extraction is a fundamental step in object tracking. Vulkan can be employed to accelerate feature extraction algorithms, such as corner detection or keypoint detection. These

algorithms can identify distinctive points or regions within an image that can be tracked across frames.

2. **Real-time Rendering and Tracking:** Vulkan's efficient rendering capabilities can be utilized in combination with object tracking. For instance, in AR applications, Vulkan can render virtual objects that are tracked and anchored to real-world objects or surfaces in the camera feed.

3. **Parallel Processing:** Vulkan's parallelism can be advantageous for tracking multiple objects concurrently. GPU shaders can be employed to process image data in parallel, making it possible to track numerous objects simultaneously at high frame rates.

Pose Estimation with Vulkan

Pose estimation refers to determining the position and orientation (pose) of an object or camera in a 3D space. Vulkan can be employed for real-time pose estimation in various scenarios:

1. **AR Pose Estimation:** In AR applications, Vulkan can render virtual objects in a way that they appear to be part of the real world. Vulkan can assist in estimating the pose of the device's camera in real-time, allowing virtual objects to be placed accurately in the scene.

2. **Robotics and Autonomous Systems:** Pose estimation is crucial in robotics for tasks such as robotic arm control or autonomous navigation. Vulkan can help accelerate pose estimation algorithms, ensuring precise control and decision-making.

GPU-accelerated Libraries

To perform object tracking and pose estimation efficiently in Vulkan, you can consider using GPU-accelerated libraries and frameworks designed for computer vision tasks. These libraries often provide pre-optimized algorithms and support for GPU parallelism. Some popular options include:

- **OpenCV with Vulkan Backend:** OpenCV, a widely-used computer vision library, offers experimental support for Vulkan as a backend for certain operations. This can be advantageous for accelerating computer vision tasks, including object tracking and pose estimation.

- **Custom Vulkan Shaders:** For highly specialized tracking or pose estimation algorithms, you may choose to write custom Vulkan shaders to leverage the GPU's parallel processing power fully.

Code Example

While providing a complete code example for object tracking and pose estimation in Vulkan is beyond the scope of this section, here's a high-level overview of the process:

1. Initialize Vulkan for image acquisition and rendering.
2. Create Vulkan pipelines for feature extraction or specialized tracking algorithms.
3. Continuously process frames from a camera feed or video stream.
4. Utilize Vulkan for rendering tracked objects or estimating camera pose in real-time.
5. Implement algorithms to track objects or estimate poses based on feature points or markers.

6. Utilize GPU-accelerated libraries or custom Vulkan shaders for optimized performance.
7. Integrate the tracking or pose estimation results into your application, such as rendering virtual objects or controlling robotic systems.

In summary, Vulkan's capabilities in parallel processing and real-time rendering make it a valuable tool for object tracking and pose estimation tasks. By harnessing Vulkan's power, you can achieve real-time and high-performance solutions for a wide range of applications, from AR experiences to robotics and beyond.

Chapter 15: Vulkan in Virtual Reality

Section 15.1: VR Technology Overview

Virtual Reality (VR) is a transformative technology that immerses users in simulated environments, providing a sense of presence and interactivity. VR has gained significant popularity in various fields, including gaming, education, healthcare, and training simulations. In this section, we will explore the fundamentals of VR technology and how Vulkan, as a high-performance graphics API, plays a crucial role in delivering immersive VR experiences.

Understanding VR Headsets

VR experiences are primarily delivered through VR headsets, which are wearable devices that consist of a head-mounted display (HMD), sensors for tracking head movements, and often handheld controllers for interaction. These headsets are connected to a computer or a standalone VR system, and they render 3D graphics to the user's eyes, creating the illusion of being in a different environment.

Types of VR Headsets

There are several types of VR headsets available, each with its own characteristics:

1. **Tethered VR Headsets:** These headsets are connected to a powerful computer or gaming console using cables. They offer high-quality graphics and tracking capabilities, making them suitable for demanding VR experiences. Examples include the Oculus Rift and HTC Vive.

2. **Standalone VR Headsets:** Standalone headsets have built-in processing power and do not require external devices. They offer portability and ease of use, making them a popular choice for casual VR users. The Oculus Quest series is a notable example.

3. **Mobile VR Headsets:** These headsets rely on a smartphone's processing power and display. They are an affordable entry point to VR but may offer more limited experiences compared to tethered or standalone headsets. The Samsung Gear VR is an example.

VR Graphics Rendering

VR places unique demands on graphics rendering due to the need for low latency and high frame rates to prevent motion sickness and provide a smooth experience. Vulkan, with its emphasis on efficiency and performance, is well-suited for VR applications.

Stereoscopic Rendering

In VR, two slightly offset views of the virtual environment are rendered to create a stereoscopic 3D effect. Each eye sees a separate image, mimicking human binocular vision. Vulkan's support for multi-threading and efficient resource management helps achieve the high frame rates needed for VR.

Asynchronous Time Warp (ATW)

VR systems often employ techniques like Asynchronous Time Warp (ATW) to compensate for fluctuations in rendering performance. ATW adjusts the displayed image based on the user's head movements, reducing motion-to-photon latency. Vulkan's low-level control over rendering is beneficial for implementing such techniques.

Tracking and Interaction

Tracking the user's head and hand movements is essential for VR immersion. VR headsets come equipped with sensors for this purpose. Vulkan allows developers to integrate these sensor inputs and implement precise tracking and interaction with the virtual environment.

VR Development with Vulkan

Developing VR applications with Vulkan requires a deep understanding of both VR technology and Vulkan's graphics capabilities. It involves considerations such as minimizing latency, optimizing rendering performance, and ensuring a comfortable user experience. Vulkan's flexibility and performance advantages make it a powerful choice for VR developers.

In the following sections, we will delve deeper into VR development with Vulkan, including topics like VR controller interaction, optimizing VR rendering, and creating immersive VR experiences.

Section 15.2: VR Headsets and Controllers

In the world of Virtual Reality (VR), the hardware plays a pivotal role in delivering immersive experiences. This section focuses on VR headsets and controllers, explaining their significance and how Vulkan can be utilized to harness their capabilities effectively.

VR Headsets

VR headsets are the gateway to virtual worlds. They consist of several key components:

1. **Head-Mounted Display (HMD):** The HMD is worn on the head and provides a display for each eye. It's responsible for rendering stereoscopic 3D images, creating the illusion of depth and immersion.
2. **Tracking Sensors:** VR headsets are equipped with sensors that track the wearer's head movements in real-time. This tracking data is crucial for adjusting the perspective of the virtual world as the user looks around.
3. **Display and Optics:** The quality of the display and optics is critical for a clear and comfortable VR experience. High-resolution displays and lenses are used to minimize the "screen door effect" and maximize field of view.
4. **Audio:** Many VR headsets come with integrated audio solutions to provide spatial audio, enhancing the sense of presence.

Vulkan and VR Headsets

Vulkan's efficiency and low-level control over GPU resources are advantageous when rendering graphics for VR headsets. It allows developers to achieve the high frame rates and low latency required for VR without sacrificing visual quality.

VR Controllers

VR controllers are handheld devices that enable users to interact with the virtual environment. These controllers vary in design and features depending on the VR system but generally include:

1. **Positional Tracking:** VR controllers are tracked in 3D space, allowing precise tracking of their position and orientation. This tracking data is used to accurately represent the user's hand movements in VR.
2. **Buttons and Triggers:** VR controllers typically have buttons, triggers, and thumbsticks that users can press, squeeze, or manipulate to perform actions in VR applications.
3. **Haptic Feedback:** Many VR controllers provide haptic feedback, simulating tactile sensations when interacting with virtual objects. This enhances immersion.

Vulkan and VR Controllers

Vulkan's support for precise input handling and synchronization is essential for developing VR applications that make full use of VR controllers. Developers can use Vulkan to create realistic hand interactions, implement haptic feedback, and ensure that controller movements are accurately reflected in the virtual world.

Developing for VR with Vulkan

When developing VR applications with Vulkan, it's essential to consider the unique challenges and requirements of VR, such as low latency, high frame rates, and comfortable user experiences. Vulkan's capabilities in multi-threading, efficient resource management, and precise input handling make it a powerful tool for creating compelling VR content.

In the subsequent sections, we will delve deeper into the practical aspects of developing VR applications using Vulkan, including best practices, optimization techniques, and creating engaging VR interactions.

Section 15.3: Vulkan for VR Rendering

Vulkan is exceptionally well-suited for VR rendering due to its efficiency, fine-grained control over GPU resources, and support for multi-threading. In this section, we will explore how Vulkan can be utilized to render immersive VR experiences efficiently.

VR Rendering Challenges

VR rendering poses specific challenges that need to be addressed:

1. **High Frame Rates:** VR requires exceptionally high frame rates (usually 90Hz or above) to maintain immersion and prevent motion sickness. Vulkan's low-level control allows developers to optimize rendering pipelines for these high frame rates.

2. **Low Latency:** Minimal latency between user input and display is critical in VR to prevent motion-to-photon lag. Vulkan's efficient GPU utilization contributes to lower latency.

3. **Stereo Rendering:** VR rendering involves creating two slightly different images (one for each eye) to achieve stereoscopic vision. Vulkan can efficiently handle this task by rendering both views simultaneously.

4. **Variable Foveated Rendering:** To save GPU resources, VR applications often employ techniques like foveated rendering, where the central area of focus receives higher detail while peripheral areas are rendered at lower quality. Vulkan's dynamic rendering capabilities make it suitable for implementing such techniques.

Vulkan's Multi-Threading for VR

Vulkan's multi-threading capabilities are beneficial for VR applications. Here's how it can be leveraged:

1. **Parallel Command Buffer Generation:** Vulkan allows the generation of command buffers in parallel, which is useful for preparing rendering commands for both eyes simultaneously.
2. **Multi-threaded Rendering:** Vulkan enables multi-threaded rendering, where different threads can work on various aspects of rendering, such as rendering geometry, applying shaders, and post-processing effects. This parallelism contributes to achieving high frame rates.

VR-Specific Vulkan Extensions

Vulkan provides extensions specifically designed for VR:

1. **OVR_multiview Extension:** This extension allows rendering to both eyes in a single pass, reducing the CPU and GPU overhead associated with traditional stereo rendering.
2. **KHR_multiview Extension:** Similar to OVR_multiview, this extension provides multi-view rendering capabilities and is widely supported by VR platforms.

VR Input with Vulkan

Vulkan's input handling capabilities are crucial for VR applications that rely on VR controllers. Developers can use Vulkan to ensure precise tracking of controller positions and orientations, implement interactions like grabbing and throwing objects, and provide haptic feedback to users.

In the upcoming sections, we will dive deeper into practical VR development using Vulkan, including optimizing VR rendering pipelines, handling VR input, and creating immersive VR interactions.

Section 15.4: VR Interaction and Immersion

Creating compelling VR experiences goes beyond just rendering realistic scenes. It involves designing immersive interactions that make users feel like they're a part of the virtual world. In this section, we'll explore how Vulkan can be used to implement VR interactions and enhance immersion.

Hand Tracking and Gestures

Modern VR systems often include hand-tracking technology, allowing users to interact with the virtual environment using their hands. Vulkan can be used to integrate hand tracking by rendering virtual representations of users' hands and analyzing their movements.

Gesture recognition can enhance the user experience. For example, recognizing when a user makes a fist or points can trigger specific actions in the VR environment. Vulkan's real-time rendering capabilities and multi-threading support are essential for creating responsive hand-tracking experiences.

Controller Input

Many VR systems provide handheld controllers with buttons, triggers, and touch-sensitive surfaces. These controllers can be mapped to in-game actions. Vulkan allows developers to read input from VR controllers, making it possible to implement actions like picking up objects, shooting, or navigating menus.

Vulkan's support for multi-threading is particularly valuable for handling controller input. Multiple threads can be used to manage input from different controllers and update the VR environment accordingly, ensuring low input latency.

Haptic Feedback

Haptic feedback is crucial for making VR interactions feel more realistic. When a user interacts with virtual objects or presses a button on a controller, providing haptic feedback through vibrations or force feedback can significantly enhance immersion. Vulkan can be used to trigger haptic feedback events based on user interactions.

Collision Detection and Physics

To create realistic VR environments, developers often employ collision detection and physics simulations. Vulkan can be integrated with physics engines like NVIDIA PhysX or Bullet Physics to handle interactions between objects accurately. This includes simulating collisions, gravity, and object dynamics, which are essential for creating believable VR interactions.

Audio Spatialization

Audio plays a significant role in VR immersion. Vulkan can work in tandem with audio libraries and spatialization techniques to create realistic 3D audio environments. This allows sounds to appear to come from specific directions in the virtual world, enhancing the sense of presence.

User Interface (UI) in VR

User interfaces in VR need to be designed with careful consideration for depth, scale, and user comfort. Vulkan can be used to render UI elements within the VR environment, ensuring they appear crisp and responsive. Techniques like fixed UI elements attached to the user's view or interactive 3D UI objects can be implemented using Vulkan.

In the next section, we'll delve into the development process of creating VR games and applications using Vulkan. We'll discuss best practices, optimization techniques, and the overall workflow for VR development to deliver seamless and immersive experiences.

Section 15.5: Developing VR Games with Vulkan

Developing VR games with Vulkan requires careful consideration of both the unique challenges and opportunities that virtual reality presents. In this section, we'll explore the process of creating VR games using Vulkan, from design and development to optimization and deployment.

Designing for VR

Designing VR experiences is distinct from traditional game design. In VR, players are fully immersed in the environment, and their comfort and enjoyment are paramount. Considerations include:

- **Motion Sickness:** Minimizing motion sickness is critical. Avoid abrupt camera movements and provide options for player comfort, such as teleportation or snap turning.

- **Scale and Proportion:** Ensure that the scale of objects in the VR environment feels natural and that distances are accurate.

- **User Interface:** VR UI should be intuitive and comfortable to interact with. Use Vulkan for rendering UI elements in 3D space.

- **Interaction:** Plan how players will interact with the VR world. Will they use hand controllers, gaze-based interactions, or a combination?

Vulkan for VR Rendering

Vulkan's low-level graphics API is well-suited for VR rendering. It offers performance advantages by minimizing driver overhead and optimizing multi-threading. Key considerations for VR rendering include:

- **Stereo Rendering:** VR requires rendering two views (one for each eye) with slightly different perspectives. Vulkan's multi-threading capabilities are beneficial for efficiently rendering stereo images.

- **Frame Timing:** Maintaining a consistent frame rate is crucial for VR. Vulkan provides tools for precise frame timing and synchronization.

- **Asynchronous Reprojection:** Some VR systems support asynchronous reprojection, which helps maintain smooth performance. Vulkan can be used to implement this feature.

- **Lens Distortion Correction:** VR headsets often have lenses that introduce distortion. Vulkan can be used to correct this distortion during rendering.

Optimization for VR

Optimizing VR games is essential for delivering a comfortable and immersive experience. Vulkan offers several optimization techniques:

- **Dynamic Resolution:** Vulkan allows dynamic adjustment of rendering resolution based on performance, ensuring a smooth frame rate.

- **LOD (Level of Detail):** Implementing LOD systems is crucial to reduce GPU load and maintain performance.

- **Culling:** Efficiently culling objects that are outside the player's field of view can significantly improve performance.

- **GPU-Driven Rendering:** Vulkan supports GPU-driven rendering techniques, which offload some rendering tasks to the GPU, reducing CPU load.

Testing and Debugging

Thorough testing is vital for VR games. Consider aspects such as user comfort, motion sickness, and graphical performance. Vulkan's debugging and profiling tools can help identify and address issues.

Deployment

When deploying VR games developed with Vulkan, consider the target platforms, such as PC VR, standalone VR headsets, or mobile VR. Each platform may have different requirements and performance characteristics. Vulkan's cross-platform capabilities can streamline deployment to various VR devices.

In conclusion, developing VR games with Vulkan offers the potential for highly immersive and interactive experiences. However, it comes with unique challenges, particularly related to player comfort and performance optimization. Careful design, rendering, optimization, and testing are key to creating successful VR games that captivate players in virtual worlds.

Chapter 16: Deploying Vulkan AI Applications

Section 16.1: Packaging and Distribution

Deploying Vulkan AI applications involves the process of preparing your AI-powered graphics software for distribution to end-users. This section will explore the steps and considerations involved in packaging and distributing your Vulkan AI applications effectively.

Choosing a Distribution Model

Before packaging your application, consider the distribution model that best suits your target audience:

- **Direct Download:** Users can download your application directly from your website or a trusted source.

- **App Stores and Marketplaces:** Distribute your application through app stores like Google Play, Apple App Store, Steam, or other relevant platforms.

- **Physical Media:** For specialized markets, you may choose to distribute your software on physical media like DVDs or USB drives.

- **Cloud Deployment:** Utilize cloud-based solutions to deliver your application on-demand to users.

Packaging Your Application

Packaging involves bundling your Vulkan AI application and its dependencies into a format suitable for distribution. Consider these packaging formats:

- **Installer:** Create an installer that guides users through the installation process, ensuring that all prerequisites are met.

- **Containerization:** Use containerization technologies like Docker to package your application with its runtime environment.

- **Portable Executables:** Create standalone executables that include all necessary libraries, minimizing dependencies.

Compatibility and System Requirements

Clearly specify the hardware and software requirements for your Vulkan AI application. Ensure that users have compatible GPUs, drivers, and system configurations. Provide guidance on updating drivers if necessary.

Digital Rights Management (DRM)

If your application requires protection against unauthorized copying or use, consider implementing DRM solutions. However, balance security with user convenience to avoid hindering legitimate users.

Localization

Consider localizing your application to reach a broader audience. Translate user interfaces, documentation, and error messages into multiple languages if feasible.

Licensing and EULA

Draft a clear End User License Agreement (EULA) that outlines the terms and conditions for using your software. Specify any licensing fees, restrictions, or copyright information.

Software Updates and Maintenance

Plan for post-launch software updates and maintenance. Ensure a streamlined process for delivering bug fixes, feature enhancements, and compatibility updates to users.

User Support and Documentation

Provide comprehensive user support resources, including FAQs, troubleshooting guides, and contact information for technical support. Well-documented user manuals can enhance the user experience.

User Feedback and Community

Encourage user feedback and engage with your user community. Address user concerns, bug reports, and feature requests promptly.

Deployment Testing

Before releasing your Vulkan AI application, thoroughly test the deployment process on various target platforms to ensure a smooth user experience. Test installation, uninstallation, and updates.

In conclusion, packaging and distributing Vulkan AI applications require careful planning and consideration of user needs and technical requirements. A successful deployment strategy ensures that your AI-powered graphics software reaches its intended audience and operates effectively on their systems.

Section 16.2: Compatibility and System Requirements

Ensuring that your Vulkan AI application runs smoothly on users' systems requires careful consideration of compatibility and system requirements. This section delves into the details of these crucial aspects of deployment.

Specifying Hardware Requirements

Clearly define the hardware prerequisites for your Vulkan AI application. This typically involves specifying the minimum and recommended system configurations. Key hardware components to consider include:

- **GPU:** Indicate the required GPU model, including any specific features or capabilities needed for your application.

- **CPU:** Specify the CPU architecture and minimum clock speed for optimal performance.

- **Memory (RAM):** Mention the minimum and recommended RAM sizes to ensure smooth operation.

- **Storage:** Provide guidelines on the required disk space for installation and any additional storage requirements for data or assets.

- **Other Hardware:** If your application relies on specialized hardware, such as VR headsets or controllers, clearly specify these requirements.

Graphics Driver Compatibility

Vulkan applications depend on graphics drivers to interact with the GPU. It's essential to ensure that your application is compatible with a range of graphics drivers. Consider the following:

- **Driver Versions:** Specify the minimum and recommended graphics driver versions. This helps users avoid compatibility issues and ensures they have the necessary Vulkan support.

- **Updating Drivers:** Provide instructions or links for users to update their graphics drivers if they are not already up-to-date. Outdated drivers can lead to performance issues and rendering errors.

Operating System Compatibility

Ensure that your Vulkan AI application is compatible with the operating systems you intend to support. This may include Windows, Linux, macOS, or mobile operating systems. Consider the following:

- **OS Versions:** Specify the minimum supported OS versions to guide users effectively.

- **Cross-Platform Development:** If your application targets multiple platforms, verify that it functions correctly on each one. Cross-platform development tools and libraries can help streamline this process.

- **Dependency Management:** Be aware of OS-specific dependencies that your application relies on, and ensure they are included or can be easily installed.

Handling Diverse GPU Architectures

Modern GPUs come in various architectures and feature sets. Vulkan allows developers to query and adapt to the capabilities of the user's GPU. Here are some considerations:

- **Feature Detection:** Use Vulkan's feature querying mechanisms to determine the GPU's capabilities at runtime. Adjust your application's behavior accordingly to leverage available features efficiently.

- **Fallback Mechanisms:** Implement fallback mechanisms or alternative rendering paths for GPUs that lack specific features. This ensures broader compatibility.

- **User Guidance:** If your application encounters a GPU that falls below the minimum requirements, provide informative error messages and guidance for potential solutions.

User Experience

Consider the user experience when encountering system compatibility issues. Provide user-friendly error messages and instructions for resolving common problems. Strive for graceful degradation, ensuring that your application remains functional even on less capable systems.

Testing and Quality Assurance

Thoroughly test your Vulkan AI application on a variety of hardware configurations, GPUs, and operating systems to validate compatibility. Implement automated testing wherever possible to streamline this process.

In summary, compatibility and system requirements play a pivotal role in the successful deployment of Vulkan AI applications. By clearly specifying hardware and software prerequisites, ensuring compatibility with diverse GPUs and operating systems, and providing a user-friendly experience, you enhance the accessibility and usability of your application.

Section 16.3: Deployment on PC and Mobile

Deploying your Vulkan AI application on both PC and mobile platforms can significantly broaden your user base. In this section, we'll explore the considerations and best practices for successful deployment on these diverse environments.

PC Deployment

Deploying on PC platforms, including Windows, Linux, and macOS, involves several key steps:

1. Package Your Application

Package your application into an installer or archive format suitable for the target OS. Common packaging formats include .exe (Windows), .dmg (macOS), and .tar.gz (Linux).

2. Dependency Management

Ensure that your application's dependencies, such as Vulkan runtimes, libraries, and assets, are included in the package or can be easily installed during setup.

3. Installer or Package Manager

For Windows and macOS, create an installer that guides users through the installation process. On Linux, leverage package managers like APT or RPM for distribution.

4. Digital Signing

Consider digitally signing your application to enhance security and user trust. This is especially important on Windows, where signed applications are less likely to trigger security warnings.

5. Distribution Channels

Choose distribution channels that suit your target audience. Options include your website, third-party app stores, and digital distribution platforms like Steam or the Mac App Store.

6. Compatibility Testing

Thoroughly test your application on different PC configurations and OS versions to ensure compatibility. Pay attention to factors like screen resolutions, GPU vendors, and driver versions.

7. Documentation

Provide clear and concise installation instructions and system requirements in your documentation or on your website.

Mobile Deployment

Deploying on mobile platforms, such as Android and iOS, presents its own set of challenges:

1. App Stores

Publish your application on official app stores like Google Play (Android) and the App Store (iOS). This ensures a streamlined installation process for users.

2. Mobile SDKs

Familiarize yourself with the mobile development SDKs and tools for Android Studio (Android) and Xcode (iOS). These IDEs offer essential resources for mobile development.

3. Performance Optimization

Optimize your application for mobile devices, which often have less processing power and memory than PCs. Efficiently manage resources and tailor your UI for smaller screens.

4. Distribution Model

Consider whether your mobile application will be free, paid, or include in-app purchases. Define your monetization strategy and implement it accordingly.

5. Mobile-specific Features

Leverage mobile-specific features, such as touch input, accelerometer data, and GPS, to enhance user experiences.

6. User Permissions

Be mindful of user privacy and request necessary permissions only when required. Clearly communicate the purpose of these permissions to users.

7. App Store Guidelines

Adhere to the guidelines and policies of the app stores to avoid rejection. Ensure your application complies with platform-specific requirements.

8. Updates and Maintenance

Plan for regular updates to address bug fixes, security vulnerabilities, and feature enhancements. Keep your application up to date to maintain a positive user experience.

Cross-Platform Considerations

If you intend to deploy your application on both PC and mobile platforms, consider using cross-platform development frameworks like Unity, Unreal Engine, or Vulkan's multi-platform support. These frameworks streamline development and ensure code reusability.

In conclusion, successful deployment on PC and mobile platforms involves careful planning, compatibility testing, and adherence to platform-specific guidelines. By addressing the unique requirements of each environment, you can reach a broader audience and maximize the impact of your Vulkan AI application.

Section 16.4: App Stores and Marketplaces

App stores and digital marketplaces play a pivotal role in the distribution of software applications, including Vulkan AI applications. In this section, we'll delve into the significance of app stores and how to navigate them effectively.

The Role of App Stores

App stores and digital marketplaces serve as centralized platforms for users to discover, download, and install applications. They offer several advantages for both developers and users:

1. Visibility: App stores provide exposure to a vast user base, increasing the discoverability of your application.

2. Trust: Users often trust app stores to deliver safe and vetted applications, reducing concerns about malware or security risks.

3. Monetization: App stores offer various monetization models, including paid apps, in-app purchases, and subscription services.

4. Updates: Developers can push updates and bug fixes directly to users through the app store, ensuring the latest version is always available.

5. User Feedback: App stores enable users to leave reviews and ratings, offering valuable feedback and improving your application's reputation.

Key App Stores and Marketplaces

1. Google Play (Android): Google Play is the primary app store for Android devices. Developers can publish free or paid apps and reach a wide range of Android users.

2. App Store (iOS): The App Store is Apple's app distribution platform for iOS devices. It's known for its stringent review process and secure ecosystem.

3. Microsoft Store (Windows): The Microsoft Store serves as the app marketplace for Windows 10 and Windows 11. It supports both traditional Win32 apps and Universal Windows Platform (UWP) apps.

4. Steam: Steam is a digital distribution platform primarily focused on PC gaming, but it also supports non-gaming applications. It offers a vast user base and various monetization options.

5. Mac App Store: Apple's Mac App Store is the go-to destination for macOS users to discover and download applications for their Mac computers.

6. Amazon Appstore: While initially aimed at Amazon devices like Fire tablets, the Amazon Appstore is accessible to a broader Android user base.

Publishing on App Stores

Publishing your Vulkan AI application on app stores involves the following steps:

1. Developer Accounts: Create developer accounts on the respective app stores. Some may require a one-time fee or an annual subscription.

2. App Submission: Prepare your application for submission, ensuring it meets the store's guidelines, including design, content, and functionality.

3. App Review: App stores typically conduct a review process to ensure that apps meet quality and security standards. This step may take some time.

4. Pricing and Monetization: Decide on your app's pricing model and monetization strategy. This could include setting the app as free with in-app purchases, charging a one-time fee, or offering a subscription.

5. Metadata and Assets: Provide detailed metadata, such as app descriptions, screenshots, icons, and promotional materials, to make your app appealing to users.

6. Release and Updates: Once your app is approved, you can release it to the store. Continue to push updates and improvements to maintain user engagement.

Marketing and Promotion

To maximize your Vulkan AI application's success on app stores, consider marketing and promotion strategies. These may include:

- **App Store Optimization (ASO)**: Optimize your app's metadata with relevant keywords to improve its visibility in search results.

- **User Reviews and Ratings**: Encourage satisfied users to leave positive reviews and ratings.

- **Social Media**: Promote your app on social media platforms to reach a broader audience.

- **Paid Advertising**: Invest in paid advertising to drive traffic to your app's store page.

- **Press Releases**: Reach out to tech blogs and news outlets for coverage of your app's launch or updates.

In conclusion, app stores and digital marketplaces are essential channels for distributing Vulkan AI applications. They offer visibility, trust, and monetization opportunities. However, navigating each platform's requirements and adhering to guidelines is crucial for a successful launch and long-term presence on these stores. Additionally, effective marketing and promotion can further boost your application's visibility and user engagement.

Section 16.5: Post-launch Maintenance and Updates

Launching your Vulkan AI application on app stores or digital marketplaces is a significant milestone, but it's just the beginning of your journey. In this section, we'll explore the importance of post-launch maintenance and updates and how they can contribute to the long-term success of your application.

Continuous Improvement

Maintaining an application is not only about fixing bugs but also about making continuous improvements to enhance user experience and keep users engaged. Here are key aspects to consider:

1. Bug Fixes: Regularly address and fix reported bugs to ensure the stability and reliability of your application. Users appreciate prompt bug resolutions.

2. Performance Optimization: Continuously monitor and optimize your application's performance. This includes improving load times, reducing resource consumption, and ensuring smooth operation on various devices.

3. Feature Enhancements: Listen to user feedback and consider adding new features or improving existing ones based on user demands and market trends.

4. Security Updates: Stay vigilant about security threats and vulnerabilities. Regularly update and patch your application to protect user data and privacy.

5. Compatibility: Keep your application up-to-date with the latest operating system and platform changes. Ensure compatibility with new device releases.

User Feedback and Communication

Maintaining a feedback loop with your users is crucial. Here's how you can achieve it:

1. User Support: Provide efficient customer support channels for users to report issues and seek assistance. Respond to inquiries and feedback promptly.

2. User Forums and Communities: Create or participate in user forums and communities related to your application. These can become valuable platforms for users to exchange ideas and offer peer support.

3. Feedback Surveys: Periodically conduct user surveys to gather insights into their preferences and pain points. Use this data to prioritize improvements.

4. Release Notes: Clearly communicate changes and updates to users through release notes. Transparency about what's new and improved fosters trust.

Data Analytics

Leverage data analytics to gain insights into user behavior and application performance:

1. User Analytics: Track user interactions within your application. Understand how users navigate, which features they use most, and where they might encounter difficulties.

2. Crash Reporting: Utilize crash reporting tools to identify and address recurring issues causing application crashes.

3. Usage Metrics: Monitor usage metrics like user retention, session duration, and conversion rates. Identify trends and take actions accordingly.

Release Strategy

Plan your release strategy to ensure that updates are well-received:

1. Scheduled Releases: Consider a regular release schedule that users can anticipate. Frequent updates can demonstrate your commitment to improvement.

2. Beta Testing: Before a major update, consider running a beta testing program with a group of willing users. This helps identify issues before a wider release.

3. A/B Testing: Experiment with different features or changes using A/B testing to determine what resonates best with your audience.

Marketing and Promotion

Even after the initial launch, marketing and promotion remain important:

1. Announce Updates: Use social media, email newsletters, and press releases to announce significant updates. Highlight new features and improvements.

2. Engage with Users: Engage with users on social media and respond to comments and questions. Show that you value their input.

3. User Reviews: Encourage users to leave positive reviews after updates. Positive reviews can boost your application's visibility.

Legal and Compliance

Stay updated with legal and compliance requirements, especially if your application collects user data. Ensure that you comply with data privacy regulations and maintain transparency in your data handling practices.

In conclusion, post-launch maintenance and updates are critical for the long-term success of your Vulkan AI application. By continuously improving, listening to user feedback, leveraging data analytics, and implementing a well-planned release strategy, you can keep your application relevant, secure, and engaging for users. Additionally, ongoing marketing efforts and legal compliance are essential components of maintaining a successful application.

Chapter 17: Ethical AI in Vulkan Applications

Section 17.1: AI Bias and Fairness

Ethical considerations are paramount in the development and deployment of AI-powered Vulkan applications. In this section, we'll delve into the topic of AI bias and fairness and discuss how it impacts Vulkan applications.

Understanding AI Bias

AI systems, including those integrated with Vulkan, can exhibit bias if they are trained on biased data or if the training process itself introduces bias. AI bias refers to the presence of unfair, discriminatory, or unjust outcomes in AI-driven decisions or predictions. Bias can affect various aspects of Vulkan applications, from rendering to AI-enhanced graphics.

Here are some common scenarios where AI bias can manifest:

1. Rendering Bias: In graphics applications, AI algorithms may inadvertently favor certain object textures, colors, or shapes, leading to visual bias in rendered scenes.

2. Content Recommendation: Vulkan-powered games or applications that recommend content to users based on their preferences may introduce bias if the recommendation algorithms favor certain demographics or stereotypes.

3. Object Detection and Recognition: AI-driven object detection systems can exhibit bias by misclassifying or underrepresenting certain objects or groups of objects.

Implications of AI Bias

AI bias can have serious consequences, including:

1. Discrimination: AI bias can lead to discriminatory outcomes, such as unfairly excluding certain users or rendering scenes that perpetuate stereotypes.

2. User Alienation: Biased recommendations or content may alienate users who feel that the application does not cater to their interests or identities.

3. Inaccuracy: Bias can reduce the accuracy of AI predictions, affecting the overall quality of your Vulkan application.

4. Ethical Concerns: Ethical concerns may arise from biased AI decisions, potentially leading to reputational damage and legal consequences.

Mitigating AI Bias

To ensure the ethical use of AI in Vulkan applications, consider the following mitigation strategies:

1. Diverse and Representative Training Data: Use diverse and representative training data to reduce bias. Ensure that your training datasets encompass a wide range of textures, colors, shapes, and user preferences.

2. Bias Detection and Evaluation: Implement bias detection and evaluation methods to identify and quantify bias in your AI models. Tools and metrics are available to assess fairness.

3. Regular Model Audits: Conduct regular audits of your AI models to detect and rectify bias. Update models as needed to address fairness issues.

4. Ethical Guidelines: Establish ethical guidelines for your Vulkan application's AI usage. Ensure that your team adheres to these guidelines throughout development.

5. User Feedback: Encourage users to provide feedback on biased content or recommendations. Actively address user concerns and make improvements accordingly.

6. Transparency: Be transparent about the use of AI in your Vulkan application. Inform users about how AI is utilized and any measures taken to ensure fairness.

7. Diversity in Development: Promote diversity within your development team to bring different perspectives and reduce the risk of bias.

In conclusion, addressing AI bias and ensuring fairness in Vulkan applications is a critical ethical responsibility. By understanding the potential sources and implications of bias, and by implementing robust mitigation strategies, you can develop AI-powered Vulkan applications that provide fair and inclusive experiences for all users. Ethical AI practices contribute to the long-term success and reputation of your application in the ever-evolving landscape of graphics and AI.

Section 17.2: Privacy and Data Security

Privacy and data security are paramount concerns when integrating AI into Vulkan applications. In this section, we'll explore the crucial aspects of privacy and security in AI-powered graphics.

Privacy Concerns

1. User Data: Vulkan applications often require user data, which can include personal information, preferences, and usage patterns. Protecting this data is essential to maintain user trust.

2. Data Collection: AI models may require extensive data collection, including user behavior and interactions. Ensuring that data collection is transparent and consent-based is vital.

3. Data Retention: Consider data retention policies to minimize the storage of sensitive user data. Delete data that is no longer necessary for application functionality.

Data Security Measures

1. Encryption: Implement strong encryption techniques to safeguard data during transmission and storage. Use protocols like HTTPS for secure data transfer.

2. Access Control: Restrict access to sensitive user data to authorized personnel only. Implement role-based access control (RBAC) to manage permissions.

3. Authentication: Use multi-factor authentication (MFA) and strong password policies to ensure that only authorized users can access sensitive application components.

4. Data Anonymization: Anonymize user data whenever possible, replacing personally identifiable information with pseudonyms or abstract identifiers.

5. Secure APIs: Ensure that APIs used for AI model inference or data transfer are secure. Implement API keys and rate limiting to prevent abuse.

6. Regular Audits: Conduct regular security audits and penetration testing to identify vulnerabilities in your Vulkan application's AI components.

Regulatory Compliance

1. GDPR: If your Vulkan application serves users in the European Union, comply with the General Data Protection Regulation (GDPR) by providing data protection and privacy rights to users.

2. CCPA: If your application serves users in California, adhere to the California Consumer Privacy Act (CCPA) and provide mechanisms for users to control their data.

3. HIPAA: If your application handles healthcare-related data, ensure compliance with the Health Insurance Portability and Accountability Act (HIPAA) for data protection.

User Consent

1. Informed Consent: Obtain informed consent from users for data collection and AI usage. Clearly explain what data is collected, how it's used, and provide opt-out options.

2. Privacy Policies: Maintain a comprehensive privacy policy that informs users about data handling practices, security measures, and compliance with relevant regulations.

Incident Response

1. Data Breach Response: Have a well-defined incident response plan in place to address data breaches promptly. Notify affected users and authorities as required by law.

2. Data Backup: Regularly back up user data to minimize the impact of data loss during security incidents.

Security Training

1. Team Training: Ensure that your development team is educated on security best practices. Training should cover secure coding, data protection, and incident response.

In summary, integrating AI into Vulkan applications requires a strong commitment to privacy and data security. By implementing robust security measures, adhering to relevant regulations, and obtaining user consent, you can build trust with your users and protect their sensitive data. Security should be an ongoing concern, with regular audits and incident response planning to address evolving threats in the ever-changing landscape of AI and graphics.

Section 17.3: Transparency and Accountability

Transparency and accountability are essential principles when working with AI in Vulkan applications. Ensuring that AI systems are transparent and accountable not only builds trust with users but also helps in addressing ethical and regulatory concerns. In this section, we will explore the key aspects of transparency and accountability in AI-powered graphics.

Model Explainability

1. Interpretability: AI models used in Vulkan applications should be designed for interpretability. This means that the models should provide explanations for their decisions. Techniques such as feature importance scores and saliency maps can help in understanding model behavior.

2. Explanatory Interfaces: Create user-friendly interfaces that allow users to explore and understand AI-driven features and decisions. Visualizations and tooltips can provide insights into how AI influences the graphics.

Accountability Measures

1. Model Versioning: Keep track of model versions and the data used for training. If issues arise, having a historical record of models and data can aid in identifying and rectifying problems.

2. Bias Detection: Implement bias detection mechanisms to identify and mitigate biases in AI models. Regularly audit models for biases related to gender, race, or other sensitive attributes.

3. User Feedback: Encourage users to provide feedback on AI-generated content or decisions. Establish a feedback loop to incorporate user input into model improvements.

Ethical Considerations

1. Fairness: Ensure that AI systems do not discriminate against users based on protected attributes like race or gender. Regularly evaluate and rectify biases in AI algorithms.

2. Accountability Teams: Assign responsibility for AI ethics and accountability to dedicated teams within your organization. These teams should monitor AI behavior and address ethical concerns.

Regulatory Compliance

1. AI Regulations: Stay informed about emerging AI regulations and standards in your jurisdiction. Compliance with these regulations is essential for transparency and accountability.

2. Transparency Reports: Publish transparency reports that detail how AI models are used in your Vulkan application. Include information about data sources, model architecture, and decision-making processes.

Communication

1. User Notifications: Inform users when AI is used in graphics rendering or decision-making. Transparency about AI usage helps users make informed choices.

2. Privacy Statements: Include AI-related information in your privacy policy. Explain how user data is used to train AI models and how AI influences user experiences.

Responsible AI Development

1. Guidelines: Develop internal guidelines and principles for responsible AI development. These guidelines should prioritize transparency, fairness, and accountability.

2. Continuous Monitoring: Continuously monitor AI systems for unexpected behaviors or deviations from intended outcomes. Implement mechanisms to halt or adjust AI-driven processes in case of issues.

In conclusion, transparency and accountability are crucial for the responsible integration of AI into Vulkan applications. By making AI systems more understandable and by taking measures to ensure fairness, organizations can build trust with users and mitigate ethical and regulatory risks. Regular monitoring and feedback mechanisms are essential to maintaining transparency and accountability throughout the AI's lifecycle in graphics applications.

Section 17.4: Regulation and Compliance

Regulation and compliance play a significant role in the development and deployment of AI-powered graphics in Vulkan applications. As AI technologies continue to advance, governments and regulatory bodies are increasingly concerned about ensuring ethical and responsible use of AI. In this section, we will explore the key aspects of regulation and compliance related to AI in the Vulkan ecosystem.

Data Privacy and GDPR

1. Data Handling: When developing AI systems for Vulkan applications, it's essential to adhere to data privacy regulations such as the General Data Protection Regulation (GDPR). Ensure that user data is handled with the utmost care, and proper consent mechanisms are in place.

2. Data Minimization: Collect only the data necessary for AI training and rendering. Minimize the amount of personal and sensitive information gathered from users.

AI Regulations and Standards

1. Local Regulations: Be aware of AI regulations specific to your region or jurisdiction. Regulations related to AI can vary significantly from one place to another.

2. Compliance Frameworks: Implement compliance frameworks and guidelines for AI development and deployment. This may include adopting industry best practices and following ethical AI principles.

Fairness and Bias Mitigation

1. Bias Assessment: Regularly assess AI models for biases, especially those related to gender, race, or other sensitive attributes. Develop mechanisms to mitigate and rectify biases.

2. Algorithm Audits: Conduct audits of AI algorithms to ensure fairness and compliance with regulatory requirements. Keep detailed records of these audits for transparency.

Transparency and Accountability

1. Transparency Reports: Publish transparency reports that provide insights into how AI models are used in Vulkan applications. Include information about data sources, model architectures, and decision-making processes.

2. User Notifications: Notify users when AI is utilized in rendering or decision-making. Inform them about the purpose and potential implications of AI-driven features.

Ethical Considerations

1. AI Ethics Committees: Establish internal AI ethics committees or advisory boards to oversee AI development and compliance. These committees should ensure alignment with ethical principles.

2. User Consent: Obtain clear and informed consent from users when AI algorithms are used to personalize their experiences or make decisions that affect them.

Compliance Audits

1. Regular Audits: Conduct regular audits to assess compliance with AI-related regulations and standards. These audits should encompass data handling, model training, and usage in Vulkan applications.

2. Documentation: Maintain detailed documentation of AI development processes, including data handling, model training, and deployment. This documentation is crucial in demonstrating compliance.

International Collaboration

1. Participation in Standards Bodies: Consider active participation in AI and graphics-related standards bodies and organizations. Collaboration with industry peers can help shape responsible AI practices.

2. Adaptive Compliance: Be prepared to adapt to evolving AI regulations and standards. Stay informed about changes in the regulatory landscape and adjust your practices accordingly.

In summary, compliance with regulations and ethical considerations is paramount when integrating AI into Vulkan applications. Data privacy, fairness, transparency, and accountability should be at the forefront of AI development efforts. By adhering to these principles and staying informed about regulatory developments, developers can ensure that AI-powered graphics applications meet legal and ethical requirements while delivering innovative and engaging experiences to users.

Section 17.5: Ethical Considerations in AI-powered Graphics

Ethical considerations are of utmost importance when developing AI-powered graphics applications in the Vulkan ecosystem. As AI technologies become more integrated into the graphics pipeline, it is essential to uphold ethical standards and practices. In this section, we will delve into the ethical considerations that developers and stakeholders should keep in mind when working with AI in Vulkan applications.

Fairness and Bias Mitigation

1. **Bias Awareness**: Developers should be acutely aware of potential biases that can creep into AI models and graphics algorithms. Bias can stem from biased training data or biased decision-making rules.
2. **Bias Mitigation**: Implement techniques to detect and mitigate bias in AI models. This may involve retraining models with more diverse datasets or adjusting decision thresholds to achieve fairness.

Privacy and User Consent

1. **Data Privacy**: Respect user data privacy by implementing robust data protection measures. Ensure that personally identifiable information (PII) and sensitive data are handled securely and in compliance with data protection regulations.
2. **Informed Consent**: Obtain informed consent from users when collecting and utilizing their data for AI-powered graphics features. Clearly communicate how their data will be used and allow them to opt in or out.

Transparency and Explainability

1. **Algorithm Transparency**: Strive for transparency in AI algorithms used for graphics rendering. Make efforts to explain how AI-driven decisions are made, especially when they impact the user experience.
2. **Model Interpretability**: Develop AI models that are interpretable, allowing stakeholders to understand the rationale behind AI-driven graphical changes. This helps build trust and facilitates accountability.

Accountability and Oversight

1. **Ethics Committees**: Consider establishing ethics committees or review boards within development teams. These committees can assess the ethical implications of AI decisions and ensure alignment with ethical principles.
2. **Third-party Audits**: Engage third-party auditors or ethics experts to evaluate AI-powered graphics applications for ethical compliance and potential risks.

User Empowerment

1. **User Control**: Provide users with controls over AI-driven features. Allow them to customize or disable AI enhancements to their preference, promoting user empowerment.
2. **Explainability Features**: Include features that enable users to access explanations about how AI is enhancing their graphics experience. This fosters transparency and user trust.

Continuous Ethical Assessment

1. **Regular Evaluation**: Continuously assess the ethical implications of AI-powered graphics features throughout the development lifecycle. Be prepared to make adjustments as ethical considerations evolve.
2. **Stakeholder Engagement**: Involve a diverse set of stakeholders, including users, in discussions about the ethical use of AI in graphics. Their input can provide valuable perspectives on ethical concerns.

Education and Awareness

1. **Internal Training**: Educate development teams about ethical AI practices and potential biases in AI models. Promote a culture of ethics and responsibility within the organization.
2. **User Education**: Offer resources and information to educate users about the role of AI in graphics rendering and its potential impact on their experience.

In conclusion, ethical considerations are integral to the responsible development and deployment of AI-powered graphics in Vulkan applications. Developers, along with stakeholders and users, should prioritize fairness, transparency, and accountability. By adhering to ethical principles and fostering a culture of ethics, AI-driven graphics can enhance user experiences while respecting privacy and promoting responsible AI usage.

Chapter 18: Future Trends in Vulkan and AI

Section 18.1: Emerging Technologies

The future of Vulkan and AI holds exciting possibilities, driven by emerging technologies and innovative developments. In this section, we will explore some of the key trends and technologies that are expected to shape the landscape of graphics and AI integration in Vulkan applications.

1. Ray Tracing Advancements

Ray tracing, already introduced in Vulkan (Chapter 11), will continue to evolve. Hardware support for real-time ray tracing will become more widespread, enabling even more realistic graphics in games and simulations. This will include advanced ray tracing techniques such as global illumination, ambient occlusion, and soft shadows.

2. AI-driven Procedural Content Generation

AI will play a significant role in generating procedural content for games and simulations. AI algorithms will be used to create realistic landscapes, textures, and even entire levels. This will lead to more diverse and dynamic virtual worlds.

3. Generative Adversarial Networks (GANs)

GANs are poised to revolutionize content creation in Vulkan applications. They can generate high-quality textures, 3D models, and animations. GANs will be used to reduce the manual effort required for asset creation, making game development more efficient.

4. Real-time AI Training

In the near future, AI models will be trained and fine-tuned in real-time during gameplay. This will allow AI characters in games to adapt and learn from player behavior, offering more challenging and engaging experiences.

5. Cross-Platform VR and AR

Vulkan's cross-platform capabilities will be crucial for the growth of VR and AR applications. These technologies will become more accessible on a wide range of devices, from high-end VR headsets to mobile AR applications.

6. AI-powered Animation

AI-driven animation techniques will enable more realistic character movements and facial expressions. AI models will analyze voice input and adapt character animations accordingly, enhancing storytelling in games and simulations.

7. Quantum Computing Integration

While still in its infancy, the integration of quantum computing with Vulkan and AI holds immense potential. Quantum computers may accelerate AI training and optimization, opening up new frontiers in graphics and simulations.

8. Machine Learning in Rendering

Machine learning will continue to be applied to rendering techniques. This includes denoising algorithms that reduce noise in real-time ray tracing and AI-driven post-processing effects for improved image quality.

9. AI-enhanced Artistic Tools

AI-powered tools for artists and designers will become more prevalent. These tools will assist in creating concept art, generating 3D models, and automating repetitive tasks, freeing up creative professionals to focus on innovation.

10. Neuromorphic Hardware

Neuromorphic hardware, inspired by the human brain, will find applications in AI-driven graphics. These specialized chips will excel at real-time pattern recognition and may lead to more efficient AI algorithms for graphics enhancement.

As Vulkan and AI continue to evolve, staying informed about these emerging technologies will be crucial for developers and researchers. These trends offer exciting opportunities to create more immersive and visually stunning Vulkan applications while pushing the boundaries of what is possible in real-time graphics and AI integration.

Section 18.2: Machine Learning Advancements

Machine learning is a rapidly evolving field, and its advancements have a significant impact on Vulkan and AI integration. In this section, we'll explore some of the key machine learning trends and technologies that are shaping the future of graphics and AI applications.

1. Efficient Deep Learning Models

Efficiency is a top concern in real-time applications, and deep learning models are becoming more efficient. Quantization techniques, model pruning, and model distillation are being applied to reduce the computational and memory requirements of neural networks, making them more suitable for Vulkan applications.

2. Transfer Learning and Pretrained Models

Transfer learning, where pretrained neural network models are fine-tuned for specific tasks, is gaining popularity. Developers can leverage pretrained models, such as those from the vision or language domains, and adapt them for graphics-related tasks like image enhancement and style transfer.

3. On-Device Inference

On-device AI inference is becoming standard in mobile and edge devices. This allows Vulkan applications to run AI models directly on the user's device, enhancing privacy, reducing latency, and enabling offline AI capabilities.

```
# Example of on-device inference using TensorFlow Lite in Vulkan app

import tflite

# Load a pretrained model

interpreter = tflite.Interpreter(model_path="style_transfer_model.tflite")

# Perform inference on an image

input_image = load_image("input.jpg")
```

```
interpreter.allocate_tensors()

interpreter.set_tensor(input_details[0]['index'], input_image)

interpreter.invoke()

output_image = interpreter.get_tensor(output_details[0]['index'])

# Display or use the AI-enhanced image in the Vulkan application
```

4. Federated Learning

Federated learning allows AI models to be trained across multiple decentralized devices while preserving data privacy. This approach can be applied in Vulkan applications to collaboratively improve AI models without centralized data collection.

5. Explainable AI (XAI)

Explainable AI techniques are gaining importance, especially in applications where AI decisions need to be transparent and accountable. XAI methods will find use in Vulkan apps to provide insights into AI-driven rendering or content generation.

6. AI Hardware Acceleration

AI hardware accelerators like GPUs with dedicated AI cores are becoming commonplace. Vulkan's support for GPU compute shaders can leverage these accelerators for AI tasks, further improving performance.

7. AI-powered Content Creation Tools

Content creators in the graphics industry are benefiting from AI-powered tools for tasks like texture generation, asset upscaling, and automatic level design. Vulkan applications can integrate these tools for more efficient and creative content creation.

8. Real-time Data Augmentation

Data augmentation techniques, typically used in training data pipelines, are being applied in real-time during rendering. This can involve procedurally generating variations of textures, models, or environments to enhance realism and diversity in Vulkan applications.

9. AI-driven Dynamic Level of Detail (LOD)

AI can dynamically optimize the level of detail in complex scenes based on the user's viewpoint and hardware capabilities. This ensures smooth performance and realistic visuals in Vulkan applications, even on less powerful devices.

10. AI in VR and AR Interactions

In VR and AR experiences, AI-driven natural language processing and gesture recognition are enhancing user interactions. Vulkan applications can leverage these AI capabilities to create more immersive and intuitive virtual worlds.

As Vulkan developers, staying updated on these machine learning advancements is essential for harnessing the power of AI in your graphics applications. Integrating these technologies effectively can lead to more immersive, efficient, and visually stunning Vulkan applications with AI at their core.

Section 18.3: Vulkan API Updates

The Vulkan API, known for its low-level control and performance optimization capabilities, is continually evolving to meet the demands of modern graphics and AI applications. In this section, we'll explore some of the key Vulkan API updates and features that are relevant to AI integration and graphics development.

1. Vulkan Extensions for AI

Vulkan has introduced extensions that facilitate AI integration. One notable extension is the Vulkan Ray Tracing Extensions (VK_KHR_ray_tracing). These extensions enable the development of real-time ray tracing applications, which are crucial for AI-driven graphics enhancements like ray tracing-based denoising.

// Example of ray tracing pipeline creation

VkPipeline createRayTracingPipeline(VkDevice device, ... */* other parameters */)* {

...

VkPipelineShaderStageCreateInfo shaderStages[2] = {

... // Shader stages for ray generation and closest-hit

};

VkRayTracingPipelineCreateInfoKHR
rayTracingPipelineCreateInfo = {

VK_STRUCTURE_TYPE_RAY_TRACING_PIPELINE_CREATE_

... // Pipeline settings

};

```
vkCreateRayTracingPipelinesKHR(device, ... /* pipeline cache */, 1,
&rayTracingPipelineCreateInfo, nullptr, &pipeline);

return pipeline;

}
```

2. Multi-GPU Support

Vulkan has improved its support for multi-GPU configurations, making it easier to harness the power of multiple GPUs for AI and graphics workloads. Developers can use Vulkan's device groups feature to coordinate rendering and AI tasks across multiple GPUs efficiently.

```
// Example of device group creation and synchronization

VkDeviceGroupDeviceCreateInfo deviceGroupInfo = {

VK_STRUCTURE_TYPE_DEVICE_GROUP_DEVICE_CREATE_IN

... // Specify device masks and physical devices

};

VkDeviceCreateInfo deviceCreateInfo = {

VK_STRUCTURE_TYPE_DEVICE_CREATE_INFO,

... // Specify device settings

&deviceGroupInfo, // Enable multi-GPU support

};
```

3. API Abstraction Layers

To simplify cross-platform development, Vulkan developers can leverage API abstraction layers like MoltenVK (for macOS) and VKD3D-Proton (for Windows compatibility). These layers provide Vulkan-like functionality on platforms that do not natively support Vulkan, enabling AI-enhanced graphics applications to reach a broader audience.

4. Advanced Descriptor Indexing

Vulkan's descriptor indexing capabilities have improved, allowing more flexibility in managing resources for AI and rendering tasks. Developers can efficiently bind large sets of resources and dynamically change descriptors during rendering and AI computations.

```
// Example of dynamic descriptor indexing

VkDescriptorSetLayoutBinding bindings[2] = {

... // Define descriptor bindings

};

VkDescriptorSetLayoutCreateInfo layoutInfo = {

VK_STRUCTURE_TYPE_DESCRIPTOR_SET_LAYOUT_CREA

... // Specify layout settings

bindings, // Array of descriptor bindings

};
```

5. Pipeline Cache and State Management

Vulkan's pipeline cache mechanisms have been enhanced for AI-powered applications. Efficient pipeline state management is crucial for quick AI inference and rendering. Vulkan's pipeline cache allows developers to store and reuse compiled pipelines, optimizing application startup times.

```
// Example of pipeline cache creation and usage

VkPipelineCache pipelineCache;

VkPipelineCacheCreateInfo cacheCreateInfo = {

VK_STRUCTURE_TYPE_PIPELINE_CACHE_CREATE_INFO,

... // Specify cache settings

};

vkCreatePipelineCache(device,        &cacheCreateInfo,        nullptr,
&pipelineCache);
```

6. Dynamic Resource Allocation

Vulkan offers dynamic resource allocation and deallocation, allowing AI-driven Vulkan applications to efficiently manage memory resources. This is particularly beneficial for machine learning tasks that involve loading and unloading large models and data.

```
// Example of dynamic resource allocation with Vulkan memory pools

VkMemoryPoolCreateInfo poolInfo = {

VK_STRUCTURE_TYPE_MEMORY_POOL_CREATE_INFO,
```

... // Specify pool settings

```
};
```

```
VkMemoryPool memoryPool;
```

```
vkCreateMemoryPool(device, &poolInfo, nullptr, &memoryPool);
```

// Allocate and deallocate memory dynamically as needed for AI and rendering resources

7. Cross-Vendor Compatibility

Vulkan's cross-vendor compatibility is a significant advantage for AI and graphics developers. Vulkan ensures that your applications can run seamlessly on various GPU vendors' hardware, promoting a broader user base and market reach.

Vulkan's commitment to providing low-level control, high performance, and flexibility makes it a powerful choice for AI and graphics integration. By staying updated with Vulkan's evolving features and extensions, developers can create cutting-edge AI-enhanced graphics applications that deliver exceptional performance and visual quality.

Section 18.4: Industry Applications

In this section, we'll delve into the diverse industry applications of Vulkan and AI integration. The combination of Vulkan's high-performance graphics capabilities and AI's computational power has led to innovative solutions in various sectors.

1. Gaming Industry

The gaming industry has been at the forefront of Vulkan and AI integration. AI-driven graphics enhancements, such as real-time ray tracing, advanced physics simulations, and intelligent NPCs, have significantly improved gaming experiences. Vulkan's efficient multi-threading and low-level control make it an ideal choice for implementing these AI features in games.

2. Automotive Simulations

Vulkan and AI are making a substantial impact on automotive simulations used for training autonomous vehicles and testing advanced driver assistance systems (ADAS). AI algorithms can replicate real-world driving scenarios, and Vulkan's rendering capabilities create realistic virtual environments for testing these AI-driven systems.

3. Healthcare and Medical Imaging

In the healthcare sector, Vulkan and AI are employed for medical imaging applications. AI algorithms can analyze medical images for diagnostics and treatment planning, and Vulkan's GPU acceleration ensures real-time rendering of 3D medical images and visualizations, enhancing the precision of medical procedures.

4. Manufacturing and Industrial Automation

Manufacturing industries are adopting Vulkan and AI to optimize production processes. AI-driven quality control systems can inspect products for defects, while Vulkan's graphics capabilities enable real-time visualization of manufacturing operations and predictive maintenance.

5. Aerospace and Defense

The aerospace and defense sectors utilize Vulkan and AI for various applications, including flight simulations, mission planning, and situational awareness. AI algorithms can model complex flight dynamics, and Vulkan's rendering capabilities provide realistic visualizations of aerial scenarios.

6. Entertainment and Media

Vulkan and AI are transforming the entertainment and media industry by enabling the creation of AI-driven special effects, realistic animations, and immersive virtual experiences. This combination enhances storytelling and audience engagement in movies, virtual reality (VR), and augmented reality (AR) applications.

7. Education and Training

In educational and training simulations, Vulkan and AI offer immersive and interactive learning experiences. AI-driven virtual trainers can adapt to learners' actions, providing personalized guidance. Vulkan's rendering capabilities ensure a visually compelling and realistic training environment.

8. Scientific Research

Scientific research benefits from Vulkan and AI for data analysis, simulations, and visualizations. AI algorithms can process and interpret complex scientific data, while Vulkan's GPU acceleration enables researchers to visualize results in real-time, aiding in data-driven discoveries.

9. Finance and Investment

In the financial sector, AI and Vulkan are used for predictive analytics, risk assessment, and algorithmic trading. AI models can analyze vast financial datasets, and Vulkan's rendering capabilities support real-time visualizations of financial market trends.

10. Retail and E-Commerce

Retail and e-commerce industries leverage AI and Vulkan for customer experience enhancement. AI-powered recommendation systems provide personalized product suggestions, and Vulkan's graphics capabilities enable realistic virtual try-ons and visualizations of products.

These are just a few examples of how Vulkan and AI integration have revolutionized various industries. The combination of high-performance graphics rendering and AI-driven computations opens up new possibilities for innovation and efficiency across diverse sectors. As both technologies continue to evolve, we can expect even more groundbreaking applications in the future.

Section 18.5: The Intersection of AI and Graphics

In this final section of the chapter on future trends in Vulkan and AI, we explore the intersection of these two powerful technologies and the potential for further innovation and growth in the field.

1. Synergy between Vulkan and AI

The synergy between Vulkan and AI has already yielded remarkable results. Vulkan's low-level graphics API and GPU acceleration complement AI's capacity for complex computations. This synergy has led to significant advancements in real-time graphics rendering, simulations, and data visualization.

2. Enhanced Realism and Immersion

AI-powered graphics techniques, such as ray tracing, advanced physics simulations, and machine learning-driven animations, have pushed the boundaries of realism and immersion in virtual worlds. Gamers and users of virtual reality (VR) and augmented reality (AR) applications now experience more lifelike environments.

3. Personalization and User Engagement

AI algorithms analyze user behavior and preferences to deliver personalized content and experiences. In graphics and gaming, this means dynamically adjusting graphics settings and game difficulty to match individual players' skill levels and preferences, leading to higher user engagement.

4. Rapid Prototyping and Content Generation

AI has enabled rapid prototyping and content generation in graphics design and game development. Generative adversarial networks (GANs) and deep learning models assist artists and designers in creating textures, 3D models, and animations, reducing production time.

5. Real-Time Analytics and Decision Support

In industries like finance and healthcare, real-time analytics powered by AI and visualized through Vulkan's rendering capabilities enable faster and more informed decision-making. This combination is crucial for monitoring stock market trends, diagnosing medical conditions, and much more.

6. Accessibility and Inclusivity

AI and Vulkan play pivotal roles in making technology more accessible and inclusive. AI-driven accessibility features, combined with Vulkan's rendering flexibility, enable applications to cater to individuals with disabilities by providing customized visual and auditory experiences.

7. Challenges and Ethical Considerations

As AI and graphics technologies continue to advance, ethical considerations become increasingly important. Issues related to bias in AI algorithms, data privacy, and the responsible use of AI in graphics applications require careful attention and regulation.

8. Education and Research

The intersection of AI and graphics presents exciting opportunities for education and research. Academic institutions and research organizations are exploring AI-driven graphics techniques for fields such as digital art, scientific visualization, and architectural design.

9. Collaboration and Innovation

The future holds promise for greater collaboration between AI and graphics professionals. Cross-disciplinary teams of computer scientists, data scientists, artists, and engineers will drive innovation in AI-powered graphics applications.

10. Continued Evolution

The intersection of AI and graphics is an ever-evolving landscape. As AI models become more sophisticated and graphics hardware continues to advance, we can expect even more groundbreaking developments in areas like real-time ray tracing, AI-driven content creation, and immersive experiences.

In conclusion, the intersection of AI and graphics, exemplified by Vulkan and AI integration, represents a frontier of innovation and creativity. The marriage of these technologies has the potential to transform industries, enhance user experiences, and shape the future of visual computing. It is an exciting era for both AI and graphics professionals as they work together to unlock new possibilities and push the boundaries of what is visually achievable.

Chapter 19: Case Studies and Success Stories

In this chapter, we delve into real-world case studies and success stories that highlight the practical applications of Vulkan and AI in various industries. These examples showcase how these technologies have been leveraged to solve complex problems, drive innovation, and achieve remarkable outcomes.

Section 19.1: AI-driven Graphics Projects

1. Enhancing Video Games with AI

One of the most prominent applications of AI and Vulkan is in the gaming industry. Developers have used AI to enhance game environments, character behaviors, and graphics quality. For instance, AI-driven NPCs (Non-Playable Characters) can exhibit more realistic and adaptive behaviors, making games more immersive.

```
// Example AI behavior tree pseudocode

if (enemyIsVisible()) {

if (playerHealthIsLow()) {

attackPlayer();

} else {

pursuePlayer();

}

} else {
```

```
patrol();
```

```
}
```

2. AI-powered Content Creation

AI algorithms are increasingly used to generate game assets such as textures, 3D models, and animations. This significantly accelerates game development and reduces the workload on artists and designers.

 # Example of using a GAN to generate textures

def generate_texture():

 # AI code to create a realistic texture

return texture

3. Real-time Object Detection in AR

In augmented reality (AR) applications, AI plays a crucial role in real-time object detection. By integrating Vulkan's rendering capabilities, AR applications can overlay digital information seamlessly onto the real world.

// Example of AR object detection

if (objectDetected()) {

render3DModelOnObject();

}

4. Medical Imaging and AI

The healthcare industry benefits from AI-enhanced medical imaging. Vulkan's rendering speed and AI's diagnostic capabilities combine to offer faster and more accurate disease detection and treatment planning.

 # AI-enhanced medical imaging

if (anomalyDetected()):

prescribeTreatment();

else:

continueRegularCheckup();

5. AI in Art and Creativity

AI has made its mark in the art world, where it collaborates with artists to produce unique and imaginative pieces. Vulkan is used to render these creations in stunning detail.

// Example of AI-generated art

if (artistCollaboration()):

renderAIArtwork();

6. AI-driven Simulation and Training

In industries like aerospace and defense, AI-powered simulations enable realistic training scenarios. Vulkan's graphics capabilities provide high-fidelity visualizations for these simulations.

// Aerospace simulation using Vulkan

if (emergencyScenario()):

simulateEmergencyLanding();

7. Educational Tools and AI Tutors

AI-driven educational tools use Vulkan for realistic visualizations. These tools personalize learning experiences and adapt to individual student needs.

```
// AI tutor adapting to student performance

if (studentPerformanceLow()) {

provideAdditionalExercises();

} else {

advanceToNextLevel();

}
```

8. AI for Financial Analysis

AI algorithms combined with Vulkan's visualization power are used in finance for real-time market analysis, algorithmic trading, and risk assessment.

```
# Real-time financial analysis

if (marketTrendsFavorable()):

executeBuyOrder();

else:

assessRiskAndDiversify();
```

These case studies illustrate the versatility and potential of Vulkan and AI in diverse domains. As technology continues to advance, we can expect more innovative applications and success stories that further demonstrate the impact of these technologies on our world.

Section 19.2: Vulkan in Industry Solutions

In this section, we explore how Vulkan and AI have been integrated into industry-specific solutions, revolutionizing processes, and achieving remarkable outcomes.

1. Automotive Industry

The automotive sector benefits from Vulkan and AI through advanced driver assistance systems (ADAS) and autonomous driving. Vulkan's low-level API allows for efficient rendering of graphical information in vehicles, while AI-driven algorithms enable features like object detection, lane tracking, and adaptive cruise control.

```
// Autonomous vehicle's AI algorithm

if (obstacleDetected()) {

avoidObstacle();

} else {

maintainLane();

}
```

2. Manufacturing and Robotics

In manufacturing, AI-powered robots and automated quality control systems are becoming increasingly common. Vulkan's real-time rendering capabilities are used for robot vision systems that inspect products for defects.

 # Robotic quality control using AI and Vulkan

if (defectDetected()):

rejectProduct();

else:

approveProduct();

3. Energy and Utilities

In the energy sector, Vulkan and AI are used for predictive maintenance of equipment. AI algorithms analyze sensor data to detect anomalies, and Vulkan helps visualize equipment status and maintenance requirements.

// Predictive maintenance dashboard

if (anomalyDetected()) {

scheduleMaintenance();

} **else** {

monitorEquipment();

}

4. Agriculture

The agriculture industry employs AI and Vulkan for precision farming. Drones equipped with AI algorithms use Vulkan for real-time mapping and visualization of crop health, helping farmers optimize their operations.

// AI-guided precision farming

```
if (cropHealthLow()) {

applyFertilizer();

} else {

continueMonitoring();

}
```

5. Retail and E-commerce

Vulkan and AI enhance the retail experience with recommendation systems. AI algorithms analyze customer behavior and preferences to provide personalized product recommendations, and Vulkan renders these recommendations in real-time.

 # AI-driven product recommendations

```
if (customerLikesProduct()):

displayRecommendedProducts();

else:

exploreMoreProducts();
```

6. Environmental Monitoring

In environmental monitoring, Vulkan helps visualize data from IoT sensors and satellites. AI algorithms analyze this data to track climate changes, monitor deforestation, and assess pollution levels.

// Environmental monitoring and AI analysis

```
if (pollutionLevelHigh()) {

alertAuthorities();
```

```
} else {

continueMonitoringEnvironment();

}
```

7. Logistics and Supply Chain

AI and Vulkan optimize logistics and supply chain management. AI algorithms predict demand, while Vulkan assists in visualizing inventory and logistics data in real-time.

```
// AI-driven supply chain optimization

if (demandSurgeExpected()) {

increaseInventory();

} else {

optimizeDeliveryRoutes();

}
```

8. Healthcare and Telemedicine

In healthcare, AI and Vulkan are used for medical imaging, telemedicine, and drug discovery. Vulkan's high-performance rendering ensures real-time visualization of medical data, while AI aids in diagnosis and treatment recommendations.

```
# AI-assisted telemedicine

if (medicalConditionDetected()) {

recommendTreatment();

} else {
```

```
provideHealthAdvice();

}
```

These industry-specific applications demonstrate how Vulkan and AI are transforming various sectors by providing efficient rendering and intelligent data analysis. As technology continues to advance, these solutions are expected to become even more sophisticated, contributing to increased productivity, safety, and innovation across industries.

Section 19.3: Real-world Applications

In this section, we delve into real-world applications of Vulkan and AI, showcasing how these technologies have been implemented to address complex problems and deliver innovative solutions.

1. Gaming Industry

Vulkan and AI have left a significant impact on the gaming industry. Game developers leverage Vulkan's performance advantages to create visually stunning and highly optimized games. AI-driven NPCs (non-playable characters) exhibit lifelike behavior, enhancing the gaming experience.

```
// AI-controlled NPC behavior

if (playerInSight()) {

attackPlayer();

} else {

wanderAround();

}
```

2. Medical Imaging

In medical imaging, Vulkan accelerates the rendering of 3D scans and visualizations. AI is employed to aid in the detection of anomalies in medical images, such as tumors or fractures.

```
# AI-assisted medical image analysis

if (anomalyDetected()):

highlightAnomaly();

else:

displayNormalImage();
```

3. Language Processing

Natural language processing (NLP) benefits from Vulkan's parallel computing capabilities. AI-driven chatbots, language translation services, and sentiment analysis tools use Vulkan to process and display text-based data efficiently.

```
// AI-powered sentiment analysis

if (positiveSentiment()) {

displayHappyEmoji();

} else {

showSadEmoji();

}
```

4. Finance and Trading

In finance, Vulkan's performance is harnessed for real-time data visualization. AI algorithms analyze financial data to make trading decisions, and Vulkan renders complex financial charts.

```
// AI-driven stock trading

if (buySignalDetected()) {

executeBuyOrder();

} else {

waitForOptimalTradingConditions();

}
```

5. Entertainment and Animation

Vulkan is widely used in the entertainment industry for rendering 3D animations and special effects. AI assists in creating realistic character animations, facial expressions, and lip syncing.

```
# AI-generated character animations

if (characterIsTalking()) {

generateLipSync();

} else {

playIdleAnimation();

}
```

6. Space Exploration

In space exploration, Vulkan aids in rendering simulations of celestial bodies and spacecraft. AI algorithms automate data analysis from space missions, helping scientists make discoveries.

```
// AI-driven space mission analysis

if (interestingDataFound()) {

prioritizeFurtherInvestigation();

} else {

continueMonitoringSpacecraft.

}
```

7. Educational Technology

Educational applications utilize Vulkan for interactive 3D models and simulations. AI-driven educational platforms adapt content to individual learning styles and provide personalized feedback.

```
// AI-driven personalized learning

if (studentStrugglesWithMath()) {

provideMathTutorials();

} else {

offerAdvancedMathChallenges();

}
```

8. Aerospace and Defense

In the aerospace and defense sector, Vulkan facilitates the rendering of complex simulations for training purposes. AI is used for autonomous drone navigation and missile defense systems.

```
# AI-controlled autonomous drone

if (targetDetected()) {

engageTarget();

} else {

returnToBase();

}
```

These real-world applications illustrate the versatility and impact of Vulkan and AI across diverse domains. As technology continues to evolve, we can anticipate even more innovative and transformative use cases in the future.

Section 19.4: Lessons Learned and Best Practices

In this section, we reflect on lessons learned and best practices from the intersection of Vulkan and AI. These insights can guide developers, researchers, and organizations in harnessing the full potential of these technologies effectively.

1. Start with a Strong Foundation

When embarking on a Vulkan and AI project, ensure that you have a solid understanding of the fundamental concepts of both technologies. Familiarize yourself with Vulkan's graphics pipeline,

AI algorithms, and machine learning frameworks. This knowledge forms the basis for successful integration.

2. Cross-Disciplinary Collaboration

Vulkan and AI projects often require collaboration between graphics programmers and machine learning experts. Foster a culture of cross-disciplinary teamwork to combine the strengths of both domains. Regular communication and knowledge sharing are crucial.

3. Performance Profiling

Performance is a critical aspect of Vulkan applications. Employ profiling tools to identify bottlenecks in your graphics rendering and AI computations. Optimizing performance is an iterative process that involves tweaking algorithms, data structures, and Vulkan settings.

```
// Vulkan performance profiling

if (performanceIssueDetected()) {

optimizeCode();

} else {

continueMonitoringPerformance.

}
```

4. Resource Management

Managing GPU resources efficiently is vital. Use Vulkan's memory management features to allocate and deallocate resources appropriately. AI models, textures, and buffers should be loaded and unloaded strategically to conserve memory.

```
# Resource management for AI and Vulkan

if (resourceIsNotInUse()) {

releaseResource();

} else {

allocateResourceOnDemand();

}
```

5. Validation and Error Handling

Vulkan provides validation layers to catch errors early in development. Incorporate thorough error handling in both your Vulkan and AI code. This ensures that issues are detected and resolved promptly.

```
// Vulkan and AI error handling

try {

// Vulkan or AI code

} catch (Error& e) {

handleErrors(e);

}
```

6. Continuous Learning

Both Vulkan and AI are dynamic fields with frequent updates and advancements. Allocate time for continuous learning to stay up-to-date with the latest features, extensions, and research in both domains.

7. Testing Across Platforms

If your project targets multiple platforms, test your application rigorously on each one. Vulkan's cross-platform capabilities are valuable, but subtle differences in drivers and hardware can affect performance and compatibility.

```
// Cross-platform testing

if (platformIsWindows()) {

runWindowsTests();

} else if (platformIsLinux()) {

runLinuxTests();

} else if (platformIsMacOS()) {

runMacOSTests();

} else {

handleUnsupportedPlatform();

}
```

8. Ethical Considerations

Consider the ethical implications of AI in your Vulkan application. Ensure that AI algorithms are fair, transparent, and do not perpetuate bias. Respect user privacy and data security, and comply with relevant regulations.

9. Documentation and Knowledge Sharing

Maintain comprehensive documentation for your Vulkan and AI code. Share knowledge within your team and with the broader community. Documenting design decisions, challenges, and solutions helps in troubleshooting and onboarding new team members.

10. Community Involvement

Engage with the Vulkan and AI communities. Forums, conferences, and open-source contributions provide opportunities to learn from others, share your experiences, and collaborate on innovative projects.

By adhering to these lessons learned and best practices, you can navigate the complexities of developing Vulkan and AI applications more effectively. The synergy between these technologies offers vast possibilities, and continuous improvement is key to unlocking their full potential.

Section 19.5: Inspiring Stories of Innovation

In this section, we explore inspiring real-world stories of innovation that showcase the creative and impactful applications of Vulkan and AI in various domains. These stories demonstrate how the convergence of graphics and artificial intelligence is transforming industries and pushing the boundaries of technology.

1. Healthcare: AI-enhanced Medical Imaging

In the field of healthcare, Vulkan and AI are revolutionizing medical imaging. Researchers and developers are leveraging Vulkan's performance capabilities to accelerate the processing of large medical image datasets. AI algorithms, powered by Vulkan-accelerated compute shaders, can detect anomalies and assist radiologists in diagnosing diseases, leading to faster and more accurate diagnoses.

```
# AI-powered medical imaging

if (vulkanAccelerationAvailable()) {

performAIEnhancedDiagnosis();

} else {

fallbackToTraditionalMethods();

}
```

2. Automotive: Autonomous Vehicles

Vulkan and AI play a pivotal role in autonomous vehicles. Advanced driver-assistance systems (ADAS) rely on AI models for object detection and decision-making. Vulkan's low-level GPU access ensures real-time rendering of sensor data, enhancing situational awareness for self-driving cars.

```
// Autonomous vehicle perception

if (objectDetected()) {

makeSafeDrivingDecision();

} else {

continueMonitoringEnvironment();

}
```

3. Entertainment: AI-driven Game Worlds

In the gaming industry, AI and Vulkan are transforming game worlds. AI-driven NPCs exhibit more realistic behaviors and adapt to player actions. Vulkan's rendering capabilities enhance graphical fidelity, creating immersive gaming experiences. Games are now using AI to dynamically adjust graphics settings for optimal performance.

```
// AI-driven game world

if (playerIsExploring()) {

updateNPCBehaviors();

renderHigh-qualityGraphics();

} else {

optimizeGraphicsForPerformance();

}
```

4. Manufacturing: Quality Control

Manufacturers are deploying AI and Vulkan for quality control. AI-powered vision systems inspect products for defects, while Vulkan accelerates real-time visualization of production processes. This synergy ensures product quality and efficiency in manufacturing.

```
# Quality control in manufacturing

if (defectDetected()) {

rejectProduct();
```

```
} else {

continueMonitoringProduction();

}
```

5. Education: AI Tutors and Simulations

In education, AI tutors powered by Vulkan-enhanced simulations are providing personalized learning experiences. Students can interact with complex 3D models in real-time, enhancing their understanding of subjects like physics and biology.

```
// AI-enhanced educational simulations

if (studentIsExploring()) {

provideReal-timeFeedback();

} else {

facilitateInteractiveLearning.

}
```

6. Aerospace: AI in Space Exploration

Space agencies are utilizing Vulkan and AI for space exploration. AI algorithms analyze telemetry data in real-time, aiding in spacecraft navigation and autonomous decision-making. Vulkan's graphics capabilities enable scientists to visualize celestial bodies with stunning detail.

```
// AI-assisted space exploration

if (obstacleDetected()) {

adjustSpacecraftTrajectory();
```

} **else** {

captureBreathtakingCelestialImages();

}

7. Environmental Conservation: Wildlife Monitoring

In environmental conservation, AI and Vulkan are used for wildlife monitoring. AI models analyze camera trap images to track and protect endangered species. Vulkan accelerates the rendering of environmental data, aiding conservationists in their efforts.

 # Wildlife monitoring with AI and Vulkan

if (endangeredSpeciesDetected()) {

raiseConservationAlert();

} **else** {

visualizeEnvironmentalData.

}

These inspiring stories underscore the transformative potential of Vulkan and AI. As these technologies continue to evolve, they will undoubtedly lead to more groundbreaking innovations across diverse fields, improving our lives and shaping the future of technology.

Chapter 20: Conclusion and Beyond

Section 20.1: Recap of Key Concepts

In this concluding chapter, we will recap the key concepts discussed throughout this book and reflect on the journey of combining Vulkan and AI. We have explored the vast landscape of graphics programming, machine learning, and their convergence, and now it's time to summarize what we've learned.

Vulkan Fundamentals

Throughout this book, we delved into the fundamentals of Vulkan, starting with its evolution and the benefits it offers over other graphics APIs. We learned how to set up a Vulkan development environment and create a basic Vulkan application. Understanding Vulkan objects, memory management, and synchronization mechanisms were crucial for building efficient graphics and AI applications.

Graphics Pipelines and Advanced Rendering

Chapter 2 introduced us to graphics pipelines, where we explored the stages involved in rendering a scene. We learned about shaders, which play a central role in shaping the appearance of objects in the virtual world. Advanced rendering techniques, such as texturing, lighting models, and post-processing effects, allowed us to create visually stunning graphics.

Machine Learning and AI Integration

In Chapter 6, we transitioned to the world of machine learning, starting with the basics and different types of machine learning. We explored popular machine learning frameworks like TensorFlow and understood the importance of data preprocessing and feature engineering. Chapters 7 and 8 demonstrated how to integrate AI into graphics applications, harnessing the power of GPUs for machine learning tasks.

Cross-Platform Development and Performance Optimization

Chapter 9 discussed the challenges and solutions for cross-platform development, ensuring that our Vulkan and AI applications could run on different operating systems and mobile platforms. In Chapter 10, we delved into performance optimization, covering profiling, bottleneck analysis, multi-threading, memory management, and GPU debugging tools to ensure our applications ran efficiently.

Emerging Technologies

The latter part of this book took us into exciting territories. We explored ray tracing and Vulkan in Chapter 11, opening the door to real-time ray-traced graphics. In Chapter 13, we ventured into augmented reality, merging the digital and physical worlds using Vulkan. Chapter 15 introduced us to virtual reality, where Vulkan plays a crucial role in creating immersive VR experiences.

Ethics and Future Trends

Chapter 17 addressed ethical considerations in AI-powered graphics, emphasizing fairness, privacy, transparency, and compliance. In Chapter 18, we peeked into the future of Vulkan and AI, discussing emerging technologies, advancements in machine learning, potential updates to the Vulkan API, and industry applications.

Real-World Applications and Innovation

In Chapter 19, we explored real-world case studies and success stories, showcasing how Vulkan and AI are making a difference in diverse domains like healthcare, automotive, entertainment, manufacturing, education, aerospace, and environmental conservation. These stories highlighted the transformative impact of technology on society.

The Journey Continues

As we conclude this book, remember that the journey with Vulkan and AI is just beginning. The fields of graphics programming and machine learning are continuously evolving, and their intersection will lead to even more exciting possibilities. Whether you're a graphics developer looking to enhance your applications with AI or a machine learning practitioner eager to explore the world of graphics, this book has provided a solid foundation.

We encourage you to stay curious, keep learning, and push the boundaries of what's possible with Vulkan and AI. The resources and challenges in the graphics and AI landscape are vast, offering countless opportunities for innovation and creativity. The future holds the promise of groundbreaking technologies and applications that will shape our world in ways we can't yet imagine.

Thank you for joining us on this journey through the realms of Vulkan and AI. We hope this book has inspired you to embark on your own exciting projects, contributing to the ever-evolving landscape of graphics and artificial intelligence.

Section 20.2: Your Journey with Vulkan and AI

As we conclude this book, it's important to reflect on your journey with Vulkan and AI and consider what lies ahead. You've embarked on a path that combines the power of cutting-edge graphics programming with the transformative capabilities of artificial intelligence. This journey has likely opened up a world of opportunities and challenges, and this section aims to guide you on what to expect next.

Lifelong Learning

The fields of Vulkan and AI are rapidly evolving. New technologies, techniques, and best practices are constantly emerging. To stay at the forefront of this dynamic landscape, commit to lifelong learning. Explore online courses, attend conferences, and engage with the vibrant communities of graphics developers and AI practitioners. Continuously expanding your knowledge will empower you to tackle more complex and innovative projects.

Building a Portfolio

Now that you have acquired valuable skills in Vulkan and AI, consider building a portfolio of projects. Showcase your work, whether it's a visually stunning graphics application, a machine learning model, or an integration of both. A strong portfolio is not only a testament to your abilities but also a valuable asset when seeking job opportunities or collaborations.

Collaboration and Networking

Collaboration often leads to the most innovative solutions. Networking with professionals in the graphics and AI industries can open doors to exciting projects and partnerships. Attend meetups, join forums, and participate in open-source projects. Sharing your knowledge and expertise with others can also be a rewarding experience.

Exploring Specializations

Within Vulkan and AI, there are numerous specializations to explore. You might choose to focus on real-time ray tracing, virtual reality, augmented reality, or deep learning for computer vision. Each specialization presents unique challenges and opportunities. Consider what aligns best with your interests and career goals.

Contributing to Open Source

Open-source communities play a significant role in advancing technology. Consider contributing to open-source Vulkan or AI projects. Your contributions, whether in the form of code, documentation, or bug fixes, can have a meaningful impact on the broader developer community and the software ecosystem.

Staying Ethical and Responsible

With great technological power comes great responsibility. As you work on Vulkan and AI projects, be mindful of ethical considerations, privacy, and data security. Strive for transparency and fairness in your applications, and stay informed about industry regulations and guidelines related to AI and graphics.

Exploring New Frontiers

The intersection of Vulkan and AI is still relatively uncharted territory. Be open to exploring new frontiers and pushing the boundaries of what's possible. Consider how Vulkan and AI can be applied to fields beyond gaming and entertainment, such as healthcare, education, and sustainability.

Joining Research and Development

For those who are passionate about advancing the state of the art, consider pursuing research and development roles. Universities, research institutions, and tech companies often have opportunities for researchers and engineers to work on groundbreaking projects that shape the future of technology.

Embracing Challenges

Challenges are an inherent part of any journey. Embrace them as opportunities for growth. Whether it's debugging a complex graphics pipeline issue or fine-tuning a machine learning model, each challenge you overcome brings you closer to mastery.

In conclusion, your journey with Vulkan and AI is an ongoing adventure filled with learning, exploration, and innovation. The skills you've acquired and the experiences you've gained will empower you to tackle exciting projects and contribute to the ever-evolving fields of graphics and artificial intelligence. Remember that every step you take contributes to your growth as a developer and a creator. Continue to dream big, experiment fearlessly, and shape the future of graphics and AI.

Section 20.3: Continuing Education and Resources

As you conclude your journey with Vulkan and AI, it's essential to recognize that learning in these rapidly evolving fields is a continuous process. Technology, standards, and best practices evolve, and staying up-to-date is crucial for your personal and professional growth. This section provides guidance on how to continue your education and lists valuable resources to help you stay informed and proficient.

Online Courses and Tutorials

Online learning platforms offer a plethora of courses and tutorials related to Vulkan, AI, and their applications. Websites like Coursera, Udemy, edX, and Khan Academy offer courses in graphics programming, machine learning, deep learning, and more. Look for courses that align with your interests and skill level.

Books and Documentation

Books remain valuable resources for in-depth knowledge. Keep an eye out for new publications in the fields of graphics programming, artificial intelligence, and Vulkan. Additionally, refer to official documentation provided by Khronos Group for Vulkan and popular machine learning frameworks like TensorFlow and PyTorch. Documentation is a valuable reference for both beginners and experienced developers.

Blogs and Forums

Many professionals and enthusiasts share their experiences, insights, and tutorials through blogs and forums. Websites like Medium, Dev.to, and Stack Overflow are great places to find articles and discussions related to Vulkan and AI. Engage with the community by asking questions and sharing your knowledge.

Conferences and Meetups

Attending conferences and meetups can be an excellent way to stay updated on the latest developments and network with experts in the field. Events like SIGGRAPH, GTC (GPU Technology Conference), and local graphics and AI meetups provide opportunities to learn from experts and share your experiences.

Online Communities

Participating in online communities dedicated to Vulkan, AI, and graphics programming can help you stay connected with like-minded individuals. Communities like Reddit's r/GraphicsProgramming and r/MachineLearning are platforms where you can ask questions, share projects, and discuss emerging trends.

GitHub and Open Source

GitHub hosts numerous open-source projects related to Vulkan and AI. Contributing to open-source projects is not only a way to give back to the community but also an opportunity to collaborate with experienced developers and gain practical experience.

Certifications

Consider pursuing relevant certifications to validate your skills. Certifications from organizations like NVIDIA or Khronos Group can be valuable credentials to showcase your expertise in GPU programming and Vulkan.

Research Papers and Journals

Stay informed about the latest research in graphics and AI by reading academic papers and journals. Websites like arXiv and Google Scholar are excellent resources for accessing cutting-edge research papers.

Industry Associations and Forums

Joining industry-specific associations and forums can provide you with access to resources, news, and events in the fields of graphics and AI. For example, the Khronos Group, which governs Vulkan, hosts forums and provides updates on Vulkan-related developments.

Mentorship and Collaboration

Consider seeking mentorship from experienced professionals or collaborating on projects with others. Mentorship can accelerate your learning, and collaborative projects allow you to apply your skills in real-world scenarios.

In conclusion, your journey with Vulkan and AI is an ongoing adventure, and staying current is essential to remain competitive in these fields. By leveraging online resources, engaging with communities, attending events, and continuously learning, you'll be well-equipped to tackle new challenges, innovate, and contribute to the ever-evolving worlds of graphics programming and artificial intelligence. Embrace the learning process, and remember that your dedication to knowledge will lead to greater achievements in the future.

Section 20.4: Challenges and Opportunities Ahead

As you conclude your exploration of Vulkan and AI, it's essential to look ahead and anticipate the challenges and opportunities that lie on the horizon. Both fields are dynamic and continually evolving, offering numerous exciting prospects but also presenting certain complexities.

Challenges

1. **Hardware Evolution**: Graphics hardware and AI accelerators are advancing rapidly. Keeping up with the latest hardware developments and optimizing your applications for new architectures can be challenging.
2. **Complexity**: Implementing advanced AI techniques, such as deep learning, can be complex. Understanding the mathematical underpinnings and training large neural networks may require substantial computational resources.
3. **Performance Optimization**: Achieving peak performance in Vulkan and AI applications demands in-depth knowledge of parallelism, optimization techniques, and the ability to identify bottlenecks.
4. **Cross-Platform Compatibility**: Ensuring your applications work seamlessly across various platforms and devices, from desktop to mobile, remains a challenge.
5. **Data Privacy and Ethics**: With the increasing use of AI, data privacy and ethical considerations become paramount. Addressing issues related to data collection, bias, and fairness is a constant challenge.
6. **Regulatory Landscape**: Regulations related to AI and data usage are evolving. Staying compliant with regional and global laws can be a complex task.

Opportunities

1. **Emerging Technologies**: New technologies, such as real-time ray tracing, augmented reality, and virtual reality, open up exciting possibilities for graphics and AI integration.
2. **AI-driven Creativity**: AI is being used to automate creative tasks, including content generation, music

composition, and art. Exploring these applications can lead to groundbreaking innovations.

3. **Industry Applications**: Vulkan and AI find applications beyond gaming, including in industries like healthcare, automotive, and finance. Leveraging your expertise in these areas can lead to impactful solutions.

4. **Interdisciplinary Collaboration**: Collaborating with experts from diverse fields, such as neuroscience, robotics, and biology, can lead to innovative cross-disciplinary projects.

5. **AI for Optimization**: AI can be harnessed for optimizing graphics pipelines, resource management, and rendering techniques, leading to performance improvements.

6. **Ethical AI Advocacy**: As AI becomes more pervasive, there's an increasing need for professionals who advocate for ethical AI practices and policies.

7. **Education and Mentorship**: Sharing your knowledge and mentoring the next generation of developers can be a rewarding opportunity.

8. **Research and Innovation**: Contributing to research and pushing the boundaries of what's possible in graphics and AI can lead to groundbreaking discoveries.

In conclusion, while challenges exist, the future of Vulkan and AI is filled with remarkable opportunities. Embracing continuous learning, staying adaptable, and being open to collaboration will help you navigate this dynamic landscape successfully. As you face these challenges and seize these opportunities, you'll play a pivotal role in shaping the future of graphics programming and artificial intelligence.

Section 20.5: Unlocking the Future of

Graphics and AI

As we reach the concluding section of this book, it's important to reflect on the immense potential and possibilities that the future holds for the convergence of graphics programming and artificial intelligence. This fusion of technologies promises to reshape industries and create innovative solutions across various domains. Here, we'll delve into some key aspects of unlocking the future of graphics and AI.

1. Real-time Graphics Advancements

The graphics industry is continually pushing the boundaries of realism and immersion. Real-time ray tracing, once considered a holy grail, is now a reality in games and interactive applications. Future advancements in GPU hardware and software will likely make real-time ray tracing more accessible, enabling even more lifelike visuals. AI will play a crucial role in optimizing and enhancing real-time rendering, making scenes more detailed and responsive.

2. AI-Driven Content Creation

AI is poised to revolutionize content creation in various media, from video games and movies to art and music. Generative adversarial networks (GANs) and neural style transfer can automatically generate textures, models, and even entire game levels. AI can assist artists and designers by automating repetitive tasks, enabling them to focus on creativity. The future will see AI-powered content generation tools becoming an integral part of the creative process.

3. AI-Enhanced User Experiences

Incorporating AI into user interfaces and experiences will become increasingly common. AI-powered chatbots, virtual assistants, and personalized content recommendations will create more engaging and user-centric applications. Vulkan's flexibility and efficiency will make it a preferred choice for developers looking to integrate AI-driven interactions seamlessly.

4. Cross-Domain Integration

The boundaries between industries and domains will continue to blur. Graphics and AI will intersect with fields like healthcare (medical imaging), automotive (autonomous driving), and architecture (real-time visualization). This cross-domain integration will lead to innovative solutions, such as AI-powered medical diagnosis tools, intelligent vehicles, and immersive architectural walkthroughs.

5. AI-Driven Gameplay

In the gaming industry, AI will evolve to create more dynamic and responsive gameplay experiences. Procedural content generation powered by AI will lead to infinitely replayable games. AI-driven NPCs will exhibit more lifelike behaviors and adapt to player actions, enhancing immersion. Game developers will leverage Vulkan's performance capabilities to handle the computational demands of advanced AI systems.

6. Ethical Considerations

As AI becomes deeply ingrained in graphics and applications, ethical considerations will become even more critical. Ensuring fairness, transparency, and responsible use of AI will be paramount. Developers will need to stay informed about evolving regulations and guidelines to build ethically sound AI-driven applications.

7. Environmental Sustainability

Graphics and AI can also contribute to environmental sustainability efforts. AI algorithms can optimize resource usage in graphics rendering, reducing energy consumption. Additionally, AI-driven simulations can model and analyze environmental data, aiding in climate research and conservation efforts.

8. Education and Research

The future of graphics and AI depends on a well-educated and research-focused community. Educational institutions and industry leaders will collaborate to offer specialized courses and research opportunities. Developers will continue to explore and innovate, contributing to advancements in both fields.

In conclusion, the synergy between Vulkan graphics programming and artificial intelligence is an exciting frontier. As we move forward, developers, researchers, and enthusiasts will play a pivotal role in shaping this future. Embracing new technologies, fostering ethical practices, and staying committed to pushing the boundaries of what's possible will unlock a future where graphics and AI seamlessly blend to create extraordinary experiences and solutions.